SECOND EDITION

Oracle PL/SQL Best Practices

Steven Feuerstein

Beijing · Cambridge · Farnham · Köln · Paris · Sebastopol · Taipei · Tokyo

Oracle PL/SQL Best Practices, Second Edition
by Steven Feuerstein

Copyright © 2008 Steven Feuerstein. All rights reserved.
Printed in the United States of America.

Published by O'Reilly Media, Inc., 1005 Gravenstein Highway North, Sebastopol, CA 95472.

O'Reilly books may be purchased for educational, business, or sales promotional use. Online editions are also available for most titles (*safari.oreilly.com*). For more information, contact our corporate/institutional sales department: (800) 998-9938 or *corporate@oreilly.com*.

Editors: Deborah Russell and Mary Treseler
Production Editor: Rachel Monaghan
Proofreader: Rachel Monaghan
Indexer: Angela Howard

Cover Designer: Karen Montgomery
Interior Designer: David Futato
Illustrator: Robert Romano

Printing History:

April 2001:	First Edition.
October 2007:	Second Edition.

 This book uses RepKover™, a durable and flexible lay-flat binding.

ISBN-10: 0-596-51410-7
ISBN-13: 978-0-596-51410-5

[M]

To the many PL/SQL programmers
around the world who have enriched my
life and made PL/SQL the amazing
success that it is.

Table of Contents

Preface

I love getting started on new projects (and I include working on new editions of existing books in that general category). It is the perfect opportunity to say to myself: "I am going to get it right this time!"

That fantasy usually persists only for days (or maybe weeks) into a project before it fades, but in the case of the second edition of *Oracle PL/SQL Best Practices*, I managed to live out my fantasy all the way through. You are holding the result in your hands, and I hope you enjoy reading and learning from it as much as I enjoyed writing it.

Here's how I managed this remarkable feat: I took a vow to not let best practices get boring.

Now, don't get me wrong. I liked the first edition of this book, and so did its many readers. Yet in hindsight, I feel as if I took a right turn when I should have kept going straight. My first book, *Oracle PL/SQL Programming*, has been extremely popular over the years, and many people have told me how much they like the sense of humor, the anecdotes, and the many detailed examples.

Several years after the publication of *Oracle PL/SQL Programming*, I wrote *Oracle PL/SQL Best Practices*. And somehow, for reasons I cannot recall, I managed to make this book a somewhat preachy and rigidly structured text. Luckily for me, developers seem to like lots of structure and don't mind *too much* being preached at by people they trust!

But as I considered revamping this book for its second edition, I found myself thinking: best practices are really important, but that doesn't mean they have to be serious—they can be fun and entertaining (as much for me to write as for you to read)!

So that's what I did: I had fun writing this book. I sacrificed some of the rigidity of structure, emphasized practicality over theoretical usefulness, and generally came down off my perch (don't worry—there are still more than enough rants and soapboxing!). In this second edition, I've tried to make the discussion a lot more interesting by sharing many of my ideas about best practices through stories about the successes and failures of the employees of the fictitious company, My Flimsy Excuse, Inc., and the adventures of its development team (the members of the team are described later in the Preface). Of course, I have also updated the text to keep pace with Oracle Corporation's implementation of new PL/SQL features, including those in Oracle Database 11*g*.

Why Best Practices?

My intention with this book is to provide you with a set of *best practices*—guidelines for building programs and applications—that will improve (and, I hope, *transform*) the PL/SQL code you write. Some of these best practices are high-level recommendations for how to approach designing and writing your overall applications. Other best practices are much more oriented to day-to-day programming practice. In most of my recommendations, I include references to code or tools that you can download that will make it easier for you to apply these recommendations.

Chapter 1, *The Big Picture*, covers the high-level recommendations for writing high-quality code. The remaining chapters of the book explore how to apply specific guidance to the everyday realities of software development. Before we delve into these specific recommendations, though, I would like to take advantage of this Preface to offer some thoughts on the role of software developers—and the nature of our jobs—in the big, wide world "out there" beyond our code.

Best Practices and the Real World

Clearly, software developers want to (and should) pay attention to best practices so that they will be able to create more successful applications. I also believe, however, that the responsibility of developers goes well beyond the specific projects on which they are working.

After all, you are one of the people who make software *possible*, who therefore make computer systems like the Internet possible. That is an awesome amount of power, but as Spider Man's uncle tells us, "With great power comes great responsibility."

From this perspective, it is very important to understand that you are not just a cog in the corporate wheel. When you are told to write a program, you should engage fully with that request. You should make sure not only that you understand in detail what it is the user wants you to write, but also that you appreciate how this program will meet its business objectives.

As a programmer, you are trained to think logically about the challenges in front of you. This rational thought process is not something to be taken for granted. Many other humans have never received such training and don't know how to reason their way through complex and thorny problems. Given this background, you can often help your users more clearly understand their own roles and their own challenges.

Your responsibility also extends beyond business objectives. You have an ethical responsibility to make sure that the software you write will not cause harm. Let's face it: executives of companies cannot always be trusted to do the right thing for their customers, for the company and its employees, and for society at large. Let's not forget the terrible lessons learned from Enron, Arthur Andersen, Union Carbide, Halliburton, and so many others. If you write software that enables executives in your firm to break the law or simply take advantage of those less fortunate, then you are complicit in that unethical behavior.

Of course, most of us will never be placed in such an ethical quandary. Instead, our main challenge will be to remember how much humanity depends on software, and how much we can all be hurt by buggy software, software that is not secure, and software that is simply badly designed—programs that waste the time of users and greatly increase their stress levels.

They Call This "Work"?

Can you really call what we do *work*? Most people on this earth work very hard in exchange for a paycheck. They drive buses, clean sewers, work in factories, pick vegetables and fruit under a blazing sun, teach children, take care of sick people—hard work that often takes a toll on their health and well-being. We, on the other hand...what do we do? Here are a variety of ways to characterize our "work":

Programming as poetry
> We sit around in nice, air-conditioned offices or cubicles. We think about things and write them down (or type them). And for this we get a paycheck. It's like getting paid to write poetry (and some of us actually do feel that our programs are a form of poetry).

Programming as Sudoku
> We play logical puzzles, similar in nature and often form to *Sudoku* or *Mastermind*, all day long. Incredible! Seriously, think about it: when your manager asks you to implement a program, it may initially sound boring and therefore like work. Here's an example: suppose you are told to write a program to calculate the mortgage payments for a customer. OK, you can be bored with it, or you can in your mind "translate" the specification for that program into the logic puzzle that it really is. The solution is the working program. The logical steps you have to go through represent the algorithm you will need to write.

Programmer as mediation
> Software generally aims to capture a small slice of the real world within cyberspace. Cyberspace is an artificial environment of our own making that is powered by computers. Computers are dumb machines that perform computations very rapidly. Because computers are dumb, humans must communicate with them using very rigid syntax and commands, following patterns that match up with the computer. Most people don't know the syntax or are not very good at thinking in these ways (procedural, object-oriented, symbolic logic, etc.). So we, the programmers, act as intermediaries between "normal people" and dumb computers.

Software is a responsibility, but it can also be a joy. So the next time you find yourself complaining about how dull your job is, or how you hate Cubicle Land and wish you could see out a window, please try to keep in perspective just how wonderful our lives really are!

And then express your gratitude for the opportunity to live a "life of the mind" by writing the best possible code and testing it thoroughly. Your users will thank you, and you will be so much more satisfied with life inside that cubicle.

The Cast of Characters

Software is still, for the most part, written by humans. So who are the humans who write the software I describe and critique in this book? Let's meet the cast of characters who inhabit the second edition of *Oracle PL/SQL Best Practices*. They work for a company called My Flimsy Excuse,* Inc. (MFE), and their web site is *myflimsyexcuse.com*. The mission statement of My Flimsy Excuse is simple and powerful:

> Provide a wide array of excuses (flimsy and otherwise) to people in need of a way to explain away questionable behavior.

The MFE founders love technology and don't want to have any flimsy excuses for failure, so they have chosen Oracle as their database technology. They have several different development teams working on various aspects of the web-deployed business plan. The team that has graciously volunteered to share its experiences with my readers is made up of the following individuals:

Sunita

> The team leader, a very smart woman with a fast, razor-sharp mind. She is always busy, always constructive, and somewhat intimidating. She was a programmer in years past, mostly trained in Fortran and then some C+. She isn't sure if that makes her a better manager or a bigger danger to the team, but she still likes to get her hands "dirty" now and then, writing code.

Delaware

> A classic anarchistic, anti-standards, big ego kind of programmer. He has a hard time learning from anyone else, and writes code that is hard to understand…but he is very productive and very bright. If you need a job done overnight (literally), Delaware is the guy to do it. He claims to read up on all the latest features of PL/SQL, but he generally programs in a rut—relying on techniques learned years past in Oracle7. He keeps his thinning hair neatly trimmed, with just a hint of a comb-over, and favors three-piece suits from the Men's Wearhouse.

---

* A "flimsy excuse" is an explanation for an action that is not very convincing and is easily exposed as a rationalization or cover-up for the real intention of the action.

The "Proper" Way to Write Code

Best practices mean different things to different people.

As I was gearing up to write the second edition, a British reader of the first edition got in touch with me. He had passed along the first edition pullout of best practice summaries and circulated it to the members of his development team. A day or two later, he received the following message.

Jason,

I don't know anything about the guy who wrote this book, but it's obvious he doesn't know anything about doing "proper" programming.

Step 1 should always be start coding, without any delay.

Then add in these steps as well. Just fit them in wherever you think they should be:

- Draw some sort of rough design on a scrap of paper (perhaps this should be near the end).
- Rewrite code, since the initial thoughts were wrong.
- Rewrite code, since the user requirements were nothing like they really wanted.
- Rewrite code, as you've just read an article on some obscure coding method/language/technology and you thought it might look good on your CV (*translation: resume*).
- Rewrite bits of code because an editor/PC/network failure has caused a loss of work.
- Rewrite code, as they've found a really cheap Sun IPX on eBay for 15 pence (*translation: roughly 30 cents*) so they're not getting the super all-singing/all-dancing PC that was mentioned in the spec. This usually involves switching language and development tools.
- Add some comments, as you've completely forgotten what a really complicated function or procedure was doing.
- Rewrite the above function, as you've found a library routine that will do it all in one call.
- Add a few days/weeks onto the plan for emailing your mates with "witty" replies to their emails.
- The final step is to always do documentation (usually some months or even years later, when you've likely forgotten whatever it is you were doing "back then").

Hope this helps bring you back to the real world.

Don't show this to anyone important, as it might ruin any future employment opportunities with our firm, unless of course they use the same methodology as me....

Lizbeth
> The anchor of the team. She used to write in Cobol and is continually shocked at the lack of strong process in the PL/SQL world. She can't understand why programmers today make fun of the Cobol programmers of the past. Didn't they write the software that made the first phase of the Information Revolution a broad success? Lizbeth is methodical and careful, but not, on the whole, the best problem solver—she too easily falls into the trap of seeing things only from her own perspective.

Jasper
> The junior member of the team. He is new to PL/SQL and new to MFE. Jasper is eager to learn from anyone and everyone and has nice thick skin, but he is not very creative (i.e., is not ready to take risks in his code). He always wears jeans, preferably of the distressed variety, complemented by polo shirts with the logos of animals on them. Lizbeth thinks of him as the son she never had, and Delaware treats him like the mascot of the team.

As you can see, each person has her or his own strengths and weaknesses. We will learn from both of these characteristics as we make our way through this book.

Structure of This Book

As I mentioned earlier, I decided to loosen up a bit structure-wise in the second edition. That does not mean, however, that you are about to start reading a chaotic and hard-to-navigate book. This section summarizes the organization.

Oracle PL/SQL Best Practices is composed of nine chapters and two appendixes. Each chapter contains a set of best practices for a particular area of functionality in the PL/SQL language or for broad programming principles (the latter are concentrated mostly in Chapter 1).

Best practices are used to overcome problems in our everyday programming life and to encourage the writing of high-quality code. To reinforce this purpose, most of the best practices in the book are presented first as a problem in the MFE environment: Sunita's team or a member of it confronts a challenge or has followed a "worst practice" into a very uncomfortable spot. We will then see how the MFE development team applies the best practice at hand to meet the challenge or repair the nasty code.

In many of the best practices, I also offer references to files available for download from the book's web site, as well as to publicly available tools (freeware, open source, and commercial) that will help you apply the best practices in a practical and efficient manner. You will find a comprehensive list of all such references in Appendix B.

Most best practices in this book are introduced by two titles: the first title is often a bit tongue-in-cheek (less than totally serious) and the second title is a more serious recommendation.

Chapter 1, *The Big Picture*, offers advice about how to improve the overall process by which you write code. The emphasis is on the application as a whole and the processes used to write that application, rather than on concrete suggestions for specific aspects of programming in PL/SQL. Please don't skip Chapter 1: if you do, it will be difficult to fully utilize the best practices in the rest of this book.

Chapter 2, *Real Developers Follow Standards*, is all about, well, standards: setting rules for how you and everyone on your team should write code. These standards range from naming conventions to standards templates from which code should be built. By the time you have finished reading this chapter, I hope that you will have overcome your ingrained resistance to standards, and instead see that rules free up more of your time to write the more interesting parts of your application.

Chapter 3, *Life After Compilation*, explores the steps that should take place *after* you get your program to compile, because, let's face it, that's just the beginning. You will learn about testing, tracing, and debugging—and the differences among these activities.

Chapter 4, *What's Code Without Variables?*, takes a close look at how you can best declare and manage data structures and variables within your PL/SQL programs. PL/SQL is a strongly typed language, which means that you need to make lots of decisions yourself in this area.

Chapter 5, *Developer As Traffic Cop*, is a "back to basics" chapter that talks about the best way to write IF statements, loops, and the new (in Oracle Database 11g) CONTINUE statement. Sure, these aren't terribly complicated constructs, but there are still right and wrong ways to work with them.

Chapter 6, *Doing the Right Thing When Stuff Goes Wrong*, covers exception management ("stuff going wrong"). We will explore defining standards for raising, handling, logging, and communicating errors back to the user. It is impossible to build a high-quality application with inconsistent error management, so be sure to read this chapter before you start your next project!

Chapter 7, *Break Your Addiction to SQL*, focuses on a crucial aspect of PL/SQL development: how you should write the SQL statements in your program to improve programmer productivity, increase performance, and make your code more maintainable. My feeling is that most PL/SQL developers are totally addicted to writing SQL—and that addiction leads to some of the biggest mistakes in how we write our code.

Chapter 8, *Playing with Blocks (of Code)*, offers advice on specifying parameters and building maintainable, readable, reusable procedures and functions—the program units that contain your business logic. It also presents recommendations for packages, the building blocks of well-designed PL/SQL-based applications, and triggers, which allow you to associate business rules with specific database objects.

Chapter 9, *My Code Runs Faster Than Your Code*, provides guidelines for improving the performance of your PL/SQL programs. These best practices range from techniques that will have an amazing impact on execution time (reducing program elapsed time from hours or days to mere minutes) to more granular recommendations whose impact will vary depending on the type of code you are writing.

Appendix A, *Best Practices Quick Reference*, compiles the best practices across all the chapters into a concise resource. Once you have studied the individual best practices, you can use this appendix as a checklist, to be reviewed both before you begin coding a new application and while you are implementing your programs.

Appendix B, *Resources for PL/SQL Developers*, offers descriptions of the files (examples and reusable code) that are referenced in the book, plus a list of the most useful books and online resources to help you take full advantage of the PL/SQL language.

How to Use This Book

My primary goal in writing this book was to create a resource that would make a concrete, noticeable difference in the quality of the PL/SQL code you write. To accomplish this, the book needs to be useful and usable not just for general study, but also for day-to-day, program-to-program tasks. It also needs to be concise and to the point. A 1,000-page text on best practices would be overwhelming, intimidating, and hard to use. The result is this relatively brief (I consider any publication under 300 pages a major personal accomplishment!) and entertaining book.

You can certainly read and apply the best practices in this book selectively. The best way to leverage best practices, however, is to start from a solid understanding of both your challenges and the high-level flows needed to break out of the current programming ruts in which you may find yourself today. So start with Chapter 1 (what a concept!) and see what you think of my "big picture" ideas. If you find yourself disagreeing with any of these ideas, think through what bothers you about them and what you would do *instead* to achieve the same results. If you like the ideas, spend some time planning how to apply them within your team. The higher level the best practice is, the more challenging it can be to get it started and ingrained in a group of developers.

Once you have absorbed (or rejected) the advice in Chapter 1, it will be easier to take advantage of the more specific best practices in the other eight chapters. I suggest that you proceed from start to end (don't panic—it's not *that* long a book!) with a light reading of each chapter, saving a full exploration of all the details until later on. Try to picture the best practices as a whole, reinforcing the following themes:

- I want to write code that I—and others—can easily understand and change as needed.
- The world is terribly complex, so I should strive to keep my code simple. I can then meet that complexity through carefully designed interaction among elements of my code.

You will then be well positioned to delve more deeply into the chapter or specific best practice that seems most critical to you at that moment.

Another very handy way to take advantage of this book is to *use the code* that is available for download. See the upcoming section "About the Code" for a discussion of the software that will help you bring your best practices to life.

Conventions Used in This Book

The following typographical conventions are used in this book:

Italic
> Used for file and directory names, for URLs, for emphasis, and for introducing a new term.

Constant width
> Used for code examples.

Constant width italic
> Indicates text that should be replaced with user-supplied values.

Constant width bold
> Indicates user input in examples showing an interaction. Also, in some examples, highlights the statements being discussed.

UPPERCASE
> Generally indicates PL/SQL keywords, names of built-in packages, etc.

lowercase
> Generally indicates identifiers (e.g., names of variables, procedures, functions, etc.).

> Indicates a tip, suggestion, or general note. For example, I'll tell you if a certain setting is version-specific.

> Indicates a warning or caution. For example, I'll tell you if a certain setting has some kind of negative impact on the system.

About the Code

The best way to learn how to write good code is by analyzing and following examples. Almost every best practice offered in this book includes a code example, both in the text and in downloadable form. I will be keeping the code up to date at my PL/SQL portal at:

> *http://www.ToadWorld.com/SF*

There you will also find training materials and additional code downloads. You can also obtain the example code, along with additional information on the book, through the O'Reilly *Oracle PL/SQL Best Practices* web page at:

http://www.oreilly.com/catalog/9780596514105

Whenever possible, the code I provide for the book can be used to generate best-practice-based code and as prebuilt, generalized components in your applications, code that you can use without having to make any modifications.

The code examples offer programs that you can use to both generate and directly implement those best practices. In some cases, the programs are rather simple "prototypes"; they work as advertised, but you will probably want to make some changes before you put them into production applications.

And you should most certainly test every single program you use from *Oracle PL/SQL Best Practices*! I have run *some* tests, of course, and my wonderful technical reviewers have also exercised the code. In the end, however, if the code goes into your application, you are responsible for making sure that it meets your needs.

Comments and Questions

I have tested and verified the information in this book and in the source code to the best of my ability, but if you find an error and want to comment on the book or the code, please notify me. By postal mail, you can contact me through O'Reilly at:

O'Reilly Media, Inc.
1005 Gravenstein Highway
Sebastopol, CA 95472
800-998-9938 (in the United States or Canada)
707-829-0515 (international/local)
707-829-0104 (fax)

You can also send messages electronically. To be put on the mailing list or request a catalog, send email to:

info@oreilly.com

To ask technical questions or comment on the book, send email to:

bookquestions@oreilly.com

For more information about books, Resource Centers, and the O'Reilly Network, see the O'Reilly web site:

http://www.oreilly.com

As mentioned earlier, the book's web site is:

http://www.oreilly.com/catalog/9780596514105

Safari Books Online

When you see a Safari Books Online icon on the cover of your favorite technology book, it means the book is available online through the O'Reilly Network Safari Bookshelf.

Safari offers a solution that's better than e-books. It's a virtual library that lets you easily search thousands of top technical books, cut and paste code samples, download chapters, and find quick answers when you need the most accurate, current information. Try it for free at *http://safari.oreilly.com*.

Acknowledgments

The second edition of *Oracle PL/SQL Best Practices* is a much improved text, largely as a result of the assistance of many fine Oracle technologists. Any errors, however, are entirely my fault and responsibility.

A special thanks to John Beresniewicz for his detailed technical review and the contribution of a fine summary of Design by Contract in Chapter 1. I hope that readers will go from the brief presentation in that chapter to the expanded description of DbC on the book's web site. I believe that using this powerful programming style will greatly strengthen your code.

My heartfelt thanks to Bryn Llewellyn, PL/SQL Product Manager at Oracle Corporation, for deepening my knowledge of PL/SQL and helping me crystallize and focus my best practices.

Technical reviewers for this second edition provided many corrections and ideas that improved the text. My deepest gratitude to Dick Bolz, Rick Greenwald, Darryl Hurley, Dwayne King, Giovanni Jaramillo, Arup Nanda, Chris Rimmer, and Bert Scalzo.

And from O'Reilly Media, thanks to my editor Deborah Russell. On the first edition, she got me off the dime and helped me turn the book around in record time; while we developed this second edition over a longer period, it was, once again, a real pleasure working with you, Debby! Thanks as well to Rachel Monaghan, the production editor; Rob Romano, who developed the figures; and Angela Howard, who wrote the index.

The second edition couldn't have happened without the first edition, which never would have hit the shelves without assistance from John Beresniewicz, Rohan Bishop, Dick Bolz, Dan Clamage, Bill Caulkins, Dan Condon-Jones, Fawwad-uz-Zafar Siddiqi, Gerard Hartgers, Edwin van Hattem, Dwayne King, Darryl Hurley, Giovanni Jaramillo, Vadim Loevski, Pavel Luzanov, Matthew MacFarland, Jeffrey Meens, James "Padders" Padfield, Rakesh Patel, Bill Pribyl, Andre Vergison (the brains behind PL/Formatter), and Solomon Yakobson.

Last and most definitely not least, I thank my wife, Veva, and my two boys, Chris and Eli, for tolerating all my time in front of a computer and for giving me endless and most excellent reasons to escape from it.

CHAPTER 1

The Big Picture

Are you happy with the quality of the code you write? Probably not, or you wouldn't be reading this book! This doesn't mean that you are a "bad" programmer. It means only that you feel that your code has room for improvement—and I'm sure that's true for every single programmer among us.

I believe that you can dramatically improve the quality of your code by following programming *best practices*. Two very interesting concepts are implicit in that term:

- It is possible to talk about a "best" way of writing code, which implies, conversely, that there is a worst or at least suboptimal way to write code.
- These "best" ways can be organized into "practices," formalized processes for writing high-quality software.

After having written software (and books about writing software) for almost 30 years, I am firmly convinced that these two concepts are both valid and fundamentally important, and that you can't have one without the other.

Humanity survived its first worldwide software crisis on January 1, 2000—but at a cost of several hundred billion dollars. Users of software, unfortunately, continue to experience localized software crises on a daily basis, as they struggle with poorly written applications that are a direct consequence of the QUAD "methodology" (QUick And Dirty).

Software has the potential to dramatically improve the quality of life of billions of human beings. It can—with the help of robotics—automate tedious and dangerous processes. It can make information and services more widely accessible. It can, should, and must play a role in halting the degradation of our environment. In short, software has an enormous potential, but that potential will never be realized unless we can find a way to substantially improve the quality of the code we write.

This book has a very simple but ambitious purpose: to help Oracle developers and development teams transform the way they write PL/SQL-based applications. To achieve this transformation in your programming life, you will need both to rethink fundamental aspects of application design and construction, and to change day-to-day programming habits.

In the chapters that follow, we'll examine a wide range of PL/SQL topics: programming standards; program testing, tracing, and debugging; variables and data structures; control logic; error handling; the use of SQL in PL/SQL; the building of procedures, functions, packages, and triggers; and overall program performance. Since this first chapter focuses on "big picture" advice for building successful applications, it seems reasonable to start off the chapter by spending some time and words defining "successful" in the context of software projects.

Successful Applications Are Never an Accident

If you have the privilege of buying a new automobile and rolling it off the dealer's lot, you don't say to yourself:

> Well, every 50 miles or so, one of my wheels might fall off. The odometer sometimes goes backward, and, oh look! My windows don't quite close. But that's all right, because the dealer said that I'll be getting version 2 in roughly six months. I can't wait!

Sounds silly, doesn't it? Yet for people who buy and use software, it has become the norm to think in precisely these terms. Now, if an automobile manufacturer really *did* deliver cars that were as buggy as many of the applications let loose upon the world, that manufacturer would likely be out of business very soon. While it is certainly possible that a software company will go belly up if its code is *too* buggy, for the most part our employers keep on going (and we keep on programming), issuing new versions that fix some bugs and introduce others.

Why is there such a difference in the way people view, use, and tolerate cars versus software? I think there are three basic reasons:

- Cyberspace, the world of software, is a world of our creation. We determine what is possible and not possible within that world. This total control gives us the ability to "upgrade" that world, fixing problems, adding possibilities, and adding constraints, with relative ease. You just can't do that with "real" products.

- Cyberspace is, at its core, an attempt by software developers to simulate a small slice of the real world, and then automate some processes to help users accomplish things in that real world. Because the world "out there" is so incredibly complex, writing software is a very hard thing to do, and even harder to do well.

- Human society (at least those societies in which the Industrial and Information Revolutions have had their way with us) is today unimaginable without computers and the software that makes computers useful. Software permeates almost every aspect of our lives. And that means that for the most part our users are a "captive audience": they *have* to use what we give them, no matter how faulty.

I am going to assume that you are reading this book because you would like to pick up some pointers about how to improve the quality of the PL/SQL code that you write. You would like to do so in order to produce applications that are more successful. Perhaps it would be helpful, therefore, to remind ourselves of what it means for an application to be successful.

I believe that for an application to be considered successful, it must satisfy the following criteria (listed in order of importance):

It meets user requirements

> This, to my mind, is the most fundamental of all. I hope the reason is obvious to you. If the application doesn't do what the user wants it to do, well, then the project is a complete or partial failure, depending on the extent to which it falls short.

It is maintainable

> The code we write today is the code that users will run tomorrow, and next year, and most likely next *decade*. The Y2K crisis drove home the point that software has a life far beyond our expectations. If we don't write our code so that it can be easily and quickly maintained, an initial success will quickly turn into a failure.

It runs fast enough to minimize user frustration

> If the application meets user needs, but runs so slowly that it makes you want to pull out the old calculator or slide rule, it cannot be deemed a success.

Now, I have a feeling that you may be reading these three criteria and feeling a stab of disappointment. "That's the most obvious thing I've ever read," you're saying to yourself. "Of course, it has to do what the user says it must, and it can't be slow as molasses, and, yeah sure, about that maintainable thing."

I agree: these characteristics are or should be obvious. In fact, they are so obvious that we don't pay them sufficient attention, with the consequence that very few of our application projects are a success! The easiest way to see what I am talking about is to consider what we developers must or should do to ensure that these criteria are met.

Successful Applications Meet User Requirements

What is the only way that we can *guarantee* that our application code meets user requirements? We must *test* our code. Without rigorous, comprehensive, and repeatable tests, we have no way of knowing that the application actually works. We simply hope for the best.

Again, this might seem obvious at first glance. But stop and think about how testing occurs in your code and in the "finished product." Testing is often the last thing we think about, and the last thing we do. That means that we never have enough time to test, and that the application goes into production full of bugs.

Those same bugs (and the process of fixing them) eat into the time required to add new functionality, so users generally always feel that critical features are missing.

Sadly, while user requirements might be more or less black and white, user expectations are not: they can and do change as users encounter the reality of programming. That is, users have come to accept applications that do not meet all their needs, and feel that they must settle for "good enough," "just barely sufficient," or, worst of all, that they have "no choice but to use this garbage."

Successful Applications Are Maintainable

I sometimes fantasize that after I retire from active development, as I live out my years in a small, isolated, and very beautiful former coffee farm near the west coast of Puerto Rico, I'll get a phone call: "Steven, they've described the Y2.1K bug in PL/SQL! All of our applications are going to crash in six months. We need you! We'll pay whatever you require—to fix the bugs you put in your code back in 2010!"

Now that, dear friends, would be quite a good deal: to be paid top dollar to fix bugs I put in my code years or decades before. Of course, it would be much nicer if I wrote my code in such a way that years from now, when bugs are discovered, it would be easy for that next generation of coders to make the necessary fixes on their own.

Sadly, as far as I can tell, most of us (and I *do* include myself in this critique) are so overwhelmed by meeting immediate deadlines that we feel we don't have the time to do things the "right way." Instead, the only option is "quick and dirty," and the code that results from taking shortcuts is generally almost impossible to maintain.

For an application to be maintainable, it must have associated with it a comprehensive *regression test,* which must be run after any changes are made to the code to ensure that no bugs have been introduced. The code must also be structured so that any developer can open up a program and feel perfectly at home in the code, even if she didn't write it, even if she's never seen it before. The code should be welcoming, rather than threatening.

Successful Applications Run Fast Enough

To ensure that users don't smash their keyboards through their monitors in frustration, we must optimize execution of our applications. This criterion usually gets the most (and the most explicit) attention, in part, I believe, because performance most directly affects our experience of using the software. We can accept that a particular feature is not yet available, or that a bug doesn't let us do what we would really like to do. We all have ways of compensating.

If minutes pass, though, whenever I (or the person running the code that is providing a service to me) press the Submit button, I tend to feel my life slipping away from me. Perhaps it is our ingrained fear of mortality, but the pain of waiting for software to finish its job is an especially sharp one.

Optimizing the performance of an application is a complex affair, in part because there are so many different moving parts in software. There has been lots of attention paid (and many tools built) to address this problem. My feeling, in fact, is that achieving adequate performance is the requirement that is most thoroughly dealt with in today's software, sometimes to the detriment of the other, more challenging criteria.

So, yes, these criteria are obvious, but meeting them can present quite a challenge. And because it can be so difficult to meet user requirements, write maintainable code, and get our applications working quickly enough, we adjust expectations downward and everyone suffers. Our users have come to expect software to be maddeningly lacking in features, ridiculously buggy, and frustratingly slow.

And that brings us directly to best practices, because without them, you can achieve success in your development project only accidentally—and that just doesn't happen!

Best Practices for Successful Applications

Best practices are the guidelines you should follow to achieve a "best" or successful application—one that meets the criteria listed in the previous sections. "Best practices" is certainly an overused term, but it is also clear enough in intent to be useful.

When programmers follow best practices, they have made a decision to work against their "quick and dirty" tendency and to consciously, with intention and purpose, seek to transform the way they write their code. Without that focus, without a deliberate act on the part of developers (and their managers as well), there is a *very* low likelihood that their applications will be successful.

Best practices also must go beyond (and deeper than) words on a page. For best practices to be successfully applied, they must be combined with tools and scripts to make them *practical*.

Best practices should operate at two levels:

Big picture
> A high-level workflow that provides an overall guide to writing code. "Big picture" best practices for constructing applications and applying fundamental principles are usually decided on before a project starts. Best practices in this category set standards for all of the code written in an application.

Day-to-day
> Concrete recommendations for specific aspects of code construction that are applied in each new program as it is written and maintained.

Both types of best practices are important. The following sections focus on the key "big picture" best practices that will set the stage for the day-to-day recommendations you will find in the rest of the book.

Software is like ballet: choreograph the moves or end up with a mess.

Put into place a practical workflow that emphasizes iterative development based on a shared foundation.

Problem: In software, the ends (production code) are inseparable from the means (the build process).

It is back in 2004. Sunita has just been promoted to development manager at My Flimsy Excuse, Inc., and has been given responsibility for both a newly assembled team (Delaware, Lizbeth, and Jasper), and a critical new application development project. She is feeling a little bit overwhelmed and intimidated. Delaware has been around forever and is famous (infamous?) for both his brilliant coding and his brittle personality. Lizbeth has more quietly, but just as firmly, established herself within the company as a valuable resource; she serves on several standards committees and sends out a monthly "What's New in the MFE Family" newsletter. Who is Sunita, compared to them?

She calls the first meeting of the team and begins to lay out her ideas for implementing the project. Delaware, attired in a very retro double-breasted suit, immediately breaks in and explains in no uncertain terms why her approach will fail. "We are all very experienced," he says sternly. "Why not leverage that experience and free us up to do what we do best?" The others nod, and Sunita feels she has little choice but to agree.

So all three developers dive in with enthusiasm, applying to their part of the application their own individual approaches to writing code. Sunita checks in regularly, but she feels more like an outsider than a manager at this stage. She reassures herself that she has a team of professionals building the application; they don't need lots of direction.

Three months into the project, problems start popping up. Delaware's code needs to talk to Lizbeth's code, but the way they have each designed their interfaces makes such communication very difficult. And not long after that, during a rare code review session (insisted upon by Sunita), they discover that they have each built their own error-management code, writing to different tables and storing different information.

But it is too late to turn back now, so the team struggles on, adding new layers of code to achieve some level of interoperability and consistency. The application grows more and more complex; deadlines are missed; performance is very uneven, with some programs running very slowly even with average quantities of data; tensions rise between developers who used to get along just fine. Finally, though, they tell Sunita that they have spent the last few days testing the code and fixing bugs; the application is now ready for QA. But the QA group finds that the application has so many low-level bugs that it can't get even halfway through an acceptance test.

Stamping "REJECTED" on the application, QA sends it back to Sunita, who admits defeat. The application will not, in its current incarnation, see the light of day.

Solution: Agree on a common development workflow built around standards, testing, and reviews.

Sunita is so disgusted with herself that she asks for a meeting with her boss and submits her resignation. To Sunita's surprise, her boss, Marguerite, is not surprised at the news of her team's failure or her intense reaction to it. She says:

> Sunita, you are right: this is very bad news, but the danger signals have been there for a while. I suppose perhaps I should have stepped in earlier and made some suggestions, but I thought it was important for you to see it through. No, I do not accept your resignation, but I would like to know what you have learned from this experience. Because now it is time for Round Two. We need this application, and you know the requirements better than anyone in the company. So what should we do now?

Sunita is stunned into silence. She thinks about what has happened over the past half-year and sums it up as follows:

* Even if every developer is excellent on his or her own, as a team we must still agree on standard approaches for the common elements of our application: error management, SQL statements, and naming conventions.
* Testing can't be short-changed, and it can't be put off until the very end of the development process. Feedback (including bad news) is needed all the way through the process.
* A manager should make sure that the developers on the team are productive and focused, but she must also make the hard decisions that no individual developer can or will make on his or her own—the developers are simply too close to the code and, hence, the problem.

With those ideas in mind, Sunita convenes her team and lays down the law: they will spend the next week (or two, if needed) researching standards and tools they can use to come up with a standard development style. With that foundation, they start again and this time are able to successfully complete the application.

While each reader, or team, may choose different tools and naming conventions, I believe that we should all follow a workflow that is based on standards and that reinforces best practices. This workflow must be simple enough to remember with ease, and must also be integrated into the tools you use. This way, you can follow the workflow without having to pay conscious attention to it every other minute of the day.

Developers need to focus on two distinct workflows:

* Application-level workflow
* Single-program construction workflow

In the next section, I'll explain my approach to the application-level workflow; then we'll delve into the recommended workflow for individual programs within that application.

Application-level workflow

You are about to start building a new application. Such a wonderful moment! If you are like me, you immediately engage in a beautiful fantasy; *this time* we are going to "do it right." We are going to write code that is easy to understand and maintain, that is thoroughly documented and tested, that is fully optimized. Sounds great, but how do you make that happen?

Figure 1-1 offers a high-level workflow that provides a framework in which we can write our code to achieve these objectives. This framework is based on the following principles:

- Software is an iterative process: anything you do today, you will need to come back and do again tomorrow.
- A shared foundation based on standards is critical to implementing best practices.

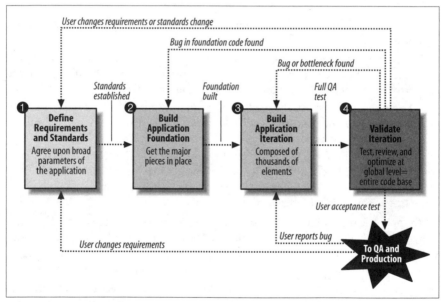

Figure 1-1. Recommended workflow for the entire application

Let's go through each of these four steps.

Step 1: Define requirements and standards.   Before writing any application code, we need the cleanest, clearest possible set of requirements from our users. I can already hear the groans emitted by readers. "Clear requirements from our users? Ha! Anything they tell us today is going to change tomorrow. Our users drive us mad!"

Yes, users can be very frustrating, but usually it isn't their fault. The requirements they give us are driven by *their* requirements, which come from the ever-changing and oh-so-complex real world "out there." So accept the fact that change is a fundamental characteristic of requirements gathering. The best you can do is freeze in place a clear vision of the application needs at this moment.

Given that constraint, however, there is something you *can* do to improve user requirements: work *with* your users to think logically through what they need. I emphasize "logically" because we programmers spend lots of time using symbolic logic to solve problems and write algorithms. Compared to most other people, our brains are highly trained instruments of rational processing. With this orientation, we are well equipped to help our users sort out their issues and work out the kinks (contradictions and points of confusion) in their requirements.

Once that is done, attention shifts to the way we will build our code to meet those requirements. Before any programs are written, you need to define the standards that are to be applied to each program. I believe that at a minimum your standards should cover these three areas:

Naming conventions and coding standards
> It is extremely important that everyone on the team write code in a similar fashion. No, we don't want to turn into Code Fascists, and insist on 100 percent conformance to a single style, but we should work to avoid wide variations.

SQL access
> SQL is so easy to write in PL/SQL that almost all of us take it totally for granted: we write SQL statements wherever, whenever, and however we like. Sound reasonable? Well, you're wrong. It doesn't make any sense at all. Think about it: SQL statements are among the most volatile elements of your code, changing along with the underlying table structures and relationships. In addition, those queries, updates, and other SQL operations are the source of most performance problems in your application. The *only* thing that makes sense about SQL in your PL/SQL code is that you proactively set guidelines for when, where, and how SQL statements are to be written into the code.

Error management
> If errors are raised, handled, and communicated inconsistently (or not at all), users will have a hard time understanding how to deal with problems when they occur, and developers will have an even harder time debugging and fixing their applications.

I am sure you can come up with other areas of standardization that are appropriate to your application, but you need rules for *at least* the above three items. So now you may be asking, "Well, what are the rules for these areas?" You will find details for each item in the chapters listed in the next section.

Step 2: Build the application foundation. Once you set some rules, you need to think about how to best and most smoothly implement those rules. I suggest that you focus on two different areas:

Formalize a process that inherently supports the rules to be followed
> If rules are nothing more than a set of checklists in a document, programmers will never be able to remember them, much less follow them. So you need to come up with clearly defined processes, backed up by tools, that make it easy for developers to follow the rules with a minimum of thought and energy.

Automate the implementation of rules
> Without a doubt, the best way to follow rules is to have them implemented automatically for you. Press a button on a screen and, *whoosh!*, here comes the code, all following the standards. Done! Whenever possible, you should also automate the *verification* of compliance with rules.

In other words, get everything ready and in place so that as a developer writes a program for your application, it can easily follow the rules.

So let's revisit the three focus areas listed in step 1, and address formalization and automation of the rules.

Naming conventions and coding standards
> The best way to formalize the process of following coding standards is to create code templates and snippets, and make them available in your editor of choice. Automation in this case would mean automated review of code to determine where that code does *not* follow best practices. Chapter 2 provides additional information.

SQL access
> The fundamental shift to be made when it comes to SQL is to think of data access as a *service*, not as code that you need to write—over and over again. In general, the rule I try to follow with SQL is: don't write it! Chapter 7 covers this concept.

Error management
> The best, perhaps only, way to implement application-wide, consistent error logging, raising, and handling is to use a single, shared package, supported by a well-designed set of tables, to do all the work for the development team. This approach makes exception management so easy that everyone follows the standards without even knowing it! See Chapter 6 for more information on this idea.

OK, the foundation is now in place. Your developers have been trained in what is available and in how to use it. This is a critical step; if developers are not informed of which libraries and utility code are available to them, your team will be doomed to minimal code reuse and maximum wasting of time and resources.

And now it's time to build an application!

Step 3: Build the next application iteration. There certainly is a lot to talk about in this step, but we will defer the discussion for now and address it (from the standpoint of workflow) in the section "Single-program construction workflow," later in this chapter, and in the detailed best practices throughout this book. The main point to consider at this level of the workflow is that after working on lots of individual programs, you eventually reach a point where you are ready to put all those pieces together into an *iteration* of the application.

Then, it's time to check whether the application meets the criteria for success—that is, to *validate* this iteration of the application.

Step 4: Validate the application iteration. If you are going to set rules, it seems only reasonable that you should go back and check to make sure that they have been followed. Let's look again at our application criteria and see what you need to do to satisfy them:

Successful applications meet user requirements
> Run *all* the regression tests for the code and make sure you get a green light at the code level. Do a round of acceptance testing (run by users and QA teams).

Successful applications are maintainable
> For all the code in your application, check whether coding standards have been followed; format the code according to the application standard (preferably using an automated "pretty printer"); identify code that is overly complex; and so on. The best way to do this is to combine peer review (people look at your code and give you feedback) with automated review.

Successful applications run fast enough
> Analyze performance of the entire application to identify bottlenecks. This analysis should be both objective (stress testing and other benchmarking) and subjective (user experience).

And what news will we get from all of this analysis? In the early iterations, we get lots of negative (uh, I mean, constructive) feedback: we've violated all kinds of rules, our code runs too slowly, and bugs have *somehow* crept into our code.

Depending on the source of the problem, we must then go back and "do it again." If a problem is identified in the requirements, we will have to return to the first step, adjust those requirements, and then work on a new iteration. If a bug is found in the foundation code, we will need to fix that. Usually, though, when we validate an iteration, we simply find that there is code that must be changed in the application-level logic, and so our attention shifts back to step 3.

We repeat this process many times, until validation gives us a green light: all is well in our application, and it can move to production. Then the phone calls come flooding in from the users: "Thank you so much for building us such a wonderful application!" and "You have made our lives so much easier!"

Ah, if only it were so. We certainly do get calls, but usually they are in the form of bug reports or along the lines of "We changed our minds and need something different." And then back we go into the application iteration. Don't think of it as a bad thing—think of it as a jobs program!

Single-program construction workflow

The high-level workflow discussed in the previous section is critical, but when you get right down to it, software is all about the details—the individual lines of code, and the identifiers and operators within those lines. I suppose you could say that about everything: our bodies are made of atoms, for example. Yet with software, we programmers are responsible for all of the details (at the level of abstraction of our particular programming language, in any case), so it is inevitable that most of our time will be spent among these details.

This section offers a high-level workflow (summarized in Figure 1-2), not for the application as a whole, but for an individual program, procedure, or function. I hope that for many of you these ideas are obvious. I find, though, that even if we *acknowledge* each of these elements of a workflow, we often shortchange critical aspects, so let's review the elements.

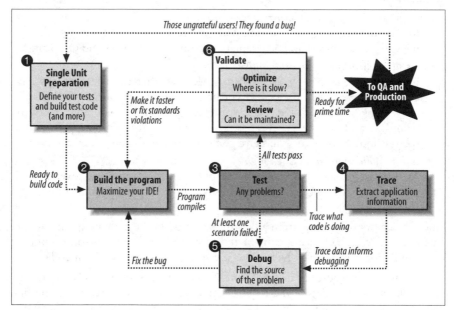

Figure 1-2. Workflow for each program you build

Step 1: Prepare for program construction.   Let's start with the most important, most neglected, and most psychologically difficult step for programmers: prepare for program construction. Why do I say that this step is difficult? Because programmers are, for the most part, human beings who like to write programs—and that really means that we like to write cool algorithms. Our brains are attracted to solving such problems. And so we feel compelled to dive in and start writing those algorithms, before we've even thought through what we need to do.

Bad idea! Instead, we need to hold off on writing the algorithms and instead *prepare* for that glorious moment of coding. We need to clarify what the user needs, and we need to think about how to verify that what we have done works. This is an important step: the time you invest here will reap benefits for the rest of the life of your program.

The program preparation step consists of four main substeps: validate requirements, construct the program header, define tests, and build test code. I won't get into the details of these substeps in this section, but I'll revisit this preparation step and make sure it gets the attention it deserves later in this chapter, in the section titled "Deferred satisfaction is a required emotion for best practices."

Step 2: Build an iteration of the program. At this point you have done all your preparation. You have clarity about what is needed. You have defined your tests and written your test code (don't worry—soon, you won't find that idea so strange). *Finally*, you are allowed to focus on those fascinating algorithms and implement an iteration of the program. At some point, you will get your program to compile and then you will have stabilized that iteration.

And the best way to do that? Ah, well, that is what most of this book is about, so check out all those chapters that come after Chapter 1 to learn how to greatly improve the code you write.

Step 3: Test the program iteration. The program compiles, which is an exciting moment in and of itself. Yet, sadly, there is more we need to do. Now it is time to test the iteration and see whether there are any problems with the program. In other words, we run the program and examine its behavior: does it do what we expect it to do? Note that when you test a program you don't care *how* it gets the job done (what kind of algorithm is used to solve the problem). The program is, from the standpoint of testing, a "black box."

The news that we usually get from our testing is simultaneously good and bad. The bad news is that our tests have identified some bugs, which means that we have to go back and fix them. The good news is that our tests have identified some bugs, which means that they can likely be fixed before our users start working with the application. Outcomes from testing are, therefore, inputs to the debugging process. Chapter 3 offers more details on the testing process.

Step 4: Trace execution of the program. Oracle offers many options for system tracing. The built-in package DBMS_TRACE, for example, provides a type of tracing that generates information about the underlying database activity. Application tracing is different. With this type of tracing, as you run your program, you record or build a trace of information about what is happening *inside* the program—for example, which company ID was passed in, what company name it found, and so on. Tracing is a form of program *instrumentation* in which you add statements to your code that either change program behavior or extract information *from* the program.

Trace output (both system and application) serves as critical raw data to the debugging process, but tracing is fundamentally different from debugging (described in the next section). Chapter 3 discusses the tracing process in detail.

Step 5: Debug the program.   When you debug a program, you take the results of testing and tracing and then step through your code, line by line (using a visual source code debugger, I hope), in search of the *source* of each problem you have uncovered. After you have used logic to narrow down a problem to specific lines of code, you make changes to your program, recompile...and then start the process over again.

At some point along the way, you run your tests and you get a big surprise: a green light! Your tests show you that your program works. You can now move on to the next stage: validation. Chapter 3 offers more details on the debugging process.

Step 6: Validate the program: optimize and review.   The validation that should eventually occur for a single program mirrors the validation for an entire application, described earlier in "Step 4: Validate the application iteration." For each particular program, you need to identify any obvious performance problems and check to make sure that you have followed the coding conventions and naming standards. Based on the feedback from these two types of validation, you go back and do the following:

- Make changes to your program.
- Run your regression tests, ensuring that you have not introduced any bugs.
- Revalidate, and go through the cycle again.

At some point, your test program returns a thumbs-up (all tests succeed) and your code review process declares your program "clean." You can now check in that program and essentially hand it off to QA, knowing that it is in good shape.

The next thing you know, the users are reporting bugs. So ungrateful! Now when a user reports a bug, she is actually reporting at least *two* bugs: the bug in your code (one or more programs) and the bug in your *test code*. After all, if your test code "worked," the bug would have been found and fixed earlier in the process.

So, whenever a user reports a bug (and really, the same goes for enhancement requirements), you will first want go back to step 1 (preparation, for which I explore more details in the next section). Add the test cases needed to describe the tests you missed, update your test code to reflect those new test cases, and then run your test code to verify reproduction of the bug. *Now* you are ready to use your debugger to track down the cause of the problem, and fix it. That way, your test definitions stay current, get more and more complete over time, and continue to help you even past the initial production release of the software.

Which steps do you perform? I expect that the steps I've discussed will make sense to most developers. From my many trainings and conversations with PL/SQL programmers, however, I have concluded the following:

- Very little preparation is done (I'll say more about what this means in the next section).
- Testing is sporadic.
- Tracing is usually based on the DBMS_OUTPUT.PUT_LINE function, which is problematic for a number of reasons, and is applied after the fact.
- Code review is hardly ever done.
- Optimization is performed manually (and rarely by the person who originally wrote the code), which means that developers need to understand EXPLAIN plans. Ugh.

In other words, for most programmers, the "workflow" of development is pretty simple: write some code and get it to compile. Run some scenarios and then spend lots of time in the debugger trying to figure out what might be going wrong and what *might* fix it.

You can do better! Full utilization of the workflow I've described, based on a solid set of tools, will result in a more balanced approach. You'll spend less time debugging and much more time writing code that *avoids* bugs and focuses on improving code quality.

Deferred satisfaction is a required emotion for best practices.

Hold off on implementing the body of your program until your header is stable and your tests are defined.

If we give in to our "base impulse" and simply start writing code, implementing interesting algorithms, we will always struggle to apply best practices. We need to start off on the right foot by preparing for the coding phase. I believe there are four key steps to preparation, shown in Figure 1-3.

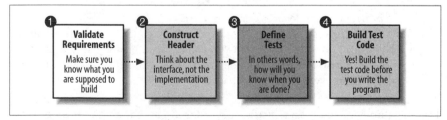

Figure 1-3. Four steps of preparing an application

Step 1. Validate program requirements

Sometimes your users give you very little documentation, and other times they overwhelm you with nice-looking documents that contain graphics, charts, and lots and lots of text. In both cases (and everything in between), do *not* assume that what the users say is right or complete. As I pointed out earlier, your users may not have developed the same ability to think clearly and logically that programmers have. So help them! Use your logical skills to help users identify illogical ideas or gaps in their requirements.

Before you start writing any code, make sure that both you and your users have a clear understanding of what is needed (and why). So ask lots of questions, shine light in the dark corners, and challenge users to make sure that they have thought through all the requirements. Remember too that what users ask for is not always the easiest way to solve a problem. Don't assume that users have already considered other approaches—and I am not talking only about programming algorithms; I am talking about business processes as well.

Step 2. Implement just the header of the program

OK, at this point let's assume that you are reasonably confident that your users know what they need and have clearly communicated those requirements to you. Now can you write your program? Yes, but just a little bit of it: only the header of the program and enough to get your program to compile.

At this stage, it's time to think *not* about how the program will be implemented (oh, but I really like to come up with clever algorithms!), but instead about:

What is a good name for the program?
> If your name does not accurately represent the purpose of the program, it will mislead anyone who reads your code.

What are the inputs (IN arguments) and outputs (OUT arguments or RETURN clause, if a function)?
> In other words, when you call this program, what information will you need to provide and what will you get back? Come up with good names for those arguments, based on your naming conventions.

Should the program be overloaded for convenience?
> One of the biggest advantages to keeping your code in packages (you are using packages, aren't you?) is that you can easily implement several different versions of a procedure or function, each having a different signature. For more details on overloading, see Chapter 8.

This may all seem rather obvious to you, but in practice, we find ourselves hurrying through naming and interface decisions, because we are so eager to move on to the "fun" part: problem solving, constructing cool algorithms, and so on. This planning will pay off, however.

Once you are happy with your header, add just enough code to get the program to compile. Usually this means adding a body with NULL; (for procedures) or

RETURN NULL; (for functions). At this stage, your program is really nothing more than a *stub*, an executable placeholder for the program.

Let's look at an example. Suppose that I need to build a program in my strings toolbox package, tb_strong_utils, that accepts a string and a start and end location, and returns the substring between those two positions. I add this header to my package specification:

```
PACKAGE tb_string_utils
IS
    /* Lots of other, existing programs above. */

    /* Return substring between start and end locations */
    FUNCTION betwnstr (
        string_in IN VARCHAR2
    , start_in IN PLS_INTEGER
    , end_in IN PLS_INTEGER
    )
        RETURN VARCHAR2;

END tb_string_utils;
```

Next, I add only the following code to the package body:

```
PACKAGE BODY tb_string_utils
IS
    /* Lots of other, existing programs above. */

    /* Return substring between start and end locations */
    FUNCTION betwnstr (
        string_in IN VARCHAR2
    , start_in IN PLS_INTEGER
    , end_in IN PLS_INTEGER
    )
        RETURN VARCHAR2
    IS
    BEGIN
        RETURN 'VALUE UNLIKELY TO BE RETURNED';
    END betwnstr;

END tb_string_utils;
```

And that is all the code I will write at this stage. Now it's time to move on to everyone's favorite activity—testing!

Step 3. Define the tests that must be run

We won't start with actual testing at this point. But we *should* think about the tests that will need to be run on the program to verify that it works. In other words, the question that should *consume* you at this stage of (pre) development is: how will I know when I am done with this program?

There is a very good chance that many readers of this book are now saying to themselves, "Why would I think about testing now? I haven't even written my program yet. How would I know what to test?" Ah, that sounds so sensible—or does it?

In fact, I believe that this perspective is total nonsense, and a significant contributor to poorly tested code! If you wait until after you write your program to (a) think about testing, (b) write your test code, and (c) run your tests, you will then face these challenges:

You won't have enough time to test
> It always takes more time than expected to write your code, and deadlines can't always be shifted. So you will usually end up short-changing the time available to test.

How will you know when you are done?
> In other words, when I say "after you write your program," I assume you have a way to tell when you are done. Without a clearly defined list of test cases that a program must pass, how will you even know you are finished?

You will tend to test for success
> If you write your tests after you implement your program, you are likely to write your test code in such a way as to show success, even when there are problems. No, I am not accusing you of cheating or intellectual dishonesty of any kind. It's just how our brains work.

This idea of thinking about and writing down tests before you write your program is known as *Test-Driven Development* (TDD). Closely associated with Extreme Programming and Agile Software methodology, TDD formalizes this idea of "test first." For detailed information on TDD, see Chapter 3 and check out *www.testdriven.com*.

You can write down your test cases in a word-processing document or a spreadsheet, but if you do, the information won't be connected to your test code or your program. Ideally, you should record test cases within a testing framework or tool. Chapter 3 also contains a list of automated testing tools for PL/SQL.

Don't worry about thinking up all your test cases in advance. That is much too difficult (even, perhaps, impossible) a task. The most important thing to do when trying out this "test first" approach is to *get started*. Testing is always very intimidating, and testing before writing code may simply feel wrong until you get used to it. So pick a relatively simple program and start the process with that. Think of just a few test cases, and then proceed through the workflow. You can always add more tests later on.

Step 4. Build your test code

Build test code before the program? Ah, now we are stepping into truly foreign territory! "Fine," you say:

> I will think about what I want to test before I write my program. I imagine that will help with my implementation work anyway. But actually write the test code? Ridiculous! That takes too long, and I don't really know how to go about it anyway. In any case, why do it now? I don't even *need* that test code until I am done writing my code.

Let me analyze and counter each of these objections.

Objection	Counter-objection
It takes too long.	This is a very valid concern. If you write the test code by hand, you will need days (at least) to complete the task. If, on the other hand, you use a tool to automate the process of writing (generating) your code, it won't take very long at all.
I don't really know how to go about it.	It's good to be honest about such things, isn't it? How do you go about writing a program to automatically test another program? It's not easy stuff. I more or less know how to answer the question because I have built several testing tools and scripts. Most PL/SQL developers, however, will be stumped and frustrated.
I don't even *need* the test code until I am done writing my code.	Yes, this is the way many of us think, and it is so very, fundamentally wrong. You see testing as something that comes *after* writing code. Instead, you should think about how you can integrate testing *into* the development process. With your test code in place at the very start, you can run your tests after each small change or added feature. You will get instant feedback on progress (another feature implemented) or setbacks (something that worked an hour ago is broken now).

No doubt about it: you need help to accomplish this step. The description of testing approaches and tools in Chapter 3 will give you a good start.

Contracts work for the real world; why not software, too?

Match strict input expectations with guaranteed output results.

Problem: What is never discussed is never agreed upon.

Sunita comes late to the weekly team meeting one Friday morning to find Delaware and Lizbeth engaged in a heated discussion over Delaware's new excuse_in_use utility function. Lizbeth says:

> The excuse_in_use Boolean function you wrote sometimes returns null and that makes it a pain to use. I always have to wrap calls to it with NVL and decide—yet again—that NULL=FALSE. Having to worry about null values in computations can really cause trouble in the form of hard-to-catch bugs. Can't excuse_in_use just return TRUE or FALSE, period?

Delaware counters:

> Well, it wouldn't be such a problem if callers like your customer_support package could be counted on not to pass null excuses into the function. But how am I supposed to know what you want when you hand me a null excuse to test? Since we've never discussed it, I figure the best policy for null is to hand out what is handed in, which is to say exactly no information. The program is more robust because it handles more input combinations without failing. It's called defensive programming.

Sunita breaks in to put a stop to the bickering:

> You are both arguing plenty, but communicating very little. Delaware, defensive programming is a fine approach when the potential callers of a module are unknown or otherwise unpredictable, but Lizbeth sits in the cube right next to you! Maybe we should defend less and cooperate more by coming up with some clear agreements about how our code should behave.

They look over Delaware's code, which tracks excuses using a package-private collection indexed by the excuse strings:

```
PACKAGE BODY excuse_tracker
IS
   TYPE used_aat IS TABLE OF BOOLEAN INDEX BY excuse_excuse_t;
   g_excuses_used   used_aat;

   FUNCTION excuse_in_use (excuse_in IN excuse_excuse_t)
     RETURN BOOLEAN
   IS
   BEGIN
      IF excuse_in IS NULL
      THEN
         RETURN null;
      ELSE
         RETURN g_excuses_used.EXISTS (excuse_in);
      END IF;
   END excuse_in_use;

   ...other programs...
END excuse_tracker;
```

Sunita goes on:

> In this case, Lizbeth does not want Delaware's excuse_in_use function to ever return a null value instead of a proper Boolean, and similarly, Delaware does not want Lizbeth's program to call his function with a null value for its input argument. So let's just satisfy both of them by requiring Delaware's function to only return TRUE or FALSE, but only under the obligation that Lizbeth's code does not pass in a null value. In fact, this is a very good rule in general for all Boolean functions, and we should probably always follow it.

Solution: Contracts capture agreements.

"I propose that we make a pact, or contract, with one another that this is how our Boolean functions will always behave," Sunita continues. "If we all agree to and stick by this contract, then there will never be any question what to expect of these functions, nor what is required to use them." The team solemnly swears (with a giggle here and there) to always both require and produce non-null data for Boolean functions. The contract is given a name: {NOT NULL IN, NOT NULL OUT} or NNINNO.

This contract is offered as a best practice in Chapter 8 in the section "Black or white programs don't know from NULL."

Just for kicks, Sunita writes up their agreement as a fancy-looking contract and tapes it to the wall of the meeting room. It's the team's first contract—simple, yet very important. And by taking this first step, they are starting down a path of implementing a powerful coding pattern as a best practice for the whole group.

About Design by Contract. The team doesn't realize it, but Sunita is introducing them to a software engineering paradigm called Design by Contract. The basic idea behind Design by Contract is to express and enforce agreements about software program behavior using the analogy of legal contracts from the domain of human affairs. Each party to a legal contract has both obligations and expected benefits under the contract. In software, the parties to a contract are a given program and its callers. The callers are expected to provide valid inputs to the program whenever they call it; if they do not, they have violated the contract. Similarly, the program is expected to guarantee correct output as long as the inputs are valid; if it does not, it has violated the contract. The program is not even required to execute when inputs are invalid.

In Design by Contract, contract elements are formally expressed as either preconditions or postconditions:

Preconditions
These capture what must be true upon entry to the program. In practice, these are often rules governing the acceptable input parameter values. Preconditions are an obligation of the caller and a benefit to the program, since the program code can count on the preconditions being true. In our example, Delaware's code benefits from the contract agreement that null inputs are not acceptable, since it does not need to specify a special case for null.

Postconditions
These capture what must be true upon exit of the program. They represent the fundamental obligation of the program to compute some well-defined result based on the preconditions having been met. Postconditions are an obligation for the program and a benefit to callers of the program. In our example, Lizbeth's code benefits when excuse_in_use agrees never to return a null value.

For more information about applying the Design by Contract paradigm to PL/SQL programming, see the link from the book's web site.

Enforcing contracts in code. Let's see what enforcing our NNINNO contract might look like in code," says Sunita. She rewrites Delaware's excuse_in_use program using contract-oriented principles:

```
FUNCTION excuse_in_use (excuse_in IN excuse_excuse_t)
  RETURN BOOLEAN
IS
   c_progname CONSTANT progname_t:='EXCUSE_IN_USE';
   l_return BOOLEAN;
BEGIN
   -- check caller obligations
   assert_precondition(condition_in => excuse_in is not null
                      ,progname_in  => c_progname
                      ,msg_in       => 'excuse_in not null');

   -- compute return value
   l_return := g_excuses_used.EXISTS (excuse_in);

   -- check return obligations
   assert_postcondition(condition_in => l_return is not null
                       ,progname_in  => c_progname
                       ,msg_in       => 'l_return not null');
   RETURN l_return;
END excuse_in_use;
```

The team members all look over the code while Sunita explains the purpose of each line:

1. First, we declare a constant self-identification token c_progname that is passed to the contract-enforcing assertion programs. This is an invaluable debugging aid when the ASSERTFAIL exception signals a contract violation, as we'll see later.

2. Next, since the program is a function, it declares a local variable of the return datatype and returns that variable in exactly one place: the very last line of the function. This enables the postcondition to be tested in a single well-defined place (i.e., immediately before the return). See Chapter 8 in the section "One way in, one way out: multiple exits confuse me."

3. The program makes use of two special assertion programs: one for testing preconditions and the other for testing postconditions.

4. The program checks precondition requirements as the first executable instructions of the main body of code. Under the contract, if precondition requirements are not met, then the program should not continue and instead should raise the ASSERTFAIL exception.

5. The program actually computes the return value and assigns it to the local variable reserved for that purpose.

6. Finally, the postcondition is checked immediately prior to the RETURN statement. In our example, this check may seem trivial and therefore unnecessary since we know that EXISTS always returns TRUE or FALSE and never null. However, consider that if a new or alternate implementation of excuse_in_use is someday created, we may want to replace the logic in this program with a call to the new program; at that point, we may not be so certain about whether l_return can be NULL or not.

Sunita continues:

> So, Lizbeth, with this new implementation you don't have to worry about getting NULL back from the function and can dispense with all those ugly NVLs in your code. However, your code must always supply non-NULL excuses to the function, or the contract precondition is violated and it is your code at fault. Let's see what will happen in that case, so you know what to expect if you violate your contract.

To test the contractual obligations in the excuse_tracker package, Sunita has Jasper write this simple "driver" procedure:

```
PROCEDURE try_excuse_in_use (excuse_in IN VARCHAR2)
IS
BEGIN
   IF excuse_tracker.excuse_in_use (excuse_in)
   THEN
      DBMS_OUTPUT.put_line ('Excuse in use: "' || excuse_in || '"');
   ELSE
      DBMS_OUTPUT.put_line ('Excuse not in use: "' || excuse_in || '"');
   END IF;
END try_excuse_in_use;
```

And then they give it a try by running this anonymous block:

```
SQL> SET SERVEROUTPUT ON FORMAT WRAPPED
SQL> BEGIN
  2     try_excuse_in_use ('lame excuse');
  3     try_excuse_in_use (NULL);
  4  END;
  5  /
Excuse not in use: "lame excuse"
BEGIN
*
ERROR at line 1:
ORA-20999: ASSERTFAIL:EXCUSE_TRACKER:EXCUSE_IN_USE:PRE:excuse_in not null
ORA-06512: at "HR.EXCUSE_TRACKER", line 68
ORA-06512: at "HR.EXCUSE_TRACKER", line 95
ORA-06512: at "HR.EXCUSE_TRACKER", line 36
ORA-06512: at "HR.TRY_EXCUSE_IN_USE", line 4
ORA-06512: at line 3
```

Sunita then points out the key aspects of this contracting exercise and the debugging information exposed by the error message sent back to the caller of excuse_tracker.excuse_in_use:

- The ASSERTFAIL exception is reserved for signaling contract violations. Nothing else raises that exception in the application. By definition, contract violations are always bugs. So this exception tells the team unambiguously that there is a bug in the code.
- The contract violation was detected by the excuse_in_use program of the excuse_tracker package. Thus, the assertion routine tells the team exactly where the contract was violated.
- The contract element violated was a precondition and therefore the bug is in the calling code. Thus the assertion routine and the unhandled exception stack tell the team exactly where to look to resolve the problem: line 4 of try_excuse_in_use.
- The specific contract condition violated is that the excuse_in parameter value is required to be non-NULL.

Delaware fusses a bit, concerned about writing all the extra code for precondition and postcondition checks, but Lizbeth counters by reminding him about all the time that will be saved by getting such clear and accurate information about misuse of program units. Sunita beams at the level of communication between her team members, but she doesn't deceive herself that everyone is now 100 percent on board with contract-driven programming. She calls the meeting to a close with a short speech:

> I think we can all agree that our contract helped clear up the ambiguity around (and simplify the code needed to run) this function. I strongly suggest that you apply these ideas to your next several programs, and then let's meet and discuss how it has gone. I'm sure you will run into rough spots and issues; the best way to address them is as a team.

Don't act like a bird: admit weakness and ignorance.

Ask for help (or at least take a break) after 30 minutes on a problem.

Problem: Steven is a hypocritical programmer.

I spend a lot of my time in public talking about best practices. In other words, I stand up in front of other developers and act "holier than thou," offering advice and admonitions along the lines of "Do this, don't do that, and certainly *never* do the other thing."

Occasionally, I am honest enough to point out that I do not always follow all my best practices. And students in my classes are, not infrequently, delighted to point out violations of best practices in my own code as I show it up on the big screen.

Why a Bird?

As the former owner of an African Grey parrot, I have learned quite a bit about the way birds behave, and have been struck by parallels with the ways programmers go about their business. Most telling for me is how sick birds instinctively hide their symptoms. When a bird gets sick, it tries to avoid letting anyone or anything know there is a problem. Why is this? In the wild, sick birds attract the attention of predators (sick birds are easier to catch). The flock maintains its strength by saying "adios" to its weakest members, and so sick birds become lunch for predators.

The parallel to programmers? We don't like to admit that we don't know everything, because we sense that admitting ignorance will diminish our position in the "flock" (development team). So we hide our ignorance, and inevitably push that ignorance (and its associated bugs) into our code.

I do think that lots of my code is at least *reasonably* well written. Sometimes, though, the way that I ignore my own recommendations is so over the top and painful that my hypocrisy is brought to the fore. Along these lines, I feel compelled to make a confession. Back in June 2007, I was in Europe presenting the Quest Code Tester product to developers, DBAs, and managers in Paris, Brussels, and Maidenhead (U.K.). When not in the public eye, I kept myself very busy debugging some of Quest Code Tester's backend code (on which I am the lead developer) as well as working on the second edition of *Oracle PL/SQL Best Practices* for O'Reilly (the book you are now reading).

Now, as I'm sure you all know, debugging code can be a frustrating and time-consuming adventure (even if you take advantage of Toad's great source code debugger). And that brings me to the source of my hypocrisy. On June 13, I sat in my room at the Holiday Inn in Maidenhead from 7 P.M. to midnight putting dents in the desk with my head. My problem? In Quest Code Tester, you can define dynamic test cases based on predefined groups of values or values retrieved via a query from a test data table. That wasn't the problem—in fact, that is a great feature. Unfortunately, the results of these tests (generated at test time) were not rolling up properly when the program being tested raised an unhandled exception. In other words, they were showing success when they should have shown failure, and vice-versa.

No doubt about it: the code that performed the rollup was complicated stuff, made more challenging by my reliance on a three-level, string-indexed, nested collection structure. Those things are not at all easy to debug. My debugging adventure also turned into one of those scenarios in which, as you fix one bug, you realize that the code you thought was working *by design* was actually working *by accident*. That is, bugs that were previously being masked were now exposed by other fixes. Wow, software can be incredibly complex!

So, I would fix one bug and then find others, fix those, and then…it was 10 P.M. and I started to encounter behavior (duplicate result rows with different outcomes) that I simply could not explain. So I struggled for two more hours, eyes tired, back sore, thirsty, and increasingly *angry*, until I gave up and went to bed.

Solution: Give your brain a break, and ask others for help.

I woke up, six hours later, with an idea hopping around excitedly in my head: I could suddenly and very clearly see why I was getting duplicates and where the problem must be occurring in my code. I hurried to my laptop (easy: it was four feet away) and 10 minutes later confirmed my analysis. I fixed that bug, found another, analyzed it, and fixed it. After 30 minutes, my code was working for all known test scenarios.

I sat back in my chair, a little bit stunned—excited, sure, at having found the solution, but also thoroughly disgusted at myself for wasting so much time the night before. How could I have done that? I knew better. But more than that, I regularly *preached* better. What a hypocrite!

So, this is what I learned (or was so painfully reminded of) from my terrible, horrible, no good, very bad* evening with the qu_result_xp package (and other similar experiences):

Apply the Thirty Minute Rule rigorously
> This rule really does work. Do *not* spend hours banging your head against the wall of your code. Ask for help. If your manager has not set up a process or fostered a culture that says it's OK to admit ignorance, you will have to do it yourself. This is especially important if you are (or are seen as) a senior developer on your team. Go to one of your junior team members and ask for help. They will be flattered, their self-esteem will increase, *and* they will help you to solve your problem.

Get help from anyone handy
> If you are stuck and cannot turn to another programmer for help, then ask a *nonprogrammer* for a sympathetic ear. My friend and Quest Code Tester codeveloper, Leonid, told me that he used to ask his grandmother (not known for her programming skills) to listen to him talk about his work. *Externalizing your thoughts*, even to someone ignorant of the content, helps you organize and clarify them.

Take a break
> If you are stuck and alone and cannot turn to another programmer—or any other human being—then STOP! Take a break. Get away from your work. Best alternative: get some exercise. Move your body. Go out for a walk or a run. Jump up and down, stretch, do sit-ups. Let your brain relax and make its

---

* I draw that phrase from my days of reading books to my son, Eli. It's a reference to the book *Alexander and the Terrible, Horrible, No Good, Very Bad Day* by Judith Viorst. If you have small children and are not already familiar with this book, I recommend that you get it.

connections—suddenly, as if by a miracle, that incredible brain of yours will start working on a solution! And when you come back from your break, try talking out loud to yourself, describing the problem. Or take out a piece of paper and write it down. The key thing is to *get it outside of your head*. You will then find it easier to visualize the problem *and* the solution.

Watch out for irrationality

You will know that you are past the point of productive work when you find yourself thinking in less than rational ways. I can still remember back in 1992 when I was building a debugger for SQL*Forms 3 on Oracle's brand-new PC implementation (the first software to use memory above the 640K limit!). I started to get runtime errors, and I discovered that if I added a tab character to the code, the location of the error would change. I sat there for hours trying to find the source of the problem (typing in extra spaces, returns, etc.), when OBVIOUSLY it was a bug down deep in Oracle. PL/SQL does *not* care about whitespace. When you find yourself saying "What my program is doing is impossible and makes no sense," you really should stop and take a break.

Team leaders and development managers have a special responsibility to cultivate an environment in which we are encouraged to admit what we do not know, and to ask for help sooner rather than later. Ignorance isn't a problem unless it is hidden from view. And by asking for help, you also validate the knowledge and experience of others, building the overall self-esteem and confidence of the team.

To be very honest with you, I don't think I am all that great a programmer. I have a quick mind and am good at *communicating* ideas. But I need lots more discipline and patience as I write my code. And I need to apply my (and others') best practices more regularly and thoroughly.

So remember: do as I say, not as I do!

Five heads are better than one.

Review and walk through one another's code; then do automated code reviews.

Problem: Sunita spent six months developing comprehensive coding standards for her group.

Huh? That's a problem? Well, not in and of itself. The problem with what Sunita did is that she produced a rather thick document (50 pages of top-notch ideas and advice), made copies, and distributed it to everyone on the team. She then assumed that the team members would diligently follow the coding standards, so she turned her attention to other pressing matters. Months went by, and Lizbeth, Delaware, and Jasper wrote lots of code in their separate cubicles, pushing hard to meet deadlines.

A few weeks before it is time to deliver the application to users, Sunita finds that she has a couple of days free from the burdens of management tasks (paperwork, for the most part). So she decides to get in touch with the code base, both to refresh her familiarity with PL/SQL and to get a comfort level about the application-specific algorithms.

She opens up a package body and starts reading through the code. As she does so, she finds herself bothered by…something…she can't quite put her finger on it, and then she realizes what it is: this code is not following the standards she defined months before! Names of variables, program comment header blocks, exception handling: none of it looks anything like the standard.

"Well," she thinks, "that package was written by Delaware." (She has always had her doubts about whether *he* would accept her ideas.) "Let's check Lizbeth's code."

So she opens another file and is immediately pleased. Lizbeth's code looks *completely* different from Delaware's. Finally, someone is following the standards! But on closer review, her sunny feelings turn to despair. It's true that Lizbeth's code is noticeably different from Delaware's, but she isn't following the group standard, either! Instead, she has her *own* naming conventions and her own approach to exception handling.

Sunita calls a meeting and asks everyone what the heck is going on. There are lots of downcast eyes and clearing of throats. "Well?" Sunita demands, "What did you do with those coding standards I put together?" It turns out that those 50-page tomes were placed in desk drawers and never looked at again.

Solution: Move beyond documents to a review process that directly engages the development team.

Sunita had the correct idea: it is crucial for everyone on a development team to write code more or less the same way (Chapter 2 offers a number of specific recommendations for what that "same way" should look like). But she was incredibly naïve to think that simply writing a document and circulating it would result in those standards being followed.

The only way to ensure that standards are followed is to review (look at, read, walk through) the code that has been written. Sunita's big mistake was that she hadn't formalized a review process—such a review would have caught problems early in the process.

Code review involves having other developers actually read and review your source code. This review process can take many different forms, including:

The buddy system
> Each programmer is assigned another programmer to be ready at any time to look at his buddy's code and to offer feedback.

Formal code walkthroughs

On a regular basis (and certainly as a "gate" before any program moves to production status), a developer presents or "walks through" her code before a group of programmers.

Pair programming

No one codes alone! Whenever you write software, you do it in pairs, where one person handles the tactical work (thinks about the specific code to be written and does the typing), while the second person takes the strategic role (keeps an eye on the overall architecture, looks out for possible bugs, and generally critiques—always constructively). Pair programming is an integral part of Extreme Programming.

Consistent code review results in dramatic improvements in overall code quality. The architecture of the application tends to be sounder, and the number of bugs in production code goes way down. A further advantage is that expertise on the development team is more broadly and evenly spread, as everyone learns from everyone else.

To make this process work, the development manager or team leader must take the initiative to set up the code review process and must give developers the time (and training) to do it right. Ideally, the most experienced and self-confident developer should go first, to demonstrate that there is nothing wrong with *being* wrong, with making mistakes and having them pointed out.

Code review should not, however, be seen simply (or primarily) as an enforcement mechanism for standards. Code review is an excellent way of sharing knowledge and ideas, as well as strengthening the sense (and reality) of teamwork.

Resources

Use the tools and books listed below to help you set up peer (manual) and automated reviews:

Automated code analysis and review options

Toad and SQL Navigator from Quest Software offer CodeXpert, the most powerful automated process for reviewing code. PL/SQL Developer also provides integrated "lint checking" of some of the most common programming mistakes.

Handbook of Walkthroughs, Inspections, and Technical Reviews (Dorset House)

This book, by Daniel Freedman and Gerald M. Weinberg, is now in its third edition. It uses a question-and-answer format to show you exactly how to implement reviews for all sorts of product and software development.

Extreme Programming Explained (Addison-Wesley)

This first book on Extreme Programming, by Kent Beck, offers many insights into pair programming.

Don't write code that a machine could write for you instead.

Generate code whenever possible.

Problem: Jasper is starting to feel more like a robot than a human being.

Lately, it seems to Jasper that he isn't using a single ounce of creativity in his brain. Instead, he finds himself relying on copy-paste-and-change to write his programs. The latest frustration in this area arises when Sunita announces that she wants him to write functions to return single rows of data from key tables for a given primary key value. He writes this one first:

```
FUNCTION excuse_for (id_in IN mfe_excuses.id%TYPE)
   RETURN mfe_excuses%ROWTYPE
IS
   retval  mfe_excuses%ROWTYPE;
BEGIN
   SELECT * INTO retval
     FROM mfe_excuses
    WHERE id = id_in;
   RETURN retval;
END excuse_for;
```

Then he has to do the same thing for customers, so he copies and pastes, changes the names of the tables, and ends up with this:

```
FUNCTION customer_for (id_in IN mfe_customers.id%TYPE)
   RETURN mfe_customers%ROWTYPE
IS
   retval  mfe_customers%ROWTYPE;
BEGIN
   SELECT * INTO retval
     FROM mfe_customers
    WHERE id = id_in;
   RETURN retval;
END excuse_for;
```

Unfortunately, he now has another 25 tables for which he needs to build these functions. How boring! But he does it, with every fiber of his soul rebelling, and finally he is done.

Then he shows the code to Sunita, who says, "What if the query raises TOO_MANY_ROWS? Don't we want to log that error? It certainly would be good to know about any violations of our primary keys!"

Holding back a scream, Jasper forces himself to nod, writes the exception section, and then does a copy-and-paste 25 more times. And all he can think about as he is doing this is, "What a terrible way to spend my time!"

Solution: If you can recognize a pattern in what you are writing, generate code from that pattern.

Life is short—and way too much of it is consumed by time spent in front of a computer screen, moving digits with varying accuracy over the keyboard. It seems to me that we should be aggressive about finding ways to build our applications with an absolute minimum of time and effort while still producing quality goods. A key component of such a strategy is code generation: rather than write the code yourself, you let some other piece of software write the code for you.

Code generation comes in particularly handy when you have to write code that is repetitive in structure (i.e., it can be expressed generally by a pattern). There is, for example, a clear pattern to the code that Jasper was writing; that's why, in fact, he could "get away with" using copy-and-paste to build the code.

Jasper had the right idea: he got angry with the wasting of his time. Programmers should have a very low tolerance for that sort of thing. Jasper's problem is that he didn't take action to *avoid* the wasting of his time. Let's take a look at what he could have done instead.

When Jasper realized that he was writing the same code over and over again, with minor changes, he should have asked himself, "Which part is changing?" He would then have seen (one would hope) that the table name and the primary key column name were the only *dynamic* parts of the pattern. Everything else stayed the same. From that basic insight, he could then write a program like this genlookup procedure:

```
PROCEDURE genlookup (tab_in IN VARCHAR2, col_in IN VARCHAR2)
IS
BEGIN
   DBMS_OUTPUT.put_line ('CREATE OR REPLACE FUNCTION ' || tab_in
                || '_row_for (' );
   DBMS_OUTPUT.put_line (    '     ' || col_in|| '_in IN ' || tab_in
                || '.' || col_in || '%TYPE)' );
   DBMS_OUTPUT.put_line ('   RETURN ' || tab_in || '%ROWTYPE');
   DBMS_OUTPUT.put_line ('IS');
   DBMS_OUTPUT.put_line ('   l_return ' || tab_in || '%ROWTYPE;');
   DBMS_OUTPUT.put_line ('BEGIN');
   DBMS_OUTPUT.put_line ('   SELECT * INTO l_return FROM ' || tab_in);
   DBMS_OUTPUT.put_line ('    WHERE ' || col_in || ' = ' || col_in ||
                '_in;');
   DBMS_OUTPUT.put_line ('   RETURN l_return;');
   DBMS_OUTPUT.put_line ('EXCEPTION');
   DBMS_OUTPUT.put_line ('   WHEN NO_DATA_FOUND THEN');
   DBMS_OUTPUT.put_line ('      l_return.' || col_in
                || ' := NULL; RETURN l_return;');
   DBMS_OUTPUT.put_line ('   WHEN OTHERS  THEN mfe_error.log_error;');
   DBMS_OUTPUT.put_line ('END ' || tab_in || '_row_for;');
   DBMS_OUTPUT.put_line ('/');
END;
```

Best Practice Housekeeping

Some programming tasks may seem incredibly mundane, but that doesn't mean they aren't also extremely important. For example, when was the last time you backed up your code? Here are two reminders of basic code housekeeping that you should make sure is in place:

Back up regularly

> I hope that your company has instituted automatic, nightly backups of all the code. You should, however, complement this process with your own quick-and-dirty backups throughout the day. Just finished a really hard algorithm? Make a copy onto a flash drive and move it away from your computer!

Use source code control (SCC)

> It's a bit hard to believe, but some of us do not use a source code tool to manage versions of our software. Some Integrated Development Environments (IDEs), like Toad, offer integrated SCC. If not, there are plenty of commercial and free products to help you in this area.

And then he could write a "driver" for this procedure that queries the table and its primary key column from the Oracle data dictionary constraint views, as follows:

```
BEGIN
   FOR l_mfe_table IN (SELECT ccol.table_name, ccol.column_name pkycol_name
                         FROM user_constraints cons, user_cons_columns ccol
                        WHERE cons.owner = ccol.owner
                          AND cons.constraint_name = ccol.constraint_name
                          AND cons.table_name LIKE '%EMP%'
                          AND cons.constraint_type = 'P')
   LOOP
      genlookup (l_mfe_table.table_name, l_mfe_table.pkycol_name);
   END LOOP;
END;
```

Once this code is in place, whenever anyone has an idea for fixing or improving these one-row lookup functions in the future, Jasper will simply run the driver block, and all the code will be regenerated. And if a new table is added, Jasper won't have to do anything except run the script to generate the code.

Now that is a whole lot better than taking a risk with repetitive stress injury (RSI) through copy-and-paste keystrokes! By the way, both of the above blocks of code may be found in the *genlookup.sp* file available on the book's web site.

I am a great believer in identifying patterns in our requirements and tasks, and then generating code to complete those tasks. My beliefs in this area are so passionate, in fact, that I have created a tool specifically to allow me (and you!) to translate abstract patterns into templates and then generate code from those templates. This freeware tool, called the Quest CodeGen Utility, is provided by Quest Software and is available at *www.qcgu.net*. If you are allergic to wasting your time and performing repetitive tasks, you will definitely want to download and check out this product. It comes with hundreds of predefined templates and also allows you to build your own via the tool's Code Generation Markup Language (CGML).

Finally, if you read this section and find yourself thinking, "Gee, I don't see all that many patterns in the code I've been writing," then you may need to strengthen your pattern-recognition skills. An excellent way to get better at recognizing patterns (and have fun while you are doing it) is to play the game of *Set* (*www.setgame.com*).

We need more than brains to write software.

Take care of your "host body": fingers, wrists, back, etc.

Science fiction is an awful lot of fun to read in books and watch in the movies. It's amazing what computers and cyborgs and so on can accomplish when they are not constrained by the economic and technical realities encountered on Planet Earth.

Well, we not only live in the real world, we write software that attempts to mimic within cyberspace a small fraction of that real world. And since the real world is always changing, there is always great pressure on us and our applications to "keep up." That results in great job security, but also tremendous challenges.

One fundamental reality we must keep in mind as we explore best practices for writing software is that our programs are written almost entirely by us, human beings. Sure, we can and should take advantage of the code-generation tools discussed earlier, but for the most part, software development doesn't happen without our sitting in front of a screen and typing. The ramifications of this simple, undeniable fact are far-reaching:

- The software we write and how we go about writing it are affected greatly by the physiology (hard-wiring) of our brains, and the psychology of humans as we interact with one another and our environment.

- Our brains can handle only so much complexity at a time (though we certainly can train our gray matter to juggle larger and larger volumes of data and structures). We need to find ways to organize our activity so that we don't get overwhelmed, confused, and lost.

- We are lucky that we are able to make a living off the product of our brains. Our brains need our host bodies in order to function, so we need to make sure we take care of those hosts. Humans didn't evolve in order to sit in front of a monitor 6, 8, or 10 hours a day.

Here are my top recommendations for taking care of your host body. You can think of these as best practices for *you*, rather than your code:

Drink lots of water

You probably hear this advice a lot. Without a doubt, you will generally be much healthier if you drink more water and less coffee, Coke, and other caffeinated, sugared products. But specifically when it comes to brain work, if you get dehydrated, it's like a car engine without enough oil. Your brain gets sluggish and dull. Here is my concrete suggestion: the next time you come back from a heavy lunch and find yourself nodding off at your desk, do *not* get a cup of coffee. Do *not* refill your cup with soda. Instead, drink down a large glass of water. You will immediately feel more awake, alive, and ready to take on your challenges.

Take lots of breaks, move around, get exercise, and go outside

If your body becomes too sedentary, it will be hard for your brain to stay focused. Plus, if you don't move around, various parts of your body will start to decay and hurt. It's a basic case of "Use it or lose it." Of course, it's hard to think about any sort of vigorous exercise routine if your lower back hurts and your knees are cracking. So start simple: do some sit-ups every day. You can do these without any special equipment, and as your abdomen gets stronger, your back will feel better. You will sit up straighter. You will feel better about yourself. Finally, spend as much time as you can out of doors. Indoor air is usually stale, recycled, and unhealthy. And if you go outside, you might even feel the sun on your face. Small joys!

Make sure your workspace is comfortable and ergonomic

Don't compromise mobility or range of motion for the sake of a few programs. I strongly recommend that you buy an ergonomic keyboard like Microsoft's Natural Keyboard. It will greatly reduce the strain on your wrists; believe me, you will adjust to its different key configuration in a matter of an hour. Make sure that your monitor, chair, and desk are properly aligned so you do not feel stress in your shoulders, neck, back, arms, or hands as you type. Don't rest your hands or wrists directly on hard desk surfaces. I recently discovered the IMAK wrist glove and now use it whenever I am away from my home office. It provides great support and comfort for my wrist.

Writing software is lots of fun, but remember to keep it in perspective: it's not worth sacrificing your physical health to write lots of exciting, cool code. Keep in mind, as well, that tradeoffs of this kind are totally unnecessary.

Is Software Programming Physically Addictive?

If you exercise a lot, then you are familiar with the "endorphin high." Your body releases special chemicals into your bloodstream that make you feel very good, that in essence reward you for the effort you are making to keep your body healthy. And if you stop exercising after having gotten used to that elevated flow of endorphins, you will feel bad.

I think the same thing happens when you write software, specifically when you solve problems in the writing of your software. How else to explain the clearly addictive behavior of programmers—staying up until all hours, eating junk food, and drinking caffeinated beverages, just so we can keep working on that gnarly algorithm and get it sorted out: this is not "normal" behavior!

Here's what I think is going on: look at the world around you, both at the geopolitical and the personal levels. The world is a mess. Wars continue to ravage several continents. Children die in the millions from easily preventable diseases. Racism, homophobia, and sexism cause tremendous pain and suffering. And we (or at least our elected leaders) don't seem to be able to solve these problems. And then there are our personal lives. I hope you are all happy and content, but chances are you have some problems. They're not very easy to sort out and resolve, are they? Life in the real world can be frustrating and depressing.

Now contrast that with cyberspace. It is a "world" entirely of our own making. We write the rules that govern what is possible and impossible, legal and illegal. It is, without doubt, a complex "virtual reality," and growing more complex every day, but still it is a known, deterministic, and closed space.

So, you read the newspaper over breakfast and shake your head at the latest uptick in violence in the Middle East. Then you drive in to work (grinding your teeth at the rush-hour traffic that also seems to have no solution). During the staff meeting, your manager gives you a new assignment: you need to solve a problem, which is framed as needing to write a program that does XYZ. Whatever that XYZ is, you know right from the start that this is a solvable problem, since it is expressed within our closed, artificial universe.

You get to work. After a while, you get your program to compile cleanly. Now, that's an exciting development and it makes you feel good. You test, debug, fix; test, debug, fix…and with each repetition of that cycle, you get closer to your solution. Finally, the moment arrives when you confirm that your program works. You have solved the problem. What a great feeling!

—continued—

I believe that this great feeling is, like any other feeling you perceive, the result of actual changes in brain chemistry. You are getting positive feedback about solving a problem, and that makes you not only want to solve more problems, but also to keep on working (maybe all through the night) to get to that end goal of a working program.

Perhaps one day scientists will set up a study of programmers, attaching electrodes to our skulls and measuring brain activity while we write our code. And then my conjecture can be tested: do we really get "high" from writing code and solving problems?

CHAPTER 2

Real Developers Follow Standards

We software developers are a very privileged bunch. We don't have to work in dangerous environments, and our jobs aren't physically taxing (though carpal tunnel syndrome is always a threat). We are paid to think about things, and then to write down our thoughts in the form of code. This code is then used and maintained by others, sometimes for decades.

Given this situation, I believe we all have a responsibility to write code that can be easily understood and maintained (and, c'mon, let's admit our secret desires, *admired*) by the developers who follow in our footsteps. Look at this way: if you have a child, she might grow up to be a programmer. She might even put in time at one of your previous employers. She might actually end up having to maintain code that you wrote.

The choice is yours: avoid mortifying embarrassment either by never putting your name in your code, or by writing code that you would be proud to show to, share with, and inflict on your own flesh and blood.

Sadly, programmers are also often a fairly arrogant and anarchistic bunch. Part of the reason for this is that those people "out there" (nonprogrammers) tend to labor under the misconception that you have to be really smart to write software. Now, I am sure that all of my readers are really, really intelligent, don't get me wrong. But you don't need to be brilliant to write software. You need to be good at acting as a translator between normal people (users) and machines (computers). You need to be good at thinking *like* a machine, putting together thoughts (commands) in logical sequences that those nonsentient computers can follow.

You know how it is with your own propaganda: after a while, you believe it yourself. And so we programmers have come to think that we are really smart, that no one can teach us anything, that we each individually know the best way to write code, format code, and structure code. The end result is often that even in a small team of developers, the code for an application will be all over the map, with everyone following different naming conventions, different coding formats, and different ways of documenting workarounds.

Tension over coding standards can also arise for a very different reason: developers on a single team are firmly committed to standards, but they are *different standards* adopted from former projects. Once you have a standard that works for you, it is hard to give it up. So at this point, it is important to remind members of a development team that the *consistent application of standards* is more important than the specific standards themselves.

I strongly believe that you don't give up individuality when you adopt standards. Instead, you free yourself to devote more effort to the most interesting and difficult challenges in your application. As my friend John Beresniewicz puts it, "We can only truly master a discipline when the required becomes automatic, allowing us to focus attention on the creative."

Best Practices for Developing and Using Standards

This section describes best practices for using standards in your code and determining ways to enforce the use of standards by your development team.

It's a free country; I don't have to use carriage returns in my code.

Adopt a consistent format that is easy to read and maintain.

Problem: Delaware writes code that no one else can read.

For a while after Sunita took over My Flimsy Excuse's development team, she thought seriously about firing Delaware. The guy was obviously brilliant in so many ways, but some forms of brilliance are best experienced in isolation—or anywhere else but where you are.

For example: Delaware adhered to the most *awful* formatting style Sunita had ever seen. *He refused to use the carriage return key.*[*] He also favored uppercase. As a result, his programs looked like this:

```
CREATE OR REPLACE PACKAGE OVERDUE_PKG IS PROCEDURE SET_DAILY_FINE (FINE_IN
IN NUMBER); FUNCTION DAILY_FINE RETURN NUMBER; FUNCTION DAYS_OVERDUE (ISBN_
IN IN BOOK.ISBN%TYPE)RETURN INTEGER; FUNCTION FINE_AMOUNT (ISBN_IN IN BOOK.
ISBN%TYPE) RETURN INTEGER; END OVERDUE_PKG;
```

Now, it really did seem that Delaware could follow and even maintain his code when it was in this format. He always got the job done. But certainly no one else could bear to lay eyes upon his work. And what would happen when Delaware moved on (assuming that anyone else would have him)?

---

[*] Yes, I know, this sounds simply ridiculous. Well, I didn't make it up! At a presentation I gave at the Oracle PL/SQL Programming 2007 conference (*www.odtugopp.com*), an attendee told me about a person in her group who manifested precisely this pathology.

Solution: Use the built-in functionality of your IDE to automatically format your code.

Rather than fire Delaware, Sunita calls everyone together one afternoon to discuss the merits of a common coding format for the team. Unsurprisingly, all the members of the team have their own personal favorites: Jasper likes to uppercase only PL/SQL keywords; Lizbeth insists on a four-space indentation; and Delaware refuses even to participate. Rather than throw her hands up in frustration, Sunita gathers the best ideas and then spends some time experimenting with the IDE that everyone on the team uses.

Almost immediately, she notices that the tool has its own automatic formatting feature. She checks with the team and soon realizes that no one uses—or even knows about—the feature. Gadzooks! In short order, she tweaks the formatting options to match what she considers to be a reasonable compromise for the team standard. She then issues the following instructions:

- We have automatic formatting available. You can pick whatever style you want for your own use as you develop your code.
- Do not spend any time manually formatting your code! It is a terrible waste of your valuable time.
- Whenever you check your code into source control, you must format it to meet the group standard (here is the options file that will do the trick).
- All code in production applications must follow the group standard that I will determine.

And she also demonstrates the power of her auto-formatter by offering to Delaware a readable version of his program:

```
PACKAGE overdue_pkg
IS
   PROCEDURE set_daily_fine (fine_in IN NUMBER);

   FUNCTION daily_fine
      RETURN NUMBER;

   FUNCTION days_overdue (
      isbn_in IN book.isbn%TYPE)
      RETURN INTEGER;

   FUNCTION fine_amount (isbn_in IN book.isbn%TYPE)
      RETURN INTEGER;
END overdue_pkg;
```

Much better, don't you think?

There is a very good chance that your IDE, unless it is Notepad, offers some degree of automatic formatting. If not, think about switching to a more mature IDE. Here are some options of which I am aware:

Toad for Oracle and SQL Navigator
Both of these tools from Quest Software use the same powerful parsing, analysis, and formatting engine (PL/Formatter).

PL/SQL Developer
This tool offers a more limited, but still quite useful auto-formatter.

Clear SQL
This is a standalone code-formatting utility.

Appendix B contains links to all of these products.

Déjà vu Code

I wrote and enacted a *PL/SQL Coding Standard* at a former client's. After two years there as a consultant, I moved on to other assignments. A year later, I returned to the previous client. I was tasked with maintaining a particular package. Looking at it, I got a strange sense of déjà vu; the code looked like something I would have written, but I could not remember having written it. Since it was laid out according to the prescribed standard, it was easy to locate sections and make the needed changes. I checked the document header to discover who wrote it, which turned out to be another fellow there. I asked him about it, and he said that he simply followed the standard. He liked how so many packages were all consistently organized, making it a breeze to read and maintain them.

—Dan Clamage, Senior Oracle Developer

Too much freedom is a very bad thing.

Adopt consistent naming conventions for subprograms and data structures.

Problem: Jasper's eagerness to help is overwhelmed by his hurry to get it done.

Jasper has always loved public libraries. In a world in which everything seems to be commercialized and privatized, the library stands as a beacon of free knowledge, free speech, and equal access. Jasper visits his local library each week and has gotten to know the head librarian (Marguerite) well. During one of his visits, Marguerite asks him if he can help with their computer system.

To Jasper's delight, the system is based on Oracle and PL/SQL. He agrees to help, and she asks him to build a program to display all the books borrowed on a certain date. He writes this procedure:

```
PROCEDURE showBorrowedBooks (date_borrowed IN DATE)
IS
   date_returned CONSTANT DATE := SYSDATE;
   minDaysBorrowed PLS_NTEGER := 10;

   TYPE bookBorrowed IS RECORD (
      dateBorrowed DATE,
      daysBorrowed PLS_INTEGER,
```

```
        isbn        book.isbn%TYPE,
        dateDue     DATE);

    bb bookBorrowed;

    CURSOR c IS
       SELECT * FROM borrowed_book
        WHERE returned = 'N';
BEGIN
    IF dateborrowed < date_returned
    THEN
       FOR rec IN c
       LOOP
          bb:= rec;

          IF bb.daysBorrowed > minDaysBorrowed
          THEN
             DBMS_OUTPUT.PUT_LINE (bb.isbn);
          END IF;
       END LOOP;
    END IF;
END showBorrowedBooks;
```

Putting aside the issue of what it is supposed to do, this is a very hard program to read! It's formatted nicely enough, but the ways in which Jasper has named and formatted identifiers are inconsistent and downright puzzling; for example:

- Some identifier names use an underscore ("_") as a break between words in the name.
- Other names rely on "camel notation," with the first letter of a new word capitalized. This style is very common in Java, but is quite dangerous in PL/SQL, since PL/SQL is not a case-sensitive language. Most PL/SQL auto-formatters will obliterate camel notation, decreasing readability.
- Even if you use camel notation in your source code for the name of a program, that name will be automatically uppercased in the data dictionary. In other words, you would not find a program named showBorrowedBooks in the data dictionary. Instead, you would find SHOWBORROWEDBOOKS.
- Some names are long and self-descriptive; others, like "bb" and "c," are cryptic.
- The format of the names does not give any clear indication of what an identifier is: is it a variable? A constant? A parameter?

Solution: Rely on naming conventions that are intuitive and easy to apply.

Adopt and promote standard ways to define names of program elements. Choose a level of "formality" of naming conventions based on your needs. If, for example, you have a team of two developers working on a small code base, you can probably get away with naming conventions that don't go far beyond the common-sense guide to "use meaningful names," plus the naming conventions in Table 2-1. If you are building a massive application involving dozens of developers, you probably need to define more comprehensive rules.

Here are some general recommendations for conventions:

Identify the scope of a variable in its name
A global variable can be prefaced with g_ , for example.

Use a prefix or suffix to identify the types of structures being defined
Consider, for example, declarations of TYPEs: of collections, objects, records, REF cursors, etc. A standard approach to declaring such a structure is *<name>*_ t. Types are quite different from variables; you should be able to identify the difference with a glance.

Use a readable format for your names
Since PL/SQL is not case-sensitive, camel notation (as in minBalanceRequired) is probably not a good choice for constructing names. Instead, use separators such as _ (underscore) to improve readability (as in min_balance_required).

Use those precious, maximum 30 characters for an identifier name carefully
You should seek a balance between descriptiveness and verbosity. I follow this guideline: the more obscure, infrequent, or complicated the meaning of an identifier, the more descriptive the name should be.

Group related declarations together
If you declare a record type and then records based on that type, put them together so it is easy to see the relationships.

You will find in Table 2-1 the naming conventions (prefixes and suffixes I place around the "root name," (*<root>*) which describes the content of the element) I use in most of my code—for example, error_code_in or excuse_out. It is a relatively simplistic approach, but that means I can usually remember to apply these rules. If you are interested in a more elaborate framework for constructing identifier names, check out the documents available at my web site at *www.ToadWorld.com/SF*.

Table 2-1. Steven's naming conventions

What I am declaring	Naming convention
IN parameter	*<root>*_in
OUT parameter	*<root>*_out
IN OUT parameter	*<root>*_inout or *<root>*_io
Constant	c_*<root>*
Global package variable	g_*<root>*
Local variable	l_*<root>*
Cursor	*<root>*_cur
Associative array type	*<root>*_aat
Nested table type	*<root>*_nt
VARRAY type	*<root>*_vat
Record type	*<root>*_rt
Object type	*<root>*_ot
Procedure and function name	None. I do not subscribe to a prefix of "p_" for procedure and "f_" for function. It seems to me that the *usage* of these subprograms clearly indicates what they are.

Here's a rewrite of the showBorrowedBooks procedure that reflects a more consistent and sensible approach to naming identifers. I use underscores in names; suffixes on parameters, records, and cursors; and prefixes to show scope ("l_" for local) and type ("c_" for constant). Carefully compare the following item names with those in the previous example:

```
PROCEDURE show_borrowed_books (
   date_borrowed_in IN DATE)
IS
   c_date_returned CONSTANT DATE := SYSDATE;
   l_min_days_borrowed PLS_INTEGER := 10;

   TYPE book_borrowed_rt IS RECORD (
      date_borrowed DATE,
      days_borrowed PLS_INTEGER,
      isbn          book.isbn%TYPE,
      date_due      DATE);

   borrowed_book_rec book_borrowed_rt;

   CURSOR all_borrowed_cur IS
      SELECT date_borrowed, isbn FROM borrowed_book
       WHERE returned = 'N';
BEGIN
   IF date_borrowed_in < c_date_returned
   THEN
      FOR book_rec IN all_borrowed_cur
      LOOP
         borrowed_book_rec := book_rec;

         IF borrowed_book_rec.days_borrowed >
            l_min_days_borrowed
         THEN
            pl (borrowed_book_rec.isbn);
         END IF;
      END LOOP;
   END IF;
END show_borrowed_books;
```

Good names lead to good code.

Name procedures with verb phrases, and functions with noun phrases.

Problem: Badly formed or inaccurate names can greatly reduce usability of programs.

Delaware builds a new package with two subprograms. Here are their headers:

```
PACKAGE misc_stuff
IS
   FUNCTION calculate_totals (...) RETURN NUMBER;
   PROCEDURE favorite_excuses (...);
END misc_stuff;
```

He then writes a block of code using their programs and it goes something like this:

```
BEGIN
    IF misc_stuff.calculate_totals (...) > 10000
    THEN
        misc_stuff.favorite_excuses (...);
    END IF;
END;
```

Putting aside the lack of arguments for the moment, don't you find yourself stumbling over this code as you read it? "If calculate totals is greater than 10,000, then favorite excuses"…huh? We can pretty well assume that the calculate_totals function calculates and returns the total of…something. Yet that is only an assumption. And what's going on with those favorite excuses? Are we displaying them, deleting them, assigning them, or what?

Solution: Construct subprogram names so they reflect both what they are and what they do.

Suppose Delaware had defined the package specification as follows:

```
PACKAGE misc_stuff
IS
    FUNCTION total_excuse_revenue (...) RETURN NUMBER;
    PROCEDURE show_favorite_excuses (...);
END misc_stuff;
```

Then his block of code would look like this:

```
BEGIN
    IF misc_stuff.total_excuse_revenue (...) > 10000
    THEN
        show_favorite_excuses (...);
    END IF;
END;
```

I wouldn't expect you to have any questions about what *this* program is supposed to be doing. The code explains itself.

Delaware achieved this effect by following these guidelines:

A procedure joins together (and runs) a series of logically related executable statements
  The name of the procedure should reflect what those statements do, and should be in the form of a verb phrase, as in *verb_subject*. "favorite_excuses," on the other hand, doesn't really tell anyone what is going on with those excuses.

A function executes one or more statements with the express intent of returning a value
  The name of a function should describe what is being returned and be in the form of a noun phrase, as in *descriptive_noun*. "calculate_totals" tells us that it is calculating totals, but doesn't explain what it is calculating and returning.

The name of the program really must be as specific as possible in describing what it does
  "calculate_totals" neglects to tell us what the totals pertain to.

The following table applies these guidelines to some *bad* names for procedures and functions.

Bad name	What's wrong?	Better name
PROCEDURE total_salary	What is the procedure doing with total salary? Displaying it? Calculating it?	display_total_salary
FUNCTION calculate_total_salary	Well, of course, you're calculating the total salary—and returning it as well.	total_salary
FUNCTION get_total_salary	What else does a function do but *get* and return things? Use of the get_ prefix is (to my way of thinking) unnecessary. The function *usage* in code makes this clear.	total_salary

Many of us are frustrated by Oracle's restriction of 30 characters for the names for all SQL and PL/SQL identifiers. This anarchistic limit certainly causes no end of problems, but John Beresniewicz offers an insight into how this limit can actually help us write better code: "Since procedure names should express the overall purpose or task they perform, the 30-character limit can help us improve modularity of code. After all, you can describe only so much activity within 30 characters."

Put your checklists into your code.

Define templates to foster standardization in package and program structure.

Problem: Checklists on paper rarely translate into changes in the way we write our code.

When Lizbeth first arrived at My Flimsy Excuse, the management team realized that she was the most experienced developer on board. So they asked her to develop some standards. Well, Lizbeth did more than that! She came up with a series of simple, easy-to-read checklists that would help the developers write high-quality code.

Lizbeth delivered her materials to management, complete with instructions on how and when they should be applied. They made lots of copies and distributed them to all of the developers. A few weeks later, when Lizbeth's development team held its monthly code review, Lizbeth was shocked to see that none of her checklists seem to have been followed. She asked around and found that everyone liked her checklists, but after reading them, they put them into their desk drawers, more or less forgot the ideas in the checklists, and went on coding as they had before.

Solution: Make your checklists *active* and directly involved in development.

Standards are a great thing, but standards that are available only in the form of a document are almost never followed. Who can remember what the document suggests? Who has time to go back and look at it?

Well, Lizbeth is a stubborn human being, so she doesn't give up right away. Instead, she realizes that to get a programmer to follow a standard, she needs to:

- Make it easier to follow the standard than to *not* follow it (who can argue with that?).
- Not tell anyone that they are following a standard (thus avoiding that ingrained, anarchistic rejection).

Lizbeth decides to take another approach. She has been using Toad for Oracle, and she remembers reading about the product's Code Templates feature. So she builds some templates that *incorporate* a number of items on her checklist, such as:

- Isolate initialization and cleanup code for packages and subprograms in their own nested blocks.
- Make sure to execute cleanup in the execution *and* exception sections.
- Make sure that all exception handlers rely on the predefined error API.
- Use a standard header comment block to describe the program.
- Use END labels to clearly identify what is ending.

 In Toad 9, it can be something of a challenge to find the code templates, so I thought I would summarize the steps here:

1. Open an edit window.
2. Right-click and choose "Editing options."
3. In the lower-right quadrant of the Options window, you will see the Languages box. Make sure that PL/SQL is the selected language and then press the Edit button.
4. Click on the Code Templates tab, and you are ready to add/change your own templates.

See? Nothing to it!

Here is the template Lizbeth created for a "generic" procedure:

```
PROCEDURE procedure_name
/*
| My Flimsy Excuse, Inc. Copyright 2007
|    All rights reserved.
| File name:
| Overview:
| Author(s):
|
| Modification History:
|   Date       Who       What
*/
```

```
IS
   PROCEDURE initialize IS
   BEGIN
      topdown.tbc('initialize');
   END initialize;

   PROCEDURE cleanup IS
   BEGIN
      topdown.tbc('cleanup');
   END cleanup;
BEGIN
   initialize;
   /*
   Main body of program
   */
   cleanup;
EXCEPTION
   WHEN OTHERS
   THEN
      /* Don't forget to clean up here, too! */
      cleanup;

      /* Standard error logging mechanism */
      q$error_manager.raise_error (
         error_code_in        => SQLCODE
       , name1_in             => 'NAME1'
       , value1_in            => 'VALUE'
                     );
END procedure_name;
```

The topdown.tbc procedure indicates that to program is still "to be completed." (This package is described in the upcoming "Resources" section.)

Of course, Lizbeth still faces the challenge of getting these templates installed on the network so everyone can use them, and of making developers aware of them. Once her co-developers realize how much time they can save by using the templates, though, utilization skyrockets and—without even being aware of it—everyone starts following the standards!

Resources

There are two templates available on this book's web site:

stdpkg_format.sql
> Standard header and format for a package, containing the standard procedure block shown above.

workaround_comment.sql
> Standard comment block to be used to explain a workaround that is written into a program.

topdown.zip
> This ZIP file contains the topdown package, which will help you write highly modular code (explained in detail in Chapter 8) and also mark subprograms as to-be-completed by calling the topdown.tbc procedure.

You will undoubtedly be able to come up with many other useful templates that are specific to your application and your standards.

One final point regarding program headers: some developers like to use highly structured comment blocks, so that the contents can be "mined" for information and reporting. Here is an example of such a header, using XML to formalize the contents:

```
/*
<VERSION>1.0.5</VERSION>
<FILENAME>stdhdr.pkg</FILENAME>
<AUTHOR>Steven Feuerstein</AUTHOR>
<SUMMARY>API to standard headers in code</SUMMARY>
<COPYRIGHT>Steven Feuerstein, 2000</COPYRIGHT>
*/
```

If you would like to use this type of header, check out the *stdpkg.pkg* script, which offers a prototype "standard header" package that *generates* a standard header (with an XML-style format) and offers programs to query such headers from stored code.

Who needs comments? My code is self-documenting!

Comment tersely with value-added information.

Problem: One person's clarity is another person's bewilderment.

Jasper is having a good time! He has just learned about collections, collections of records, and collections of collections, and he is enjoying himself tremendously using these complex data structures. He is deep into his program, fully conceptualizing the structures—what they mean, how they relate. And while he is in "the zone," he writes code like this without giving it a second thought:

```
IF master_list(l_curr_index).properties_flag.field1 = 'N' THEN
```

And at that moment, he understands exactly what it means. A few months later, however, a user reports a bug in the application, and it is traced back to the program containing this line of code. Jasper is on holiday, so Lizbeth is assigned the job of fixing this bug.

When she looks at the code, she gets really angry. What does it mean? How is she supposed to have *any* idea how to fix the program when she can't even figure out what is going on? Well, there is nothing to do but push through her frustration. But she sends off a somewhat nasty note to Jasper telling him, "You should put in some comments if you are going to write such cryptic stuff, Jasper!"

Jasper comes back to work and is surprised by the email. He remembers with joy the clarity of the moment when he wrote that code. What was hard to understand? To his utter dismay, however, when he opens up the file and looks at the code himself, he realized that even *he* can't understand the intent of that line of code...how embarrassing!

Solution: Sometimes you really do need to add comments.

Well, Jasper knows he has lots to learn, and he has clearly made a mistake here. A comment is needed. And so he changes the code to this:

```
/* If the first field of the properties record is N... */
IF master_list(l_curr_index).properties_flag.field1 = 'N' THEN
```

Unfortunately, when he shows this to Lizbeth, she gets even *more* irritated. "Jasper, this doesn't help. It doesn't tell me anything beyond what the code already says!" Jasper sighs, "So I should *explain* what my code is doing, right? OK, how about this?"

```
/* If the customer is not eligible for a discount... */
IF master_list(l_curr_index).properties_flag.field1 = 'N' THEN
```

Lizbeth exclaims:

> Much better! That would have helped me tremendously last week, but it's never too late to improve one's code. Of course, there are still some problems. For one thing you've got that hardcoded "N" sitting there. Also, frankly, while it's nice to provide the comment, it would be even *nicer* to write your code so that it truly *is* self-documenting.

"For example," continues Lizbeth, taking control of Jasper's keyboard, "rather than expose all that very low-level structural code, why not create a function whose name describes the activity and whose body contains the complicated logic?"

```
/* If the customer is not eligible for a discount... */
IF customer_not_eligibility (l_curr_index) = 'N' THEN
```

"Now we don't really need the comment," points out Jasper, getting into the swing of things, "Hey, and we could even avoid the hardcoded 'N' by making the function a Boolean that returns TRUE or FALSE."

```
IF customer_not_eligible (l_curr_index) THEN
```

Jasper is very pleased with himself. Not only has he written some really cool code, but now it's even possible to understand that code!

Wait a minute, though! Does this mean that, in fact, you don't really ever *need* to put comments in your code? Well, certainly, if you can write code that speaks for itself without additional comments, that is ideal. There are, however, some scenarios in which comments really are required; these include:

Program headers
> An example is given in the previous best practice. A standard header makes it easy for a person to get a basic orientation to what the program is supposed to do. In addition, the modification history for a program is critical.

Special steps
> These include explanations of workarounds, patches, operating system dependencies, and other "exceptional" circumstances. If you have to take special steps when you are writing your code, you should include an explanation or "tag" to point out the special nature of that code.

Complex or opaque logic

Let's face it, lots of what we write really is quite complicated. When you are implementing a very challenging algorithm, you should include a comment offering insights to everyone coming along later (including yourself!) so that they are not totally baffled by what you have done.

To be completed

Sometimes we only partially complete a program, and then have to break off and work on something else. How can we be sure to remember to go back and finish later (this is especially a problem if the incomplete program actually *compiles*)? Leave yourself a note via a comment, like /* TO DO */, or a call to a program like topdown.tbc.

CHAPTER 3

Life After Compilation

It's nothing short of amazing how excited we programmers can get when our newly built program simply *compiles* for the first time. What a great achievement! It makes us feel as if we're almost done implementing that program.

Well, sure, a clean compile is an important milestone (one we are sure to experience again and again, as we apply fixes to our code). But it is also just the beginning of a long journey that will someday lead to our program being placed into *production*, which is sort of like being voted into the Hall of Fame. Real users will now be using our code. We rock!

You've probably heard sayings about how the journey is more important than the destination. That's sort of true with software, but also false. The only reason to embark on the journey is to produce that production-ready piece of code that normal human beings will use (after all, if you write a program and no one ever runs that program, does the program really exist?).

The journey from a clean compile to a fully tested and optimized program is important—don't get me wrong. If you follow the wrong path, you will never get to your destination. And if you take lots of shortcuts on the journey, the end point (the completed program) will be so deeply flawed that it will be rejected or, perhaps worse, *detested* by your users.

This chapter looks at several key phases in the journey from compilation to production. In particular, I focus on several different activities that every programmer engages in, to widely varying extents, so he or she can reach that golden moment: testing, tracing (also known as *instrumentation*), and debugging. Another key aspect of post-compilation activity is *reviewing code*, which I discuss in Chapter 1.

Testing, Tracing, and Debugging

Before diving into the details, let's explore some high-level thoughts concerning the different terms related to identifying and fixing bugs in your code:

Testing

> Test your code to identify bugs that occur under a certain set of circumstances (a "test case" with specific inputs to arguments in the program).

Tracing

> Turn on tracing to obtain what is usually a substantial amount of "raw data" about what the program did as it ran.

Debugging

> Use your debugger to isolate the specific lines of code that caused the bug (and that correspond to the flow indicated by the trace data).

Then use your Integrated Development Environment (IDE) to fix the bug, and start the cycle all over again!

Testing

When you test a program, you run test code that exercises the program (usually, but not always, to verify the functionality of the program—in other words, does it do X?). That test code then tells you whether or not the test succeeded. Alternatively, you will have to manually go through the results of the test code and deduce for yourself whether it worked. Generally, the more you can automate the testing process the better. Automation saves you time, and most programmers are rarely able to "set aside" much time for testing.

A test identifies a problem in your code, but it usually doesn't give you a whole lot more information than that ("You passed in 16 and should have gotten back 12; instead, you got 10."). You then need to figure out which lines of code are causing that problem. Both tracing and debugging can help you do that.

Tracing

When you trace execution of your program, you run that program and as it is running, you record or build a trace of information about what is happening *inside* the program.

In Oracle PL/SQL, the most common (and also the crudest) type of tracing is a call to the DBMS_OUTPUT.PUT_LINE procedure, which sends information to the screen after the program has finished running. A more elaborate built-in tracing mechanism is the DBMS_APPLICATION_INFO package.

It is not at all rare to come across PL/SQL applications that are full of (littered with?) calls to DBMS_OUTPUT.PUT_LINE. I generally avoid ever making a direct call to this built-in. For example, in the Quest Code Tester backend, I use a tracing utility, adapted from the Quest CodeGen Utility qd_runtime package, to allow me to flexibly turn tracing on and off, and write information to the qu_log table.

From there, I can extract the data to display on the screen, fill up a file, and so on. Here is a simple example from the Quest Code Tester backend:

```
IF qu_runtime.trace_enabled
THEN
    qu_runtime.trace ('get_attribute_ex datatype guid'
                      , ret_attr.test_element.data_type_guid
                      );
END IF;
```

Notice that I call the trace_enabled function to determine whether tracing is on before I call the trace subprogram. qu_runtime.trace will, itself, check whether tracing is enabled, but by that time it will also have evaluated the arguments. To achieve the lowest possible runtime overhead, I call trace_enabled, which simply checks the value of a Boolean flag.

Conditional compilation (CC), a feature added to PL/SQL in Oracle Database 10g Release 2, can come in very handy with tracing, because you can use CC to automatically compile the trace logic out of your programs when you don't want it showing up and possibly slowing down the application.

Now, between the "data" you get from testing and tracing, you are ready to figure out what you did wrong in your program and fix it.

Debugging

Debugging is not the same thing as tracing, and it definitely should *not* be confused with testing. You will generally start a debugging session after your tests have identified a bug. You might have also turned on tracing to get a "dump" of information about the overall flow of the application leading up to the bug.

With this "raw data" (specific test-case failure information and trace data), you then need to find the specific lines of code that are causing the bug, and also figure out how to change those lines of code to fix the bug.

Given the maturity of the PL/SQL IDE market, most serious editors now include a visual source code debugger. For example, in Toad for Oracle, you click in the "gutter" of the editor next to the line on which you want execution to "break" or pause. You start up your program and it runs to the breakpoint. You can then examine the values of variables, change values (in some debuggers), and then step through the code, line by line, examining the program flow and how data structures are affected.

PL/SQL source code debuggers are incredibly useful, and some are very powerful, flexible implementations. Make them a part of your toolset when searching out the causes of bugs in your code!

Best Practices for Testing, Tracing, and Debugging

In the following sections, you will find descriptions of the best practices that I recommend you follow after your programs compile. I discuss both processes and tools for testing, tracing, and debugging.

Thanks, but no thanks, to DBMS_OUTPUT.PUT_LINE!

Avoid using the DBMS_OUTPUT.PUT_LINE procedure directly.

Problem: DBMS_OUTPUT.PUT_LINE is inadequate for tracing.

As I noted earlier, DBMS_OUTPUT.PUT_LINE is the most common tracing mechanism employed by PL/SQL developers—and it is one of the worst from which you can choose (or make yourself).

I am very glad that Oracle provided DBMS_OUTPUT in version 2 of PL/SQL. Before that, it was difficult to debug code, because there was no easy way to trace program execution to the screen. However, the implementation of DBMS_OUTPUT leaves much to be desired. Here are my complaints:

It's a productivity disaster
You have to type 20 characters (and a typo or two) just to ask PL/SQL to show you something. Hey, what can I say? Life is short and every character counts.

The overloading is inadequate
You can pass only single strings, dates, or numbers. You can't pass it a Boolean value, nor can you pass it multiple values to be displayed (without doing the concatenation yourself).

The string length is limited
Prior to Oracle Database 10g Release 2, if you try to display a string with more than 255 characters, you get one of two errors: ORA-20000 (a.k.a. ORU-10028 line length overflow) or ORA-06502 (numeric or value error). I don't know about yours, but a whole lot of my strings are longer than 255 bytes.

The number of lines is limited
For releases before Oracle Database 10g Release 2, your program can display a maximum of 1 million lines—and it can be lots less if you forget to specify a high number in your SET SERVEROUTPUT command in SQL*Plus (resulting in an out-of-buffer error). Starting with Oracle Database 10g Release 2, you can now request that the buffer size be unlimited.

There is no incremental feedback
You don't see anything on your screen until your PL/SQL program has finished executing—whether that takes five minutes or five hours.

Solution: Build a layer of code over DBMS_OUTPUT.PUT_LINE.

When you are faced with a utility such as DBMS_OUTPUT that is simultaneously necessary and faulty, you should say out loud (it will make you feel better):

I am fed up, and I am not going to take it anymore!

Specifically, set a rule that you will never call DBMS_OUTPUT.PUT_LINE directly but instead build (or use) a layer of code over DBMS_OUTPUT.PUT_LINE that corrects most, if not all, of the previously listed problems.

You can take a number of different approaches to encapsulating and improving upon DBMS_OUTPUT.PUT_LINE. In the next section, I reference files containing implementations for each of these approaches; all are available on the book's web site.

Display procedures

You can use one simple procedure to display strings, dates, and numbers, and a second procedure to display Boolean values—taking care of problems 1, 2 (partly), and 3 above. The *pl.sp* and *bpl.sp* files offer this capability.

Package replacement

I provide a package replacement for DBMS_OUTPUT that offers a variety of overloadings of datatypes for display, such as a Boolean, a string and a Boolean, two numbers, etc. This implementation takes care of problems 1–4 above (you can avoid buffer overflow problems when a small buffer size has been set). My favorite replacement is the "p" package. You type just three characters, "p.l", to ask Oracle to display information to the screen. Check out the *p.pks* and *p.pkb* files.

General trace package

A more general trace package hides DBMS_OUTPUT, but also allows the user to redirect the "target" of the output. If, for example, you know that you will be generating 5 MB of information, you might want to send output to a file. If your program runs for two hours, you might want to send output to a data-base pipe, so you can "watch" from another session. The *watch.pkg* file contains such a generalized trace utility that can write output to the screen, a file, a table, or a pipe.

q$error_manager package

Another very flexible tracing option is the q$error_manager.trace program that comes with the freeware Quest Error Manager, available at *www.ToadWorld.com*.

Assume the worst, and you will never be disappointed.

Instrument your code to trace execution.

Problem: We live in the moment, and don't think about what it will take to maintain our code.

For the past few years, Sunita has overseen the development of an application made up of hundreds of tables and even more packages. It has grown like a rather ugly pearl, with layer upon layer of new code, patches to existing code, etc. Of course, almost all of this structure is hidden from user view. A user can simply type a value into a field and press the Submit button; a second later, some information is displayed on the screen. But that field is like the tip of an iceberg floating above the water line. By pressing Submit, the user has actually triggered the execution of thousands of lines of code, performing all sorts of really complicated activities.

And today, a user typed in something new and different, pressed Submit, and received an unhandled exception. She calls Support; Support notifies Sunita; then Sunita asks Lizbeth to track down the source of the problem. It is a new one, and they really have no idea why or where it is occurring. Lizbeth then takes these steps:

1. She analyzes the code to determine which programs are being called.
2. She compiles those programs in debug mode.
3. She runs the code (emulating user input) and uses the source code debugger to step through the application line by line to identify the problem.

And four hours later, there she is: still stepping through the code line by line. Now, Lizbeth is a disciplined and determined programmer, so she shows no signs of weariness, but it sure is taking a lot longer to track down the problem than Sunita had originally thought. Why is this taking so long?

General Solution: Build instrumentation (tracing) into your application from the start.

The problem is that Lizbeth is relying on the wrong technique (debugging) to track down the source of the issue, or she has started that debugging process too early.

Just about any substantial production application will execute thousands and thousands of lines of code. An interactive debugger that lets you set breakpoints and step through code is a fantastic tool (and is discussed later in this chapter). Debuggers pretty much assume, however, that you have localized the source of your problem and are now ready to zoom in. Since Lizbeth is starting from scratch in her analysis, she finds herself moving step by step through all of that code, which is very tedious and unproductive.

A better general solution at this stage of bug analysis is to rely on *tracing*. With tracing, you simply set a flag that turns it on. Then you run your application just as a user would (that is, you do not take it step by step), and it generates oodles of trace information. Now you have lots of data that will (I hope) help you narrow down your search for the bug's cause. Then you can switch to debug mode: set a breakpoint at the beginning of the call stack in which the bug surfaces, and step *from there*.

Assuming that you see the value of tracing as a complement and a "raw data feed" to your debugging session, the next questions you then ask are:

• Where should you put trace calls?
• How should you implement tracing?

I suggest that you add tracing as follows:

On startup of a subprogram
    Call trace to register the values of parameters passed to the program, as well as any other "state" you wish to record.

When an error occurs
    You may want to supplement error information with additional trace data.

Before and after key computational steps
    These are the parts of your code where most errors will occur.

As for the implementation of your trace mechanism, follow these guidelines:

Don't use DBMS_OUTPUT.PUT_LINE as your primary tracing mechanism
This is explained in the previous best practice.

Use conditional compilation (CC) if running Oracle 10g Database Release 2 or higher
Conditional compilation allows you to conditionally include or exclude tracing information based on a conditional compilation flag that is set outside of the program itself.

Consider using DBMS_APPLICATION_INFO
This is a built-in package that sends trace information to the V$SESSION, V$SESSION_LONGOPS, and V$SQL views. Check out the Oracle documentation for lots of details on this package.

Build your own trace facility
You can also use one of my packages, referenced in the previous best practice. Doing so will give you lots more flexibility than DBMS_OUTPUT—for example, allowing you to write to a file, a table, or a pipe.

Specific Solution 1: Embed trace calls in Boolean expressions to minimize overhead.

Whether you use DBMS_OUTPUT.PUT_LINE or some other program to do tracing, you may also want to consider adding an "is tracing enabled?" function, and then call your tracing program only if tracing is, indeed, enabled.

Let's use the qd_runtime tracing API to demonstrate why embedding trace calls can be helpful. Suppose that I need to trace the value returned by the big_calc function. I can call qd_runtime.trace as follows:

```
BEGIN
    qd_runtime.trace ('BIG_CALC', big_calc (arg1, arg2));

    l_calc_result := big_calc (arg1, arg2);
```

The first argument is the context and the second is the value passed to the trace repository.

That all looks fine, except that big_calc normally requires at least 10 seconds to complete its calculations. Even if tracing is disabled, big_calc will be called twice, doubling the elapsed time of these lines of code. I certainly don't want that to happen when the code is running in production.

So, I usually write my trace code as follows:

```
BEGIN
    IF qd_runtime.trace_enabled ( )
    THEN
        qd_runtime.trace ('BIG_CALC', big_calc (arg1, arg2));
    END IF;

    l_calc_result := big_calc (arg1, arg2);
```

Now I will incur that additional overhead only when I have explicitly turned on tracing.

Alternatively, in Oracle 10g Database Release 2 and higher, you can use conditional compilation (in a sense, a "meta-Boolean" expression) to include or remove tracing logic from your code. Here is a simple example:

```
PROCEDURE my_procedure IS
BEGIN
   $IF $$app_tracing_enabled
   $THEN
      qd_runtime.trace ('BIG_CALC', big_calc (arg1, arg2));
   $END

   l_calc_result := big_calc (arg1, arg2);
```

When I am in test mode and need to see the tracing, I compile my program unit as follows:

```
ALTER SESSION SET PLSQL_CCFLAGS = 'app_tracing_enabled:true'
/
ALTER PROCEDURE my_procedure COMPILE
/
```

And then when the program is run, the call to the trace function will be present and executed. The downside to this approach is that you need to recompile the program unit, which may not be advisable with a running application in production.

Specific Solution 2: Include standardized modules in packages to dump package state when errors occur.

When an error occurs in one of your PL/SQL blocks, it's often useful to determine the values of persistent package variables at the time of the failure. One way to obtain this information is to write a "dump" procedure in each of your packages. This dump procedure displays or records the contents of any relevant variables or data structures—whatever you determine is of value inside that package. You can then feed this information to an error handler, to provide as much information as possible to the person debugging your code.

Providing such dump procedures can dramatically reduce the time spent inserting debug messages only to remove them later, and it can also record problems that appear intermittently and are hard to reproduce.

This approach obviously relies on conforming to standards established in advance, so that method names and stack formats can be interpreted, but all of these details can be hidden from view in a package, such as the error_pkg package included in the *callstack.sql* file on the book's web site. This package (provided by Dwayne King, ace reviewer and PL/SQL developer) keeps track of the call stack by recording in a PL/SQL table each piece of code as it "announces" itself. It then uses that stack to determine which dump methods need to be called when an error occurs.

Unfortunately, there is no reliable (and supported) way right now to easily determine which packages "have state" even if they aren't in the call stack, but this may be possible in the future. Another straightforward exercise is to extend this package to write to a logfile or pipe instead of just using the standard DBMS_OUTPUT package.

The demo_pkg file shown here, also defined in the *callstack.sql* script, demonstrates this "dumping process" by including a procedure named instantiate_error_context in the specification:

```
CREATE OR REPLACE PACKAGE demo_pkg
IS
     PROCEDURE proc1;

     PROCEDURE instantiate_error_context;
END;
```

The proc1 procedure sets the module name in the stack, assigns a value to a variable, and then calls proc2, which also "announces" itself and modifies a package variable. It then, however, raises an exception:

```
PROCEDURE demo_pkg.proc1 IS
BEGIN
     --announce entry into this module
     error_pkg.set_module_name ('demo_pkg.proc1');

     -- Application processing here.
     application.field_1 := 'test string';

     proc2;

     error_pkg.remove_module_name;
EXCEPTION
     WHEN OTHERS
     THEN
          error_pkg.set_err_msg ('DATO23');
          error_pkg.raise_error ('Failed Operation');
END;
```

The instantiation procedure (invoked by the error_pkg.log_error subprogram) passes the values of the package data (the package state) to the error package:

```
PROCEDURE demo_pkg.instantiate_error_context
IS
BEGIN
     error_pkg.add_context (
          'DEMO_PKG', 'Field #1', application.field_1);
     error_pkg.add_context (
          'DEMO_PKG', 'Field #2', application.field_2);
     error_pkg.add_context (
          'DEMO_PKG', 'Field #3', application.field_3);
END;
```

When you run demo_pkg.proc1, you see the following output:

```
SQL> EXEC demo_pkg.proc1
Adding demo_pkg.proc1 to stack
Adding demo_pkg.proc2 to stack
Error Log Time:          13:15:33
Call Stack:              demo_pkg.proc1 --> demo_pkg.proc2
Comments:                Failed Operation
CFRS Error No:           DAT027
Oracle Error:            ORA-01403: no data found
----------DEMO_PKG---------------------
Field #1:                test string
Field #2:                -37
Field #3:                NULL
```

 The error_pkg used in the example and found in the *callstack.sql* file requires you to explicitly list the packages that contain instantiate_error_context procedures. An improved implementation is to rely on dynamic SQL (either DBMS_SQL or native dynamic SQL) to automatically construct the program call and execute it.

Specific Solution 3: Build trace "windows" into your packages using standardized programs.

On the one hand, it's very helpful to use packages to hide complexity. On the other hand, when you are trying to figure out why a package is not behaving as expected, it can be very helpful to peek inside it and watch what's going on.

You can easily build a "read-only" window into a package. Programmers can open the window when and if they want to, watch what the package is doing (or at least what the author of the package claims the package is doing), and then shut the window when that information isn't needed.

To build a window, you will need to:

- Add tracing code inside the package body.
- Supply an on-off switch in the specification so that users can open and close the window.

For example, my overdue_pkg (overdue fines) package allows a programmer to set the daily fine rate, as shown by this partial package body:

```
CREATE OR REPLACE PACKAGE BODY overdue_pkg
IS
   g_daily_fine NUMBER := .10;

   PROCEDURE set_daily_fine (fine_in IN NUMBER) IS
   BEGIN
      g_daily_fine :=
         GREATEST (LEAST (fine_in, .25), .05);
   END set_daily_fine;
   ...
```

I now want to add a trace to this package so that a programmer using overdue_pkg can see what the daily fine is being set to when her application runs. First, I add an on-off switch to the package specification and body:

```
CREATE OR REPLACE PACKAGE overdue_pkg
IS
   ... other elements in package

   PROCEDURE trc;
   PROCEDURE notrc;
   FUNCTION tracing RETURN BOOLEAN;
END overdue_pkg;
```

Then, I add my trace to the set_daily_fine procedure:

```
PROCEDURE set_daily_fine (fine_in IN NUMBER)
IS
BEGIN
   IF tracing
   THEN
      watch.action ('set_daily_fine', fine_in);
   END IF;

   g_daily_fine :=
      GREATEST (LEAST (fine_in, .25), .05);
END set_daily_fine;
```

Rather than call DBMS_OUTPUT.PUT_LINE or even my enhanced pl procedure, notice that I call watch.action. The watch package is a more robust tracing mechanism. Among other features, it allows you to direct output to a database pipe, bypassing the buffer limitations of DBMS_OUTPUT.

Now, when I want to watch what is happening inside my overdue package, I simply turn on tracing for my session before I run my application code:

```
SQL> EXEC overdue_pkg.trc
SQL> EXEC library_test
```

 As noted earlier in this section, you can also consider using Oracle Database 10g Release 2's conditional compilation feature for your tracing. The only drawback is that you will have to recompile your package before the tracing can be enabled.

Users really don't want to be programmers.

Test your programs thoroughly, and as automatically as possible.

"Of course," you say. "Users certainly don't want to be programmers. That's a silly title for a best practice."

Ah, but I believe that most of us do actually (though subconsciously) treat our users as if they were programmers. Why do I say this? Because....

- A fundamental task of a programmer is to test the individual programs that he writes. These are called *unit tests*.
- Most programmers do not test individual units, and barely test higher-level units, before they are integrated into the application as a whole.
- Most applications are, therefore, handed off to users for acceptance testing, with lots of untested program units.
- The end result: users find bugs that should have been found through unit testing, which means they are, in effect, performing unit tests, and that means they are, in effect, acting as programmers.

…which we all agree they don't want to do, so maybe we shouldn't force them to!

Problem: Sunita's team is dragged down off its pedestal of semi-godliness.

When Sunita first joined My Flimsy Excuse, the users all but bowed to her as they passed in the hallways. Sunita was a programmer, a wizard who made computers dance to her tune and made it possible for MFE to sell its products. Five years later, Sunita has noticed that she is more likely to get a surly glance and an abrupt nod, rather than a bright, thankful smile.

What's changed in that time? Well, her team has released 20 production applications. Surely that should be cause for celebration in the Land of the Users. So much functionality! So many screens!

And so many bugs.

As with so many other development organizations, Sunita's group has always worked under extremely tight deadlines and inadequate headcount. They struggled to implement all the functionality requested by the users. When it came to testing, they did what they could, but it was all done by hand and was very incomplete. They knew this, but what could they do?

What they did is what we all do: they gave the application to the users for "acceptance testing" and kept their fingers crossed in the hope that the users would not find *too* many bugs.

Fat chance. So the users find tons of bugs and after a while they find themselves muttering, "Those programmers aren't so smart, and they don't even seem to be very good at their jobs." And that's when users stop treating programmers like wizards, like special people.

All because we expected *them* to act like programmers. Not a good idea.

General Solution: Don't make testing an option, and don't just "try" a few things.

Sunita realizes that something has to be done when, during budget meetings, the Queen of All Users raises concerns about the amount of money to be allocated to IT in the next fiscal year. This has never happened before. Sunita is determined to change the users' perspective on her team. She spends some time exploring the literature on unit testing and is shocked to find that all the experts agree that for every line of code you need to test, you will need to write 10 or more lines of test code.

An order of magnitude more code just to test your code? Impossible! Her team can barely find time to finish writing the actual programs. Rather than despair, however, she realizes that what is needed is a way to *automate* testing, most especially automation of the writing of the test code. After a few hours of searching the Internet, she comes up with the following options for automated testing in the world of PL/SQL:

Quest Code Tester for Oracle
> This tool offers the highest level of test automation in the Oracle tools market. Describe the tests you need to run in a graphical interface, and Quest Code Tester then generates the test code and runs the test, automatically reporting all the results. For more information on this tool, see the upcoming section, "Specific Solution 2: A brief introduction to Quest Code Tester for Oracle." For details, go to *http://www.quest.com/code-tester-for-oracle*.
>
> Disclaimer: I (Steven Feuerstein, not Sunita) designed this tool. I led the development team and wrote lots of its backend. It is also sold by my employer, Quest Software.

utPLSQL
> This open source framework is modeled after the same Extreme Programming unit testing principles on which Junit was designed, and for years it has been just about your only option for automated unit testing. The problem with utPLSQL is that you still have to write the vast majority of the test code yourself. For more information, see the upcoming section, "Specific Solution 1: A brief introduction to utPLSQL." The project page for utPLSQL at Source-Forge is at *http://utplsql.sourceforge.net/*.
>
> Another disclaimer: I (Steven Feuerstein, not Sunita) wrote this tool back in 1999 (it has been enhanced further since then).

PL/Unit
> This tool is very similar to utPLSQL, but it offers less testing coverage. PL/Unit predefines a backbone of testing assertion routines, which programs may then code to, taking some of the burden off the individual developer. Because PL/Unit is so similar to utPLSQL (but more limited), I don't describe the details in this book. For more information, go to *http://www.apollo-pro.com/help/pl_unit.htm*.

Before describing Quest Code Tester for Oracle and utPLSQL in greater detail, let's summarize the most critical points of this best practice:

- I believe that the entire software industry suffers from an ongoing, deep crisis—namely, that we force our users (a captive market, if there ever was one) to endure the pain, frustration, and expense of our inadequate testing. The National Institute of Standards and Technology (NIST) estimated back in 2002 that software bugs cost the U.S. economy approximately $60 billion each year, and it has only gotten worse.

- If we don't address this problem ourselves (self-regulate or self-police), the user community will eventually scrap that incredible shrinkware license (which in effect says: "Our software could destroy your company overnight and it is neither our problem nor our fault.") and force us to pay for our poor testing.

- It cannot be left up to individual developers to write their test code in whatever manner they see fit. Few developers even really know how they should go about writing their test code (ask yourself: "Do I know how to write a program to test a procedure that inserts into table A, deletes from table B, and passes back three OUT arguments, one of which is a collection or an array?"). And almost certainly they would evaluate the results of running that test *manually*. In other words, we scan the results (rows in tables, output to the screen, etc.) and try to figure out by ourselves whether or not the test succeeded. Manual verification takes much too long, is error-prone, and is not sufficiently repeatable.

- Automated code testing tools play a critical role in helping us resolve this crisis, but even more important is addressing the human psychology behind the lack of testing. We programmers will avoid testing (and documenting and performance tuning and...) whenever possible, because it simply isn't as much fun as writing code (and more code).

The conclusion is clear: group leaders like Sunita (and IT managers up the chain from development team leaders) should set two unbreakable rules for developers:

- No code should be allowed to be checked into the code repository, and certainly not allowed to be passed on to the QA organization, unless it has a repeatable, automatically verifiable test script defined for it.

- All the automatically verifiable tests should be run on a regular basis (many groups perform them nightly) to make sure that no bugs have crept back into the code base. In other words, make sure the code has not regressed—hence the term "regression test" for this kind of testing.

So let's look at how utPLSQL and Quest Code Tester for Oracle can help you resolve the crisis of inadequate testing in your environment.

Specific Solution 1: A brief introduction to utPLSQL.

utPLSQL is a unit testing framework for programmers using the PL/SQL language. It is based on the unit testing principles of Extreme Programming and is essentially PL/SQL's analog to the Java language's wildly popular Junit.

utPLSQL is often described as a "cooperative paradigm." What this means is that if you cooperate with the API and processes of utPLSQL, it will then give you back some clear benefits. Here are the key elements of that cooperation:

- You write test code as PL/SQL packages that conform to the naming conventions expected by utPLSQL (the default is that if your program is named xyz, then your test test package should be named ut_xyz).

- In your test package, when you want to check whether a particular test succeeded, you call one of the programs in the ut_assert package.

- What do you get back? You call the utPLSQL.test program, pass it the name of your program, and utPLSQL will run your test for you. These ut_assert routines will automatically perform the test requested and write the information to the built-in utPLSQL test results repository.

- Finally and most wonderfully, utPLSQL will display the results of your test on your screen.

Here is an example of calling the ut_assert.eq program within a test package to determine if the string returned by a function matches the expected value:

```
PROCEDURE ut_betwnstr
IS
    -- Verify and complete data types.
    against_this   VARCHAR2 (2000);
    check_this     VARCHAR2 (2000);
BEGIN
    -- Define "control" operation for "zero start"
    against_this := 'ab';

    -- Execute test code for "zero start"
    check_this :=
        betwnstr (string_in    => 'abcdefgh'
                , start_in      => 0
                , end_in        => 2
                , inclusive     => TRUE
                );

    -- Assert success for "zero start"
    utassert.eq ('zero start', check_this, against_this);
    -- End of test for "zero start"
```

Here is an example of the output from running the entire ut_betwnstr test package; notice that it automatically shows which test cases failed and which succeeded:

```
SQL> EXEC utplsql.test ('betwnstr')
> FFFFFFF    AA      III  L       U       U RRRRR    EEEEEEE
> F          A  A    I    L       U       U R    R E
> F         A    A   I    L       U       U R    R E
> F         A    A   I    L       U       U R    R E
> FFFF      A    A   I    L       U       U RRRRRR  EEEE
> F         AAAAAAAA I    L       U       U R    R  E
> F         A    A   I    L       U       U R    R  E
> F         A    A   I    L       U   U   R       R E
> F         A    A  III LLLLLLL  UUU      R       R EEEEEEE
.
FAILURE: "betwnstr"
.
> Individual Test Case Results:
>
FAILURE - betwnstr.UT_BETWNSTR: EQ "normal" Expected "cde" and got ""
FAILURE - betwnstr.UT_BETWNSTR: EQ "zero start" Expected "ab" and got ""
SUCCESS - betwnstr.UT_BETWNSTR: ISNULL "null start" Expected "" and got ""
SUCCESS - betwnstr.UT_BETWNSTR: ISNULL "null end" Expected "" and got ""
FAILURE - betwnstr.UT_BETWNSTR: EQ "neg start and end" Expected "efg" and got ""
```

This is certainly nothing more than a brief glimpse of utPLSQL, but I can tell you that it is in use by dozens, if not hundreds, of development organizations, and is a substantial step beyond writing your own home-grown test code that relies on manual verification of results. Again, the home page for utPLSQL is *http://utplsql.sourceforge.net/*.

I could introduce you to PL/Unit as well, but it is the same concept and code flow as utPLSQL, only with fewer options and a smaller user base. So, let's move on to something that is dramatically different.

Specific Solution 2: A brief introduction to Quest Code Tester for Oracle.

I wrote utPLSQL back in 1999, and there I was in 2006 writing a new testing tool. Why would I do such a thing? Well, for all that utPLSQL helps you automate the testing process, you still have to write almost all of the test code yourself (the same holds true for Junit). I have met developers who have proudly told me about (and shown me) the tens of thousands of lines of utPLSQL test package code they have written.

I have been very impressed with the level of dedication and discipline required to do this. I have also found that I personally do not have this level of dedication and discipline. In other words, I never got into the habit of using utPLSQL myself.

Now, some people might think that because I write about PL/SQL and, in particular, about best practices, that I must follow them all myself and be a really great programmer. Not true. I believe that in many ways I am a very typical programmer: short of time, not very disciplined, much preferring to "play" (write new programs) than "work" (document and test what I have already written).

Realizing that I was never going to use utPLSQL in any big way, and noticing that it was being used by a tiny percentage of the total PL/SQL community, I decided to try again. This time around, I set a very ambitious goal for my second testing tool:

> Rather than having to write test code, I want to describe my tests to the tool through a visual interface, and let it build the appropriate test code based on those descriptions.

Of course, I also want it to run the tests for me with the click of a button, and automatically compute and display the results. Finally, I need to be able to customize the test logic, because no tool could possibly handle 100 percent of my complicated, specialized testing requirements.

So that was the dream…and Quest Code Tester is the reality: the first truly automated testing tool for PL/SQL programs.

The screenshot in Figure 3-1 showcases some of the power of Quest Code Tester's declarative approach. In the Test Builder Outcome Grid, I have specified three different tests that I want Quest Code Tester to run for my test case:

- Does the string returned by the function equal "cde"?
- Does the program complete in no more than five seconds?
- Is the employees table empty after this program has run?

All of these tests, and many more, can be selected and executed, without the developer having to write any test code at all.

| 2c. Outcomes | | Describe the behavior that verifies correct program execution. | | |

A. Data changed by program		B. Test Type		C. Expected results	
Argument or RETURN Clause		=		Same type as [Function return value]; provide value below	
[Function return value] - VARCHAR2(32767)	[...]			abc	[...]
Table		=		Table	
EMPLOYEES	[...]			'Q##COPY_1316397409'	[...]
Elapsed Time	⌄	<=		Pls_Integer	⌄
Returned in 100ths of seconds	[...]			500	◯

Figure 3-1. Describing tests in the Quest Code Tester Outcome Grid

Resources

This book is not the appropriate place to provide a detailed explanation of the Quest Code Tester, but I encourage you to check out the following resources:

Main product page
> http://www.quest.com/code-tester-for-oracle

Online community web site
> http://unittest.inside.quest.com/index.jspa

Tutorial Library
> http://www.unit-test.com/Presentations/library.php

> If you want to quickly get a sense of the power of Quest Code Tester, this is probably the most useful link. The Tutorial Library contains dozens of short videos that I have recorded to show you how to use Quest Code Tester.

Do you take road trips without a destination in mind?

Follow the test-driven development methodology.

Problem: We cannot trust our own minds to fully and objectively test our code.

Delaware has done it again! On Monday, Sunita assigned him the task of writing a program to gather excuses from various web sites, collect them within an Oracle table, and then use PL/SQL to analyze and categorize those excuses. Just two days later, Delaware announces that he has completed the task. Amazing! Sunita thought it would take a week. "And you tested it?" she asks him warily. "Absolutely! I ran it through its paces," he answers.

Sunita nods and asks him to email her the code along with the test script. It arrives in moments, and when she runs the script against some dummy web sites it seems to work. But then she decides to change the test environment. All the dummy web sites now hold nary a single excuse on them—there is no data to mine and retrieve. When she runs Delaware's excuse_me_now program, it raises an unhandled exception: NO_DATA_FOUND.

When Sunita asks Delaware about this, he slaps his forehead: "Duh! How could I forget to test that?" And he looks rather silly in front of his boss. Hey, at least his sloppiness wasn't caught by the *users*!

Surely you've had a similar experience. You write a program. And then you test it. Lots. You really do. And yet, still, when you hand it off to QA, or to the users, or to *anyone else*, they hit bugs right away, and you look like a total amateur. What's going on here?

Basic human psychology is the culprit, in three ways:

We tend to take the path of least resistance (effort) whenever possible
> Without an automated tool, testing is a tedious, seemingly endless, and quite difficult task. Consequently, we put it off for as long as we possibly can. We tell ourselves that we need to write the program before we can even think about testing. And with that rationalization, we sneak back to our comfortable world of algorithms (logic puzzles). Later for testing!

We so badly want/need our programs to work that we practice avoidance
> Even with a good tool, we still avoid testing if at all possible, because testing is all about the *negative*, about failure (at least with my code, that's what testing seems to be about). Who wants to dwell on the negative? It is all we can do to stay focused sufficiently on the positive (implementing user requirements correctly). Later for testing!

We test what is most likely to succeed
> When we focus on testing only after the program has been finished (more or less), our tests tend to focus on the parts of the program on which we worked the hardest and in which we have the most confidence. We avoid—usually quite subconsciously—the areas of code that are least likely to be used and have gotten the smallest amount of our attention.

Solution: Decide before you implement your program how you will know when it works correctly.

So…later for testing. OK, why not? As long as it gets done, right? Well, not really. First of all, if we leave all of our testing to the very end, that test phase will be much more difficult and time-consuming, because our code will be absolutely chock-full of bugs. If, on the other hand, we test *iteratively* (make one change, test the impact of that change), when we finally enter the concentrated test period, our code will be much cleaner and easier to test.

Second, and more fundamental, if we wait to think about and write our tests until after our programs have been implemented, we will prejudice that test code to show success. This doesn't happen because we are cheaters or maliciously fudging our tests (well, I will speak for myself, anyway). It happens without our realizing it; it's just the way our brains work.

That's what happened to Delaware. How could he miss such an obvious test as "web sites with no excuses?" Because deep down inside, he *knew* that (a) his code hadn't dealt with that case very well; (b) it was *so* unlikely to happen (yeah, right), and (c) well, let's stay positive, shall we?

You can stay positive all you want, but that won't make the bugs go away.

So how can you avoid this problem? Simple: write your tests first, and use those test definitions to *drive* your development. That is, follow the Test-Driven Development (TDD) methodology. TDD, as defined in Wikipedia *(http://en.wikipedia.org/wiki/Test_driven_development)*, is:

> A computer programming technique that involves repeatedly first writing a test case and then implementing only the code necessary to pass the test. The goal of Test-Driven Development is to achieve rapid feedback. The technique began to receive publicity in the early 2000s as an aspect of Extreme Programming, but more recently is creating more general interest in its own right. Practitioners emphasize that Test-Driven Development is a method of designing software, not just a method of testing. Along with other techniques, the concept can also be applied to the improvement and removal of software defects from legacy code that was not developed in this way.

For many programmers, the mantra of "test first" seems at first glance to be nonsensical. We are convinced that we cannot test our program until after the program is written. But, really, when you think about it, just the opposite is true. Here's what doesn't make any sense:

> I start writing my program without any clear idea of how I will know when I am done, when the program works. I determine this moment through a loosey-goosey, subjective feeling (and then start thinking about testing).

What kind of sense does that make?

Resources

For more information about TDD, visit the following web sites:

Home base for the TDD movement
  http://www.testdriven.com

Good, basic introduction to TDD
  http://www.agiledata.org/essays/tdd.html

Quest Code Tester community site
  http://www.agiledata.org/essays/tdd.html

> This site offers resources that will show you how to follow TDD using this tool for PL/SQL testing.

For every test you can think of, there are 10 tests waiting to be performed.

Don't worry about getting to 100 percent test coverage.

Problem: Lizbeth has entered a medical condition called the Test-By-Hand Coma State.

Sunita recognizes that Delaware is not a very good tester, so she turns to Lizbeth and asks her to finish testing the excuse_me_now program. Being very diligent,

Lizbeth sits down and thinks about what else must be tested. She implements these test cases in Delaware's script, and runs the expanded test.

While doing that, she thinks of a few more tests, writes the code for those, and tests again. She changes excuse_me_now when she finds bugs, runs the test again, and then thinks of even more test cases. Everyone else goes home, and she keeps on testing. The hours slip by, she forgets to eat, thinks of more test cases....

And when Sunita arrives at work the next morning, there's Lizbeth, breathing shallowly, staring blankly at her monitor, which displays the ever-lengthening list of test cases, and not responding to external stimuli.

Another victim of the Test-by-Hand Coma State; time to dial 911.

Solution: When it comes to testing, be happy with getting started and with steady progress.

The Test-by-Hand Coma State is just the flip-side of another indication of an unhealthy perspective on testing: the Why Bother Syndrome (WBS). WBS goes like this:

> I'll never be able to think of *all* the test cases for this program; thus, I will never be able to fully test the program. So why bother testing at all?

The underlying reality of WBS (you'll never think of—or implement—*everything*) is true, but the conclusion is very faulty.

For any nontrivial program, you could spend the rest of your life just sitting around and thinking up test cases (well, that's a little bit of an exaggeration). But even a trivial program can easily have dozens, if not hundreds, of test cases. Still, you should never use that as an excuse to avoid getting started. And you definitely should not worry about getting to 100 percent coverage today.

Instead, you should choose your testing tool and get started. Once you create your test program with even a single test case, you will find it much, much easier to add another, and then 10 others, to that test case. And you will so appreciate the feedback you get from those tests, that you will think of and want to add more. Over time, your test code will grow into a very substantial regression test of your program.

That's great! Just don't let test cases take over your programming life. And remember that you should think in terms of general conditions, not necessarily specific values, when you set up your tests.

For example, if my program accepts a string, start location, and end location, and returns the substring between those two locations, I shouldn't really need to set up a test case for each permutation of integer values. There is an infinite number of those. Instead, I will think in terms of distinct logical variations, such as start location and end location within the string, start location of 0, end location past the end of the string, start bigger than end, and so on.

When coming up with test cases, make sure you cover these broad categories:

Boundary condition tests
> Test those "weird" or extreme values that often expose bugs in algorithms. Examples include NULL, 0, $2^{31} - 1$ (largest allowable value for PLS_INTEGER), strings of 32,767 characters (maximum length allowed in PL/SQL), etc.

Requirements coverage
> Every specific requirement should be covered by its own test case. And every time the user adds a new requirement, make sure you have test cases to cover it. For example, suppose I want to built a test for SUBSTR. It treats a starting position of 0 as if the user provided 1 instead. I need a test case for this particular scenario.

Verification of bugs with test cases
> Every time a user reports a bug, you should immediately create a test case that reproduces the bug. Then work on fixing it. By taking this step, you ensure that the bug cannot creep back into the code later without causing a test failure.

Sherlock Holmes never had it so good.

Use source code debuggers to hunt down the cause of bugs.

Problem: Jasper writes some complicated code and has no idea what it is doing.

Jasper is excited. He's been on the development team for a year now, and has gained Sunita's confidence. She rewards his efforts by assigning to him a very complicated task. The mathematicians over at the secret research center of My Flimsy Excuse have finally come up with an algorithm that they believe will accurately describe the flimsiness of an excuse. Now the team must implement that program. Jasper will be given that job.

With the implicit promise of a promotion behind the assignment, Jasper dives in. He concentrates really, really hard on the logic, pouring out line after line of code. He ends up with more than 200 lines of densely packed statements, coursing through the many steps of the algorithm. And now it is time to test his work! He sets up a simple test script (anonymous block), runs the code, and gets the wrong answer.

Unfazed, he goes back to his code, laboriously reads through the statements, and after about 30 minutes finds the line of code that might be causing the problem. He makes a change, runs his script, and gets the wrong answer. Of course. So he repeats this process another eight times. Hours go by.

Sunita drops by and asks, "How's it going?" Jasper puts on a brave face, but he is clearly discouraged and all but moans: "My code is so complicated, I can't really follow what it is doing—and I just wrote it!"

Solution: Use the built-in, interactive source debuggers available in almost every PL/SQL IDE.

Sunita feels horrible. How could she have forgotten to review with Jasper when to test, when to trace, and when to debug? Here we have a perfect use case for debugging:

- Jasper knows the program doesn't work.
- Now he needs to find the lines of code that cause the problem.
- The code is complicated and convoluted. He really needs to "get inside" the program and follow along as it is running.

Every PL/SQL IDE worth its salt has some kind of interactive debugger these days. Some of these debuggers are built on top of Oracle Corporation's own built-in DBMS_DEBUG package; others utilize the Java Debug Wire Protocol (JDWP). Features and sophistication vary widely, but all such debuggers allow you to do the basics:

- Set breakpoints.
- Step into and over program invocations.
- Look at the values of local variables and parameters.

Figure 3-2 shows an example of the Set Watch window in Toad for Oracle, which offers many options for setting a watch on a particular variable. Check out *www.quest.com/toad* for details.

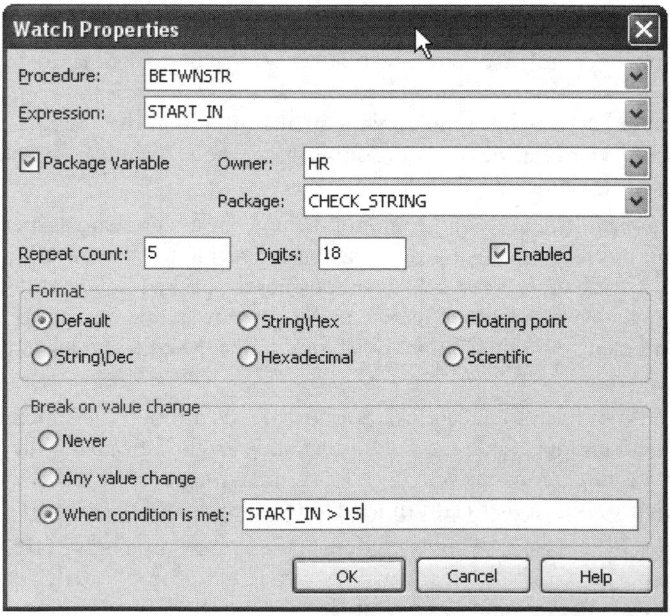

Figure 3-2. Setting watch properties in the Toad for Oracle Debugger

CHAPTER 4

What's Code Without Variables?

PL/SQL is a *strongly typed* language. This means that before you can work with any kind of data structure, you must first declare it. And when you declare it, you specify its type and, optionally, an initial or default value. All declarations of these variables must be made in the declaration section of your anonymous block, procedure, function, or package. I've divided the best practices in this chapter into three main categories, described in the following sections:

Best Practices for Declaring Variables and Data Structures
Presents best practices for specifying %TYPE and %ROWTYPE, declaring SUBTYPEs, and localizing variable initialization.

Best Practices for Using Variables and Data Structures
Presents best practices for simplifying the specification of business rules and data structures and avoiding implicit datatype conversions.

Best Practices for Declaring and Using Package Variables
Presents best practices aimed particularly at the use of variables in packages.

Best Practices for Declaring Variables and Data Structures

Use the best practices described in this section when you declare your variables and data structures.

That column's never going to change!

Always anchor variables to database datatypes using %TYPE and %ROWTYPE.

Problem: Lizbeth writes a "quick-and-dirty" program.

Lizbeth *hates* doing anything the quick-and-dirty way. In fact, she generally hates to be in a hurry at all. But Sunita comes by with an urgent request: "I need you to write a program to scan through all the flimsy excuses in our system, and display the title and description of each excuse. I need it in 30 minutes, but we're going to run it only once, so you don't have to worry about following all the usual best practices."

Gritting her teeth, Lizbeth puts aside her good judgment and quickly familiarizes herself with the structure of the table:

```
CREATE TABLE flimsy_excuses (
     id INTEGER
   , title VARCHAR2(50)
   , description VARCHAR2(100)
   , ... and many more columns ...
);
```

She then throws together the following program:

```
PROCEDURE show_excuses
IS
    CURSOR quick_cur IS SELECT title, description FROM flimsy_excuses;

    l_title VARCHAR2 (50);
    l_desc  VARCHAR2 (100);
BEGIN
    OPEN quick_cur;

    LOOP
        FETCH quick_cur INTO l_title, l_description;
        EXIT WHEN quick_cur%NOTFOUND;

        DBMS_OUTPUT.put_line (
           'Title/description: ' || l_title || ' - ' || l_desc);
    END LOOP;
END show_excuses;
```

Lizbeth runs some tests—it appears to do the job. She finishes in well under 30 minutes and hands over the code to Sunita, who is delighted and hurries off to do whatever she needs to do with it. Quickly putting show_excuses out of her mind, Lizbeth returns to her *real* work, and slows way down.

Years go by, and one day Lizbeth gets a call from Support: "We're getting reports of unhandled VALUE_ERROR exceptions in the reporting module. Can you take a look?" She does take a look and much to her combined horror, dismay, and disgust, she finds that old quick-and-dirty, one-off, never-to-be-used-again show_excuses program integrated directly into the production reporting subsystem.

That's bad enough, but it seems that it has been working for years. Why would it suddenly be experiencing "technical difficulties?" It takes Lizbeth two very frustrating hours, but she finally figures it out: the DBAs just yesterday put in a number of changes to the base tables so that My Flimsy Excuse could support multiple languages (many of which are much more verbose than English).

In particular, the maximum length of the flimsy_excuses.title column was increased to 1,000 and the description column to 4,000. Once the new data went into the table and the program was run, those quick-and-dirty declarations of l_title and l_description were suddenly wholly inadequate.

Solution: Assume that everything will change and that any program you write could be around for decades.

Lizbeth never should have compromised her programming principles. Everyone's always in a hurry, but we all know that doing things in a hurry doesn't really save time—it just *shifts* where the time is spent.

Furthermore, we always underestimate the staying power of our code. We can't really imagine that the program we write today will be around for years (heck, we don't even really believe that our code can continue working year after year without our paying any attention to it!). Yet it does. Applications have incredible staying power. And the shortcuts we take today come back to bite us (or whichever poor fool now must maintain the application) later on.

So we should always write our programs expecting them to last a long, long time—and also expecting everything they depend on and use to change.

In the particular case of the show_excuses program, Lizbeth's big mistake was getting lazy about declaring the two variables. She hardcoded the maximum length of the variables to the *current* maximum size of the table's columns. Instead, she should have declared the variables using the %TYPE attribute, as you see in this rewritten declaration section:

```
PROCEDURE show_excuses
IS
    CURSOR quick_cur IS SELECT title, description FROM flimsy_excuses;

    l_title  flimsy_excuses.title%TYPE;
    l_desc   flimsy_excuses.description%TYPE;
```

Now this program will automatically adapt to changes in the underlying table. It won't have a choice in the matter. Whenever the data structure against which a declaration is anchored changes, the program containing the anchoring is marked INVALID. Upon recompilation, it automatically uses the new form of the data structure.

These declarations are also "self-documenting": a %TYPE declaration tells anyone who reads it what kind of data this variable is supposed to hold.

You can also use the %ROWTYPE attribute to anchor an entire record to a cursor, table, or view. In fact, this kind of declaration makes much more sense for show_excuses. Let's rewrite the program using %ROWTYPE:

```
PROCEDURE show_excuses
IS
    CURSOR quick_cur IS SELECT title, description FROM flimsy_excuses;
    l_record quick_cur%ROWTYPE;
BEGIN
    OPEN quick_cur;
    LOOP
        FETCH quick_cur INTO l_record;
        EXIT WHEN quick_cur%NOTFOUND;

        DBMS_OUTPUT.put_line ( 'Title/description: '
```

```
             || l_record.title || ' - ' || l_record.description);
      END LOOP;
   END show_excuses;
```

Now Lizbeth can declare just a single variable, a record, that has the same structure as the cursor. This code is even more resilient. The lengths of columns can, of course, change without causing the program to raise errors. But Lizbeth can even add more values to the SELECT list of the query, and the record will automatically (after recompilation) have an extra field corresponding to that new element.

Lizbeth could simplify this code even further by using a cursor FOR loop. Since she is iterating through every row, she can avoid the record declaration entirely as follows:

```
PROCEDURE show_excuses
IS
   CURSOR quick_cur IS SELECT title, description FROM flimsy_excuses;
BEGIN
   FOR l_record IN quick_cur
   LOOP
      DBMS_OUTPUT.put_line ( 'Title/description: '
           || l_record.title || ' - ' || l_record.description);
   END LOOP;
END show_excuses;
```

 If your variable holds data that is coming from a table or a cursor, use %TYPE or %$ROWTYPE to declare that variable. Aim for a single point of definition for the datatypes that you are using for declarations. And if you can get the Oracle database to do the work for you (implicitly declaring the variable or record), all the better!

There's more to data than columns in a table.

Use SUBTYPEs to declare program-specific and derived datatypes.

Problem: Lizbeth learns her lesson but then cannot apply it.

No doubt about it, Lizbeth has learned her lesson: even when she is told to hurry, she will take her time and use %TYPE and %ROWTYPE to declare her variables.

Sure enough, Sunita is soon back at her cubicle, asking her to write another program. This time, she needs to display the names of all the people who have requested flimsy excuses. The name of a person must be displayed in the form "LAST, FIRST." The excuser (a person who makes excuses) table has these columns, among others:

```
CREATE TABLE excuser (
   id INTEGER
 , first_name VARCHAR2(50)
 , last_name VARCHAR2(100)
 , ... and many more columns ...
);
```

She then starts writing the function to construct the full name:

```
FUNCTION full_name (
   last_name IN excuser.last_name%TYPE
 , first_name IN excuser.first_name%TYPE
 )
   RETURN VARCHAR2
```

But then it is time to declare a local variable to hold the full name, and she tries to write something like this:

```
IS
   l_fullname excuser.????%TYPE;
```

But what can she use for the column name? There is no column for "full name": it is a derived value. Lizbeth sighs. Will she just have to hardcode another maximum length and run into another bug years from now?

Solution: Create a new datatype with SUBTYPE and anchor to that.

The SUBTYPE statement allows you to create "aliases" for existing types of information, in effect creating your own specially named datatypes. Use SUBTYPE when you want to standardize on a set of named datatypes that aren't anchorable back to the database. You can then anchor to those new datatypes instead, and achieve the same, desired goal: if a change must be made to, or takes place in, a datatype, you will have to make that change in only one place.

Let's apply this technique to Lizbeth's challenge. Stepping back for a moment, the full_name function really is an encapsulation of a business rule: how to construct the full name for an excuser.

Rather than write a standalone, schema-level function to return that full name, it would make much more sense to create a separate package to hold all the rules-related activity for an excuser. So, Lizbeth can create a package specification like this:

```
PACKAGE excuser_rp
IS
   FUNCTION full_name (
      last_name_in IN excuser.last_name%TYPE
    , first_name_in IN excuser.first_name%TYPE
    )
      RETURN VARCHAR2;
END excuser_rp;
```

In addition, she can create a new datatype that is designed to hold full names:

```
PACKAGE excuser_rp
IS
   SUBTYPE full_name_t IS VARCHAR2(1000);

   FUNCTION full_name (
      last_name_in IN excuser.last_name%TYPE
    , first_name_in IN excuser.first_name%TYPE
    )
      RETURN full_name_t;
END excuser_rp;
```

The SUBTYPE command simply defines another name, an alias, for VARCHAR2(1000). She can then use that type as the return type of the function to clearly document what *type* of string is being returned.

Now attention shifts to the package body:

```
PACKAGE BODY excuser_rp
IS
    FUNCTION full_name (
        last_name_in IN excuser.last_name%TYPE
      , first_name_in IN excuser.first_name%TYPE
    )
        RETURN full_name_t
    IS
        l_fullname   full_name_t;
    BEGIN
        l_fullname := last_name_in || ',' || first_name_in;
        RETURN l_fullname;
    END full_name;
END excuser_rp;
```

And when Lizbeth calls this function, she will also use the full name type:

```
DECLARE
    l_my_name excuser_rp.full_name_t;
BEGIN
    l_my_name := excuser_rp.full_name (
        l_person.last_name, l_person.first_name);
```

Notice that Lizbeth no longer hardcodes her datatype in the declaration; she simply refers back to her subtype. If 1,000 characters are not enough, she can change the definition of that subtype in the package specification and recompile. Everything will automatically adjust to the new size.

Clearly, Lizbeth could have written this function without declaring a local full name variable altogether, but the example illustrates an important point. Note, however, that you will certainly run into this requirement with much more complex code in which local variables will be required.

I take exception to your declaration section.

Perform complex variable initialization in the execution section.

Problem: The exception section of a block can only trap errors raised in the execution section.

That is a little fact that many PL/SQL developers don't realize, and one that causes lots of headaches. Delaware writes the following packaged function, a classic "getter" of a private variable:

```
PACKAGE fe_config
IS
    FUNCTION get_worst_excuse  RETURN VARCHAR2;
END fe_config;
/

PACKAGE BODY fe_config
IS
    c_worst_excuse CONSTANT VARCHAR2 (20) :=
        'The dog ate my homework. Really.';

    FUNCTION get_worst_excuse  RETURN VARCHAR2
    IS
    BEGIN
        RETURN c_worst_excuse;
    END get_worst_excuse;
BEGIN
    DBMS_OUTPUT.put_line ('Initialization logic here');
    ... lots of initialization code ...
EXCEPTION
    WHEN OTHERS
    THEN
        fe_errmgr.log_and_raise_error;
END fe_config;
/
```

As far as Delaware can tell, he has set things up so that if anything goes wrong while initializing the package, he will trap and log the error. Yet when he tries to call the function, he gets an unhandled exception:

```
SQL> BEGIN
  2     DBMS_OUTPUT.PUT_LINE (fe_config.get_worst_excuse ());
  3  END;
  4  /
BEGIN
*
ERROR at line 1:
ORA-06502: PL/SQL: numeric or value error: character string buffer too small
ORA-06512: at "HR.FE_CONFIG", line 3
```

For a solid five minutes, Delaware stares at this simple package, stumped. Then he groans and smacks his forehead. Of course! The exception section that is underneath the package initialization section will trap only exceptions that occur in that initialization section (the execution section of a package). And 20 characters simply aren't enough for the world's worst excuse.

Now Delaware could simply raise the length of that constant's VARCHAR2 declaration. But he would rather fix the problem in a more long-lasting and fundamental way.

Solution: Don't trust the declaration section to assign default values.

As we've seen, the exception section of a block can trap only errors raised in the execution section of that block. So if the code you run to assign a default value to a variable fails in the declaration section, that error is propagated unhandled out to the enclosing program. It's difficult to debug these problems, too, so you must either:

- Be sure that your initialization logic doesn't ever raise an error. That's hard to guarantee, isn't it?
- Perform your initialization at the beginning of the execution section, preferably in a separate "initialization" program.

Here's what Delaware did with his package:

- He did no more hardcoding of the VARCHAR2 length. He anchored to a database column instead.
- He moved the assignment of the default value into a separate procedure, and called this procedure in the package's initialization section.

 It is particularly important to avoid assigning default values in the declaration section if they are function calls or expressions that make it hard to predict the value that will be returned.

Here is Delaware's new code:

```
PACKAGE BODY fe_config
IS
    g_worst_excuse flimsy_excuse.title%TYPE;

    FUNCTION get_worst_excus RETURN VARCHAR2  IS
    BEGIN
        RETURN g_worst_excuse;
    END get_worst_excuse;

    PROCEDURE initialize IS
    BEGIN
        g_worst_excuse := 'The dog ate my homework. Really.';
    END initialize;
BEGIN
    initialize;
EXCEPTION
    WHEN OTHERS
    THEN
        fe_errmgr.log_and_raise_error;
END fe_config;
```

Now if that string is too long, the exception section will catch the problem and the error logging will come into play.

Best Practices for Using Variables and Data Structures

Use the best practices described in this section when you reference the data structures you have declared in your programs.

This logic is driving me crazy!

Replace complex expressions with well-named constants, variables, or functions.

Problem: Business rules can be complicated, and it's hard to keep them straight.

While it's possible to train our brains to manage and keep straight a very large amount of information, we all have limits. Unfortunately, application requirements don't always respect those limits. You'll often encounter business rules with 5, 10, or 20 individual clauses in them. And you'll have to put all of those together in a way that works and, ideally, can be understood and maintained. And therein lies the rub.

Consider the code below. I need to figure out whether an employee is eligible to receive a raise, so I faithfully translate the various conditions from the requirements document to the code:

```
IF l_total_salary BETWEEN 10000 AND 50000
   AND emp_status (emp_rec.employee_id) = 'H'
   AND (MONTHS_BETWEEN (emp_rec.hire_date, SYSDATE) > 10)
THEN
     give_raise (emp_rec.empno);
END IF;
```

This code compiles, I do some testing, and it seems to be working all right, so I move on. A week later I come back to this area of my program to fix a bug, and realize: Wow, that's hard to understand! And because I can't immediately understand it, I also can't be very confident of what it does or whether it is correct.

Lucky for me, I don't *need* to understand that code right now. It's not part of the bug. But it does distract me, and make it hard to find and read the code that *was* causing the problem.

Solution: Simplify code to make the criteria for the business rules more obvious.

So, I put my bug-fixing on hold for a moment and create a local function named eligible_for_raise and simply move all the code there. Then my main execution section is simplified to do nothing more than this:

```
IF eligible_for_raise (l_total_salary, emp_rec)
THEN
     give_raise (emp_rec.empno);
END IF;
```

With this approach, I have hidden all the detailed logic behind a function interface. If a person working in this program needs to get the details, she can visit the body of the function.

Yet this function still has all the same problems of readability and maintainability, so the best approach of all is to go inside that function and make the criteria behind the rule more obvious:

```
FUNCTION eligible_for_raise (
    total_salary_in IN NUMBER
  , emp_rec_in IN employees%ROWTYPE
)
    RETURN BOOLEAN
IS
    c_salary_in_range CONSTANT BOOLEAN
         := total_salary_in BETWEEN 10000 AND 50000;

    c_hired_more_than_a_year CONSTANT BOOLEAN
         := MONTHS_BETWEEN (emp_rec.hire_date, SYSDATE) > 10;

    c_hourly_worker CONSTANT BOOLEAN
         := emp_status (emp_rec.employee_id) = 'H';
    l_return BOOLEAN;
BEGIN
    l_return :=    c_salary_in_range
               AND c_hired_more_than_a_year
               AND c_hourly_worker;

    RETURN NVL (l_return, FALSE);
END eligible_for_raise;
```

Certainly my code has gotten longer, but now it is so much easier to understand. I don't have to deduce or infer anything from the code. Instead, it tells me, directly and explicitly, what is going on.

Go ahead and splurge: declare distinct variables for different usages.

Don't overload data structure usage.

Problem: World weariness infects Lizbeth's code.

Lizbeth is a good citizen of the world. She read *The Nation* each week (which is, by the way, the oldest weekly newspaper published in the United States), votes in every election, and contacts her Congressperson about any number of issues. She is, in short, well informed and intelligent, and consequently tends to get rather depressed about the state of affairs in the world.

Usually, she puts that aside when she comes to work (in fact, she looks to her world of programming as a refuge). Today, however, she just feels tired of it all, and still, she must work on a "scan and analyze" that takes a list of excuses and perhaps performs analysis on them. She needs to get the number of excuses in the list, get the length of each title, and so on. So many integer variables, so little time! With a big sigh, she writes the following code:

```
PROCEDURE scan_and_analyze (
   excuses_in IN excuses_tp.excuses_tc -- a collection type
)
IS
   intval   PLS_INTEGER;
BEGIN
   intval := excuses_in.COUNT;

   IF intval > 0
   THEN
      FOR indx IN 1 .. excuses_in.COUNT
      LOOP
         intval := LENGTH (excuses_in (indx).title);
         analyze_excuse_usage (intval);
      END LOOP;
   END IF;
END;
```

Sure, the code will compile. But who would want to maintain code that looks like this?

Solution: Don't let your weariness show in your code—and don't recycle!

This is just one entry of a more general category: "Don't be lazy (in the wrong way)!"

The problem with Lizbeth's code is that it's pretty much impossible to look at any use of the intval variable and understand what is going on. You have to go back to the most recent assignment to make sense of the code. Compare that to the following:

```
PROCEDURE scan_and_analyze (
   excuses_in IN excuses_tp.excuses_tc  -- a collection type
)
IS
   l_excuse_count   PLS_INTEGER;
   l_title_length   PLS_INTEGER;
BEGIN
   l_excuse_count := excuses_in.COUNT;

   IF l_excuse_count > 0
   THEN
      FOR indx IN 1 .. excuses_in.COUNT
      LOOP
         l_page_length := LENGTH (excuses_in (indx).title);
         analyze_excuse_usage (l_page_length);
      END LOOP;
   END IF;
END;
```

When you declare a variable, you should give it a name that accurately reflects its purpose in a program. If you then use that variable in more than one way ("recycling"), you create confusion and, very possibly, introduce bugs.

The solution is to declare and manipulate separate data structures for each distinct requirement. With this approach, you can also make a change to one variable's usage without worrying about its ripple effect to other areas of your code.

Here is a final, general piece of advice: reliance on a "time-saver" shortcut should raise a red flag. You're probably doing (or avoiding) something now for which you will pay later.

Didn't your parents teach you to clean up after yourself?

Clean up data structures when your program terminates (successfully or with an error).

Problem: Sometimes you really do need to clean up in a PL/SQL block.

PL/SQL does an awful lot of cleanup for you automatically, but there are a number of scenarios in which it's absolutely crucial for you to take your own cleanup actions.

Consider the following program: it manipulates a packaged cursor, declares a DBMS_SQL cursor, and writes information to a file:

```
PROCEDURE busy_busy
IS
    fileid UTL_FILE.FILE_TYPE;
    dyncur PLS_INTEGER;
BEGIN
    dyncur := DBMS_SQL.OPEN_CURSOR;
    OPEN book_pkg.all_books_by ('FEUERSTEIN');
    fileid := UTL_FILE.FOPEN ('/apps/library', 'bestsellers.txt', 'R');

    ... use all that good stuff in here ...

EXCEPTION
    WHEN OTHERS
    THEN
        err.log;
        RAISE;
END busy_busy;
```

At first glance, you might want to congratulate the author for including an exception section that logs the error and then raises that exception again. Hey, at least he gave some thought to the fact that *something* actually could go wrong.

With a second glance, however, we uncover some drawbacks: after this program terminates (even without an error), the dynamic SQL cursor floats away, uncloseable, because the handle is erased from memory. Yet the cursor itself continues to consume SGA memory, which could cause serious problems if this kind of error is widespread. And that's not all. The package-based cursor (all_books_by) stays open, which means that the next time this program is called, the still-open packaged cursor causes an *ORA-06511: PL/SQL: cursor already open* error. Wait, there's more! The file is not closed, but the handle to the file is cleaned up, thereby making it impossible to close this file without closing all files with UTL_FILE.FCLOSE_ALL or with a disconnect.

Yuck! That program is as messy as my son's bedroom when he was a teenager. Clearly, we need to do some cleanup. How about this?

```
PROCEDURE busy_busy
IS
   fileid UTL_FILE.FILE_TYPE;
   dyncur PLS_INTEGER;
BEGIN
   dyncur := DBMS_SQL.OPEN_CURSOR;
   OPEN book_pkg.all_books_by ('FEUERSTEIN');
   fileid := UTL_FILE.FOPEN ('/apps/library', 'bestsellers.txt', 'R');

   ... use all that good stuff in here ...

   DBMS_SQL.CLOSE_CURSOR;
   UTL_FILE.FCLOSE (fileid);
   CLOSE book_pkg.all_books_by;
EXCEPTION
   WHEN OTHERS
   THEN
      err.log;
      RAISE;
END busy_busy;
```

Now, that's really great—as long as no error is raised. Because if the program terminates with an exception, then all the same problems occur. No problem! I will simply copy and paste those three cleanup lines into the exception section. Really? No! Terrible idea! Whenever you find yourself thinking about copying and pasting code, ask yourself: do I *really* want to have multiple copies of this code running around in my application?

Maybe, just maybe, it would be better to create a single program and call it wherever it is needed. I have taken that approach in my third implementation of busy_busy (below). I now have a local procedure that performs all cleanup operations. I call it at the end of the execution section (clean up on success) and in the WHEN OTHERS clause (clean up on failure).

```
PROCEDURE busy_busy
IS
   fileid UTL_FILE.FILE_TYPE;
   dyncur PLS_INTEGER;

   PROCEDURE cleanup IS
   BEGIN
      IF book_pkg.all_books_by%ISOPEN THEN
```

```
            CLOSE book_pkg.all_books_by;
        END IF;

        IF DBMS_SQL.IS_OPEN (dyncur) THEN
            DBMS_SQL.CLOSE_CURSOR (dyncur);
        END IF;

        IF UTL_FILE.ISOPEN (fileid) THEN
            UTL_FILE.FCLOSE (fileid);
        END IF;
    END cleanup;
BEGIN
    dyncur := DBMS_SQL.OPEN_CURSOR;
    OPEN book_pkg.all_books_by ('FEUERSTEIN');
    fileid := UTL_FILE.FOPEN (
        '/apps/library', 'bestsellers.txt', 'R');

    ... use all that good stuff in here ...

    cleanup;
EXCEPTION
    WHEN NO_DATA_FOUND
    THEN
        err.log;
        cleanup;
        RAISE;
END;
```

Notice that as I moved my cleanup logic into its own program, I also took the time to enhance it, so that I close only those things that are actually open. This increased attention to detail and completeness often happens quite naturally when you focus on creating a single-purpose program.

A common cleanup procedure offers several important advantages:

- Your programs are less likely to have memory leaks (open cursors) and to cause problems in other programs by leaving data structures in an uncertain state.

- Future developers can easily add new cleanup operations in one place and be certain that they will be run at all exit points.

- When and if I add another WHEN clause, I will be very likely to follow the "model" in WHEN OTHERS and perform cleanup there as well.

Resources

The *stdpkg_format.sql* file on the book's web site contains a template for a package specification and body) that you may find useful as a starting point.

Programmers are (or should be) control freaks.

Beware of and avoid implicit datatype conversions.

Problem: PL/SQL performs implicit conversions—but they're not always what you want.

Sometimes, PL/SQL makes life just *too* darn easy for us developers. It will, for example, allow you to write and execute code like this:

```
DECLARE
    my_birthdate DATE := '09-SEP-58';
```

In this case, the runtime engine automatically converts the string to a date, using the default format mask.

You should, however, avoid implicit conversions in your code (Figure 4-1 shows the types of implicit conversions that PL/SQL attempts to perform). There are at least two big problems with relying on PL/SQL to convert data on your behalf:

Conversion behavior can be unintuitive
> PL/SQL may convert data in ways that you don't expect, resulting in problems, especially within SQL statements.

Conversion rules aren't under the control of the developer
> These rules can change with an upgrade to a new version of Oracle or by changing database-wide parameters, such as NLS_DATE_FORMAT.

You can convert explicitly using one of the many built-in functions, including TO_DATE, TO_CHAR, TO_NUMBER, and CAST.

Solution: Perform explicit conversions rather than relying on implicit conversions.

Let's see how I would move from implicit to explicit conversion of the previous declaration.

This code raises an error if the default format mask for the instance is anything but DD-MON-YY or DD-MON-RR. That format is set (and changed) by a database initialization parameter—well beyond the control of most PL/SQL developers. It can also be modified for a specific session. A much better approach, therefore, is:

```
DECLARE
    my_birthdate DATE :=
        TO_DATE ('09-SEP-58', 'DD-MON-RR');
```

Taking this approach makes the behavior of my code more consistent and predictable, since I am not making any assumptions about factors external to my program. Explicit conversions, by the way, would have prevented the vast majority of Y2K issues found within PL/SQL code.

From \ To	CHAR	VARCHAR2	NCHAR	NVARCHAR2	DATE	DATETIME/ INTERVAL	NUMBER	BINARY_ FLOAT	BINARY_ DOUBLE	BINARY_ INTEGER	PLS_ INTEGER	SIMPLE_ INTEGER	LONG	RAW	ROWID	CLOB	BLOB	NCLOB
CHAR		•	•	•	•	•	•	•	•	•	•	•	•	•	•	•	•	•
VARCHAR2	•		•	•	•	•	•	•	•	•	•	•	•	•	•	•		•
NCHAR	•	•		•	•	•	•	•	•	•	•	•	•	•	•	•		•
NVARCHAR2	•	•	•		•	•	•	•	•	•	•	•	•	•	•	•		•
DATE	•	•	•	•														
DATETIME/ INTERVAL	•	•	•	•									•					
NUMBER	•	•	•	•				•	•	•	•	•						
BINARY_ FLOAT	•	•	•	•			•		•	•	•	•						
BINARY_ DOUBLE	•	•	•	•			•	•		•	•	•	•					
BINARY_ INTEGER	•	•	•	•			•	•	•		•	•	•					
PLS_ INTEGER	•	•	•	•			•	•	•	•		•	•					
SIMPLE_ INTEGER	•	•	•	•			•	•	•	•	•		•					
LONG	•	•	•	•	•			•	•	•				•		•		•
RAW	•	•	•	•									•				•	
ROWID		•	•	•														
CLOB	•	•	•	•									•					•
BLOB														•				
NCLOB	•	•	•	•									•			•		

Figure 4-1. Implicit datatype conversions attempted by PL/SQL

Resources

bool.pkg is a package file available on the book's web site that you can use to convert between Booleans and strings. You will find this code useful particularly since the Oracle database doesn't offer any built-in utilities to perform these operations.

Best Practices for Declaring and Using Package Variables

Use the best practices described in this section when you are declaring variables for use in packages.

Danger, Will Robinson! Globals in use!

Use package globals sparingly and only in package bodies.

Problem: Jasper needs Lizbeth's program data. Delaware needs Jasper's program data.

Everyone is working very hard in the final week or two of the coding cycle. Packages are constructed quickly, and everyone needs to reference "stuff" in everyone else's packages. Here's one example:

Lizbeth creates a package named mfe_reports to consolidate all reporting-related functionality, including a function that returns the standard header for a report. This header is composed of a top line, a bottom line, and a report-specific string sandwiched in between. Here is Lizbeth's package specification:

```
PACKAGE mfe_reports
IS
    topline VARCHAR2(100) := 'My Flimsy Excuse - We Report for You!!!!!!';
    bottomline VARCHAR2(100) := '== Report Generation Engine Version 4.3 ==';
    ...
END mfe_reports;
```

Jasper builds a report in his mfe_acceptability package. He doesn't like the exclamation marks at the end of the top line, but he can't get Lizbeth to change it ("Sorry, Jasper, that's the standard."). He also thinks putting "=" at the beginning and end of the bottom line is dumb. So he writes the following code:

```
PACKAGE BODY mfe_acceptability
IS
    PROCEDURE acceptance_report IS
        c_carriage_return CONSTANT VARCHAR2(1) := CHR(10);
    BEGIN
        mfe_reports.topline := replace (mfe_reports.topline, '!', '');
        mfe_reports.topline := replace (mfe_reports.bottomline, '=', '');
        DBMS_OUTPUT.PUT_LINE (
            mfe_reports.topline || c_carriage_return ||
            'Acceptance Report' || c_carriage_return ||
            mfe_reports.bottomline);

        ... rest of report logic ...
    END acceptance_report;
```

And now Jasper can create the report just the way he likes it.

Unfortunately for Jasper, the users are dismayed. They *like* the exclamation marks and the equals signs. They *asked for* those characters. And so they complain to Sunita, and Jasper gets in trouble. Jasper's response? "If you didn't want me to change it, why didn't you *stop* me from changing it?"

A very good question.

Solution: Don't expose program data in package specifications, letting everyone see and change it.

Lizbeth realizes now that she should have ensured that neither Jasper nor any other developer could change the elements of the header. At first, she thinks to herself: "Well, fine. I will make the variables constants and then Jasper will not be able to change the values."

```
PACKAGE mfe_reports
IS
    topline CONSTANT VARCHAR2(100) :=
        'My Flimsy Excuse - We Report for You!!!!!!';
    bottomline CONSTANT VARCHAR2(100) :=
        '== Report Generation Engine Version 4.3 ==';
END mfe_reports;
```

This is true. Now Jasper has no choice: he will have to accept the top and bottom lines and use them as is. Otherwise, he will get this error:

```
PLS-00363: expression 'MFE_REPORTS.TOPLINE' cannot be used as an assignment
target
```

Looking at Jasper's code, though, Lizbeth realizes that she needs to do more. If she is truly supposed to help people produce standard headers, it doesn't make any sense for them to be concatenating the various pieces together with line breaks.

So she decides to take things a step further and build a function that does all the work for the user of the mfe_reports package:

```
PACKAGE mfe_reports
IS
    FUNCTION standard_header (text_in in VARCHAR2) RETURN VARCHAR2;
END mfe_reports;

PACKAGE BODY mfe_reports
IS
    FUNCTION standard_header (text_in in VARCHAR2) RETURN VARCHAR2
    IS
        c_carriage_return CONSTANT VARCHAR2(1) := CHR(10);
        c_topline CONSTANT VARCHAR2(100) :=
            'My Flimsy Excuse - We Report for You!!!!!!';
        c_bottomline CONSTANT VARCHAR2(100) :=
            '== Report Generation Engine Version 4.3 ==';
    BEGIN
        RETURN c_topline
            || c_carriage_return
            || text_in
```

```
            || c_carriage_return
            || c_bottomline;
      END standard_header;
   END mfe_report
```

With this function in place, Jasper can add the header to his report with nothing more than this:

```
PACKAGE BODY mfe_acceptability
IS
   PROCEDURE acceptance_report IS
   BEGIN
      DBMS_OUTPUT.PUT_LINE (
         mfe_reports.standard_header ('Acceptance Report'));

      ... rest of report logic ...
   END acceptance_report;
```

Sure, he might still gripe a bit about the lack of control over the report header, but at least now he doesn't have to write nearly as much code. Instead, the central report package does most of the work for him.

Jasper's direct references (and changes) to the package variables in mfe_reports demonstrated some of the problems associated with global variables. A *global variable* is a data structure that can be referenced outside the scope or block in which it is declared. A variable declared at the package level (outside any individual procedure or function in that package) is global at one of two levels:

- If the variable is declared in the package body, then it is globally accessible to all programs defined within that package.
- If the variable is declared in the package specified, then it is accessible to (and directly referenceable by) any program executed from a schema that has EXECUTE authority on that package.

Globals can also be defined in any PL/SQL block. In the following block, for example, the l_publish_date is global to the local display_book_info procedure:

```
DECLARE
   l_publish_date DATE;
   ...
   PROCEDURE display_book_info IS
   BEGIN
      DBMS_OUTPUT.PUT_LINE (l_publish_date);
   END;
```

Globals are dangerous and should be avoided, because they create hidden "dependencies" or side effects. A global doesn't have to be passed through the parameter list, so it's hard for you to even know that a global is referenced in a program without looking at the implementation.

Furthermore, if that global is a variable (not a constant) and is declared in the package specification, then you have in effect *lost control* of your data. You cannot guarantee the integrity of its value, since any program run from a schema that has EXECUTE authority on the package can change the package however the developer of that program desires.

You can avoid using globals, and uncontrolled modifications to globals, in a number of ways:

Pass the global as a parameter in your procedures and functions
> Don't reference it directly within the program (circumventing the structure and visibility of the parameter list).

Declare variables, cursors, functions, and other objects as "deeply" as possible
> That would be in the block nearest to where, or within which, that object will be used). Doing this will reduce the chance of unintended use by other sections of the code.

Hide your package data behind "gets and sets"
> These are subprograms that control access to the data. This approach is covered in the next best practice.

Scope declarations as locally as possible
> If your variable is used only in a single subprogram, declare it there. If it needs to be shared among multiple programs in a package body, declare it at the package level (but never put the declaration in the package specification).

Packages should have a strong sense of personal space.

Control access to package data with "get and set" modules.

Problem: Data structures declared in a package specification may end up bypassing business rules.

Data structures (scalar variables, collections, cursors) declared in the package specification (not within any specific program) are able to be referenced directly from any program run from a session with EXECUTE authority on the package. This is almost always a bad idea and should be avoided.

Solution: Declare data in the package body, and hide the data structures via functions in the package specification.

Instead, declare all package-level data in the package body and provide "get and set" programs—a function to GET the value and a procedure to SET the value—in the package specification. Developers can then access the data through these programs, and automatically follow whatever rules you establish for manipulating that data.

Suppose that I've created a package to calculate fines for overdue books. The fine is, by default, $.10 per day, but it can be changed according to this rule: the fine can never be less than $.05 or more than $.25 per day. Here's my first version:

```
PACKAGE overdue_pkg
IS
    g_daily_fine NUMBER DEFAULT .10;
```

```
FUNCTION days_overdue (isbn_in IN book.isbn%TYPE)
    RETURN INTEGER;

-- Relies on g_daily_fine for calculation
FUNCTION fine (isbn_in IN book.isbn%TYPE)
    RETURN INTEGER;
END overdue_pkg;
```

You can easily see the problem with this package in the following block:

```
BEGIN
    overdue_pkg.g_daily_fine := .50;

    DBMS_OUTPUT.PUT_LINE ('Your overdue fine is ' ||
        overdue_pkg.fine (' 1-56592-375-8'));
END;
```

Here I bypassed the business rule and applied a daily fine of $.50! By "publishing" the daily fine variable, I lost control of my data structure and the ability to enforce my business rules.

The following rewrite of overdue_pkg (available on the book's web site) fixes the problem; for the sake of the trees, I show only the replacement of the g_daily_fine variable with its "get and set" programs:

```
PACKAGE overdue_pkg
IS
    PROCEDURE set_daily_fine (fine_in IN NUMBER);
    FUNCTION daily_fine RETURN NUMBER;
```

and the implementation:

```
PACKAGE BODY overdue_pkg
IS
    g_daily_fine NUMBER DEFAULT .10;

    PROCEDURE set_daily_fine (fine_in IN NUMBER)IS
    BEGIN
        g_daily_fine :=
            GREATEST (LEAST (fine_in, .25), .05);
    END;

    FUNCTION daily_fine RETURN NUMBER IS
    BEGIN
        RETURN g_daily_fine;
    END;
```

Now it's impossible to bypass the business rule for the daily fine.

In this particular example, by the way, you will be even *better* off if you put your maximum and minimum fine information in a table. You could then use the package initialization section to load these limits into package data structures. This way, if (more likely when) the data points change, you won't have to change the program itself, just some rows and columns in a table.

The only way to change a value is through the set procedure. The values of your data structures are protected; business rules can be enforced without exception.

By hiding the data structure, you also give yourself the freedom to change how that data is defined without affecting all accesses to the data.

CHAPTER 5

Developer As Traffic Cop

There are many ways to conceptualize the job of a software programmer. One is that we sit around and play logic puzzles all day long—and get paid for it! Another is that we perform translation services between "normal people" and computers.

Yet another way to look at what we do is that we control the flow of data traffic between users and semiconductors. This is a very important job. If we let a chunk of data make a right turn when it should make a left turn—watch out! Someone could get fired when he or she should get promoted. A stock price could dive when it should rise slightly, and so on.

In this chapter I explore best practices related to the constructs that Oracle PL/SQL offers to control the flow of processing in your programs; these are presented in the following sections:

Best Practices for Conditional and Boolean Logic
    Presents best practices for using the IF and CASE statements.

Best Practices for Loop Processing
    Presents best practices for using FOR, WHILE, and simple loops.

Best Practices for Branching Logic
    Presents best practices for using the GOTO and CONTINUE statements.

These constructs are relatively straightforward in syntax and usage. There are, however, several best practices you should take into account when you work with these kinds of statements.

Best Practices for Conditional and Boolean Logic

Follow the best practices in this section when you are using PL/SQL's IF and CASE statements. Ah, perhaps you didn't even know that PL/SQL supports CASE! This feature was introduced in Oracle9i Database in two forms: the CASE expression and the CASE statement.

The CASE expression (just as you will conclude from its name) is an *expression* that fits inside a PL/SQL statement. The CASE statement is a standalone executable statement. Here is an example of a CASE expression:

```
BEGIN
    l_value :=
        CASE l_selection
            WHEN 'A' THEN 'Apple'
            WHEN 'O' THEN 'Orange'
            ELSE NULL
        END;
END;
```

And here is an example of a CASE statement, performing the same logic as the above expression:

```
BEGIN
    CASE l_selection
        WHEN 'A' THEN l_value := 'Apple';
        WHEN 'O' THEN l_value := 'Orange';
        ELSE          l_value := NULL;
    END CASE;
END;
```

OK, enough instruction in the basics. Let's take a look at some recommendations for how best to use these statements.

Reading your code should not require mental gymnastics.

Use IF…ELSIF only to test a single, simple condition.

Problem: IF-statement logic can become complex and confusing.

The real world is very complicated; the software we write is supposed to map those complexities into applications. The result is that we often end up needing to deal with convoluted logical expressions.

You should write your IF statements in such a way as to keep them as straightforward and understandable as possible. For example, expressions are often more readable and understandable when they are stated in a positive form. Consequently, you are probably better off avoiding the NOT operator in conditional expressions.

It's not at all uncommon to write or maintain code that's structured like this:

```
IF condA AND NOT (condB OR condC)
THEN
    proc1;
ELSIF condA AND (condB OR condC)
THEN
    proc2;
```

```
    ELSIF NOT condA AND condD
    THEN
        proc3;
    END IF;
```

It's also fairly common to get a headache trying to make sense of all that.

Solution: Simplify by specifying clauses at multiple levels.

You can often reduce the trauma of headache by trading off the simplicity of the IF statement itself (one level of IF and ELSIF conditions) for the simplicity of clauses within multiple levels:

```
    IF condA
    THEN
        IF (condB OR condC)
        THEN
            proc2;
        ELSE
            proc1;
        END IF;
    ELSIF condD
    THEN
        proc3
    END IF;
```

Don't forget, by the way, to take into account the possibility of your expressions evaluating to NULL. This can throw a monkey wrench into your conditional processing.

Of course, there are always tradeoffs. Multiple levels of nested IF statements can decrease readability, so you will need to strive for a workable balance.

KISS (Keep it Simple, Steven).

Use CASE to avoid lengthy sequences of IF statements.

Problem: Lizbeth needs to construct a string conditionally from a number of pieces.

Lizbeth is writing a function that generates a flimsy excuse in a format that can then be used in email. One particular chunk of the report displays details on the usage of a specific flimsy excuse. She needs to include or exclude data based on a variety of conditions. Her code looks like this:

```
    FUNCTION excuse_as_email (
        excuse_in IN mfe_excuse.ID%TYPE
      , target_in IN VARCHAR2 DEFAULT NULL
    )
        RETURN VARCHAR2
```

```
    IS
        l_excuse        mfe_excuse%ROWTYPE    := mfe_excuse_qp.onerow (excuse_in);
        l_email_text   VARCHAR2 (32767);
    BEGIN
        /* Initialize the email text with the excuse's description. */
        l_email_text := l_excuse.description;

        /* If the excuse has a "target" add a "Dear..." */
        IF target_in IS NOT NULL
        THEN
            l_email_text := 'Dear ' || target_in || ', ' || l_email_text;
        END IF;

        /* If the excuse has a URL reference, include that inside double quotes,
           otherwise add nothing to the string. */
        IF l_excuse.url_reference IS NOT NULL
        THEN
            l_email_text := l_email_text || ' "' || l_excuse.url_reference || '"';
        END IF;

        RETURN l_email_text;
    END excuse_as_email;
```

Notice that with this approach Lizbeth also must declare a local variable to hold the string as it is built through the sequence of IF statements.

Solution: CASE will greatly simplify the code.

Lizbeth's excuse_as_email function gets the job done, but it is very awkward and verbose code—so many IF statements, so many concatenations.

This type of logic (conditionally adding logic to strings—in particular, if it is NULL, don't add anything) is perfectly suited to the use of the CASE expression. The above function could be written much more simply as:

```
    FUNCTION excuse_as_email (
        excuse_in IN mfe_excuse.ID%TYPE, target_in IN VARCHAR2 DEFAULT NULL
    ) RETURN VARCHAR2
    IS
        l_excuse   mfe_excuse%ROWTYPE := mfe_excuse_qp.onerow (excuse_in);
    BEGIN
        RETURN CASE
                   WHEN target_in IS NOT NULL
                       THEN 'Dear ' || target_in || ', '
                   ELSE NULL
               END
           || l_excuse.description
           || CASE
                  WHEN l_excuse.url_reference IS NOT NULL
                      THEN ' "' || l_excuse.url_reference || '"'
                  ELSE NULL
              END;
    END excuse_as_email;
```

Now I no longer need to declare a container for my return value; I simply construct the value directly and entirely within the RETURN statement, and back it goes!

More to the point, though, all of my conditional logic, which previously required separate IF statements, may now be contained within the single assignment, using CASE expressions.

Solution: Don't forget the ELSE in the CASE!

When you use a CASE statement, you should always include an ELSE clause. If you do not and the CASE statement does not find a match for your expression, then the Oracle database will raise an ORA-06592 error:

```
ORA-06592: CASE not found while executing CASE statement
```

Consider the following function:

```
FUNCTION fruit_translator (letter_in IN VARCHAR2) RETURN VARCHAR2
IS
    retval VARCHAR2(100);
BEGIN
    CASE
        WHEN letter_in = 'A' THEN retval := 'Apple';
        WHEN letter_in = 'B' THEN retval := 'Banana';
    END CASE;
    RETURN retval;
END fruit_translator;
```

If I run this function and pass it "O" for "Orange", I will see the following error:

```
SQL> BEGIN DBMS_OUTPUT.put_line (fruit_translator ('O')); END;
  2  /
*
ERROR at line 1:
ORA-06592: CASE not found while executing CASE statement
```

Note that this error will *not* be raised with a CASE *expression*. In other words, if I change my fruit_translator function to this:

```
FUNCTION fruit_translator (letter_in IN VARCHAR2) RETURN VARCHAR2
IS
    retval    VARCHAR2 (100);
BEGIN
    RETURN CASE
        WHEN letter_in = 'A' THEN 'Apple'
        WHEN letter_in = 'B' THEN 'Banana'
    END;
END fruit_translator;
```

then the function will simply return NULL if I pass in anything but "A" or "B" for the letter.

Beware the hidden costs of NULL.

Treat NULL conditions explicitly in conditional statements.

Problem: Why is Lizbeth's IF statement doing that?

Lizbeth writes a program that needs to either use an excuse or send a reminder to customers that they previously indicated that they wanted to use an excuse. She writes the conditional statements as follows:

```
IF l_action_type = 'EXCUSE'
THEN
    use_excuse;
ELSE
    send_reminder;
END IF;
```

When she runs the program, however, she finds that she keeps sending a reminder when she does not expect it (she certainly didn't specify an *excuse* in her test run).

After half an hour, though, she lets out a strangled cry, one that is often heard in Oracle development shops around the world: "Oh, how I hate those NULLs!"

Solution: Remember that a NULL is not equal to anything else, even another NULL, and code explicitly for that case.

When Lizbeth wrote this code, she said to herself: "Well, if it's not an excuse, it must be a reminder." And that makes perfect sense—unless, for some reason, l_action_type is set to NULL.

That situation is definitely occurring here, and so Lizbeth must change her conditional logic to explicitly address a NULL value scenario. She can do this either with an explicit check for NULL or by adding an ELSE clause:

```
IF l_action_type = 'EXCUSE'
THEN
    use_excuse;
ELSIF l_action_type = 'REMINDER'
THEN
    send_reminder;
ELSIF l_action_type IS NULL
THEN
    <respond to the NULL>
ELSE
    <general catch-all for other values>
END IF;
```

Lizbeth then must make a choice: is a NULL value a legitimate alternative or an indication of a problem? If it is a legitimate alternative that means "don't do anything," she might write this:

```
ELSIF l_action_type IS NULL
THEN
    /* Nothing to do in this case. */
    NULL;
```

In other words, even if nothing happens, you should add the code and comment to make explicit what is going on here. If you leave such processing implicit in the code, someone might come along later, decide that you didn't think about this situation at all, and write an ELSE or ELSIF clause that results in a bug.

If NULL (or any other value, for that matter) indicates a problem in the application, Lizbeth will then log and raise an error in the ELSE clause using the common error management package:

```
ELSE
    q$error_manager.raise_error (
        , error_name_in => 'UNANTICIPATED-ERROR'
        , text_in => 'Action type must be EXCUSE or REMINDER.'
        , name1_in => 'ACTION TYPE', value1_in => l_action_type);
END IF;
```

> You can also use an assertion program at the beginning of this block of code (or at least before the IF statement) to immediately raise an error if the action type is not an acceptable value. See Chapter 6 for more details on assertion routines.

Best Practices for Loop Processing

Follow the best practices in this section when you are using any of PL/SQL's looping statements:

FOR loop
Iterate through either a range of integer values or all the rows fetched from a cursor.

WHILE loop
Check a boundary condition before executing the body of the loop.

Simple loop
Use when the exit logic is coded within the body of the loop.

When you need to write a loop, you have a choice to make regarding the type of loop. Whenever you have a choice, you can make a wrong choice. Therefore, it is important to understand the differences among these loops, so you can make an informed (and, I hope, correct) decision!

Here are the high-level guidelines I use to make my determination on type of loop:

Numeric FOR loop
I use this type of loop when I know that I want/need to iterate through *every* integer value between low and high—and I will not conditionally terminate the loop early (except possibly by an exception being raised).

Cursor FOR loop
I use this type of loop when I know that I want/need to fetch *every* row identified by the cursor—and I will not conditionally terminate the loop early (except possibly by an exception being raised).

WHILE loop

I use this type of loop when I do not know in advance the number of iterations of my loop; when I need to conditionally terminate the loop based on some Boolean expression; and when I may not want the body of the loop to execute even once.

Simple loop

I use this type of loop when I do not know in advance the number of iterations of my loop; when I need to conditionally terminate the loop based on some Boolean expression; and when I want the body of the loop to execute *at least once*.

Now let's take a look at some best practices related to loops.

There's a right way and a wrong way to say goodbye.

Never EXIT or RETURN from WHILE and FOR loops.

Problem: Jasper writes a loop that offers many exit paths.

Jasper needs to write a program to loop through a set of flimsy excuses used by a customer and stored in an operating system file, and process the data according to these rules:

- If any excuse has been used more than three times, mark that excuse as off-limits in the future and terminate the loop immediately.
- If the title of the excuse contains the first name of the customer, issue a warning regarding possible lack of deniability and terminate the loop immediately.

The program he writes looks like this:

```
1   PROCEDURE analyze_excuses (customer_id_in IN mfe_customer_tp.id_t)
2   IS
3      l_customer   mfe_customer_tp.mfe_customer_rt;
4      l_excuses    mfe_excuse_tp.mfe_excuse_tc;
5      /* Keep track of the number of times this excuse was used. */
6      TYPE usage_count_by_id_t IS TABLE OF PLS_INTEGER
7         INDEX BY mfe_excuse_tp.id_t;
8      l_usages     usage_count_by_id_t;
9
10     PROCEDURE initialize IS
11     BEGIN
12        /* Get customer row and all excuses used by that customer. */
13        l_customer := mfe_customer_qp.onerow (customer_id_in);
14        l_excuses := mfe_excuse_qp.ar_cust_excuses_fk (customer_id_in);
15     END initialize;
16
17     PROCEDURE increment_usage (index_in IN PLS_INTEGER) IS
18     BEGIN
```

```
19          IF l_usages.EXISTS (l_excuses (index_in).ID)
20          THEN
21             l_usages (l_excuses (index_in).ID) :=
22                    l_usages (l_excuses (index_in).ID) + 1;
23          ELSE
24             l_usages (l_excuses (index_in).ID) := 1;
25          END IF;
26       END increment_usage;
27    BEGIN
28       initialize;
29
30       FOR indx IN l_excuses.FIRST .. l_excuses.LAST
31       LOOP
32          increment_usage (indx);
33
34          IF l_usages (l_excuses (indx).ID) > 3
35          THEN
36             mfe_excuse_xp.set_off_limits (l_excuses (indx).ID);
37             EXIT;
38          END IF;
39
40          IF INSTR (UPPER (l_excuses (indx).title), l_customer.first_name) > 0
41          THEN
42             mfe_excuse_xp.issue_warning
43                    (l_excuses (indx)
44                    , l_customer
45                    , 'Potential lack of deniability; name is mentioned!'
46                    );
47             EXIT;
48          END IF;
49       END LOOP;
50    END analyze_excuses;
```

There are, without a doubt, many fine aspects to this program, including:

Consistent table API

> The program relies on a consistent table API to retrieve information from the excuses and customers table. For more information about generating and using this API, check out Chapter 7.

Initialization module

> The program creates a separate local module, initialize, to consolidate all initialization of data used in the main body of the program.

Hiding of low-level logic

> The program hides the logic used to increment the usage counter. This logic is critical for one of the business rules of this program, but it is also very low-level stuff that is best hidden away until Jasper (or someone else) actually needs to work with it.

By taking the above steps, Jasper ensures that his executable section is smaller and is devoted almost entirely to implementing the rules for this program. And that's where the problem with this code lies.

On line 30, Jasper codes a numeric loop that states quite clearly that he should iterate through all the elements in the collection. Then within that loop, he conditionally short-circuits the loop if either of two rules is violated. Jasper has, in other words, *lied* in his code. The use of the FOR loop states that we will iterate through all elements in the collection. His EXIT statements inside the loop tell a different story. Whenever you have disconnects like this, maintainability suffers.

In a program this small, it is easy to see all of the logic in one glance, so the worrisome aspects of the program are not so obvious. Suppose, though, that the program is much longer, hundreds of lines spanning multiple pages, with several *other* conditional exit points. And suppose further that I have a problem in my code. The loop is terminating when it should not. With all these different exit points, it's hard to track the flow of the program and hard to figure out where the termination is taking place and why. What's more, the program is also inflexible because of its hardcoded exit points.

Solution: One way in, one way out.

A classic guideline from the days of structured programming is "one way in, one way out." That is, there should be only one way to enter a loop and only one way to exit it. In our example, you can never enter a loop in more than one way, but as you have seen, you can certainly exit in as many different ways as you want, resulting in the problems I described above.

Whenever you encounter this situation or are about to write a program with a FOR loop, ask yourself: do I really always want to iterate through all values or records? If so, keep the EXITs out of the loop; they clearly don't belong. If, on the other hand, you realize that you *might* need to exit under some circumstances, then do *not* use the FOR loop. Instead, switch to a WHILE or simple loop.

Here is a rewrite of analyze_excuses (focusing on the changed lines, in bold) that employs a WHILE loop with just a single exit (through the boundary condition):

```
 1   PROCEDURE analyze_excuses (customer_id_in IN mfe_customer_tp.id_t)
 2   IS
 3      l_keep_checking BOOLEAN DEFAULT TRUE;
 4
 5      ...same declarations as before...
 6   BEGIN
 7      initialize;
 8
 9      l_index := l_excuses.FIRST;
10
11      WHILE (l_index IS NOT NULL and l_keep_checking)
12      LOOP
13         increment_usage (l_index);
14
15         IF l_usages (l_excuses (l_index).ID) > 3
16         THEN
17            mfe_excuse_xp.set_off_limits (...);
18            l_keep_checking := FALSE;
19         ELSIF INSTR (UPPER (l_excuses (l_index).title)
20            , l_customer.first_name) > 0 AND l_keep_checking
```

```
21         THEN
22             mfe_excuse_xp.issue_warning (...);
23             l_keep_checking := FALSE;
24         END IF;
25         l_index := l_excuses.NEXT (l_index);
26     END LOOP;
27 END analyze_excuses;
```

Jasper now scans through the contents of the excuses collection from first to last with the NEXT method (lines 9 and 25). He uses the l_keep_checking Boolean variable to determine whether he should continue (line 11). And instead of issuing an EXIT statement in the loop, he simply assigns FALSE to this variable (lines 18 and 23).

While the change in this code might seem trivial, it is now easier to debug and understand the code. Jasper knows that the only way out of the loop is with an exception or by having line 11 evaluate to FALSE. And this approach is so much more *scalable*. As the logic becomes more complex (and usually convoluted), it is easier to incorporate this logic because he knows that he can use this single variable to control loop execution.

Finally, this piece of advice applies to the use of the RETURN and GOTO statements within a loop. Do not code multiple exit points of any sort. Treat the body of a loop as a subprogram, with a clearly defined and single path out of that loop. The person maintaining your code in years to come will thank you!

Don't take out "programmers' insurance"...and don't worry about SkyNet.*

Never declare the FOR loop index or any other implicitly declared structure.

Problem: The previous developer wrote some code just in case.

Long before Lizbeth joined My Flimsy Excuse, a developer named Oscar (whose last name, personality, and current whereabouts have been lost to the fog of history) wrote a program to remove all excuses from the system if they matched the provided title filter. The program looked like this:

```
PROCEDURE remove_excuses (filter_in IN mfe_excuses.title%TYPE)
IS
    CURSOR excuses_cur
    IS
      SELECT id, title FROM mfe_excuses
      WHERE title LIKE filter_in;
    excuse_rec mfe_excuses%ROWTYPE;
```

---

* SkyNet is the name of the computer system that attains sentience in *Terminator* (the movie in which Arnold Schwarzenegger reached the pinnacle of his acting career)—and immediately acts to wipe out the human race.

```
BEGIN
   FOR excuse_rec IN excuses_cur
   LOOP
      mfe_excuses_cp.del (excuses_rec.id);
   END LOOP;
END remove_excuses;
```

It's worked just fine for years (at least, no bugs were reported), but Lizbeth has now been asked to modify the procedure to display the last excuse removed. So she adds this code after the FOR loop:

```
   END LOOP;
   DBMS_OUTPUT.PUT_LINE (
      excuse_rec.id || ' - ' || excuses_rec.title);
END;
```

The code compiles, but Lizbeth spends the next two hours banging her head against the wall (not literally!) trying to figure out why the last excuse information keeps coming up NULL. She doesn't think to question the existing code, since it worked and was written by the legendary Oscar. It must be Lizbeth's fault, but she cannot figure it out.

Just then, Jasper wanders by in his neatly pressed Sonoma Summer jeans and every hair in place. Noticing her frustration, he stops, peers at her screen, and asks, "Hey, Lizbeth, why are you declaring that record right after the cursor? Doesn't the cursor FOR loop do that for you?"

Lizbeth takes another look at the program, groans, and lowers her head to her desk. How could she not have realized that?

Solution: Cyberspace is a world of our making. Remove all uncertainty from your code.

While Oscar is long gone and thus not available to question, it has now become clear to Lizbeth that Oscar didn't really understand how cursor FOR loops worked. So, *just to make sure,* or to put it another way, *just in case,* he added the declaration of the record to the block. That wasn't necessary; PL/SQL implicitly declares the loop index you name in your FOR loop header.

It didn't do any harm in his version of the program, but it laid the foundation for the introduction of buggy code later. Oscar thought he was declaring the loop index variable, but instead he was actually declaring a completely *different* variable with the same name.

How is that possible, you might be wondering. PL/SQL is not supposed to let us declare multiple variables with the same name in the same scope. That's true, and indeed in this situation, the variables are *not declared in the same scope.* The scope of the loop index variable is restricted to the *body* of the loop (between the LOOP and END LOOP statements). Inside this loop, any reference to excuses_rec is resolved to the loop index variable.

But when the loop terminates, any reference to excuses_rec is resolved to the explicitly declared variable, which is initialized to NULL and remains NULL.

Bottom line: rather than making sure he understood how PL/SQL works, Oscar took the easy way out and "covered all his bases," a form of insurance: "Gee, I don't know if I need to declare that or not, so I'd better declare it." This laziness made the remove_excuses program vulnerable to bugs.

There is no reason to tolerate any seeming "mysteries" in code. Software is nothing more than a series of commands that control the behavior of a silicon chip. We made up all the rules when we (the collective computer industry) made the chip and wrote the many layers of code required to control it. There is no AI lurking inside our computers, bending them to its will. There is no SkyNet about to take over our networks and launch a nuclear attack on humanity!

So, the next time you find yourself wondering, "How does that statement behave in PL/SQL?" or "What are the consequences of doing it *this* way?", take the time to write a script to explore the functionality and get actual answers to your questions.

Remove all ambiguous and unnecessary code from your programs, and that code will behave much more reliably and be more easily maintained by the next generation of programmers. Make sure, however, that your source code control system has copies of the old versions, available on demand

There is more than one way to scan a collection.

Use FOR loops for dense collections, WHILE loops for sparse collections.

Problem: It's so hard to write code without making assumptions!

Delaware is in heaven. He thought he knew all there was to know about PL/SQL… and then he discovered collections. Collections indexed by integers and indexed by strings (oh, the possibilities!). Collections that contain within them other collections! Collections used with FORALL to allow his code to run faster than he ever thought possible!

He decides to stay late and help all of the team's programmers by providing a package that offers a standard collection type (list of strings) and some utility programs to manipulate collections defined on that type. Here is the package specification Delaware creates:

```
PACKAGE stringcoll_utils
IS
    TYPE string_tt IS TABLE OF VARCHAR2 (32767)
        INDEX BY PLS_INTEGER;

    PROCEDURE show (list_in IN string_tt);

    FUNCTION eq (list1_in IN string_tt, list2_in IN string_tt)
        RETURN BOOLEAN;
END stringcoll_utils;
```

By using this package, all of the programmers will be able to easily declare a collection, display its contents, and even compare two collections of the same type to see whether they are equal. That sounds handy! In just a few moments, Delaware has thrown together this package body:

```
PACKAGE BODY stringcoll_utils
IS
    PROCEDURE show (list_in IN string_tt)
    IS
    BEGIN
        FOR indx IN list_in.FIRST .. list_in.LAST
        LOOP
            DBMS_OUTPUT.PUT_LINE (list_in (indx));
        END LOOP;
    END show;

    FUNCTION eq (list1_in IN string_tt, list2_in IN string_tt)
        RETURN BOOLEAN
    IS
    BEGIN
        IF list1_in.COUNT <> list2_in.COUNT OR
           list1_in.FIRST <> list2_in.FIRST OR
           list1_in.LAST <> list2_in.LAST
        THEN
           RETURN FALSE;
        END IF;
        FOR indx IN list_in.FIRST .. list_in.LAST
        LOOP
            IF list1_in (indx) <> list2_in (indx)
            THEN
                RETURN FALSE;
            END IF;
        END LOOP;
        RETURN TRUE;
    END eq;
END stringcoll_utils;
```

"Looking good," Delaware mutters to himself. He throws together a test script and is pleased with the results (note that he takes advantage of the boolean_utils package (see the *boolean_utils.pkg* file) to display the Boolean value):

```
DECLARE
    family    stringcoll_utils.string_tt;
    pets      stringcoll_utils.string_tt;
BEGIN
    family (1) := 'Veva';
    family (2) := 'Eli';
    family (3) := 'Chris';
    family (4) := 'Steven';
    stringcoll_utils.show (family);
    pets (1) := 'Micah, the Three Legged Cat';
    pets (2) := 'Moshe Jacobawitz, the Fat and Friendly';
    pets (3) := 'Sister Itsacat, the Dinosaur Kitty';
```

```
        boolean_utils.put_line (stringcoll_utils.eq (family, pets));
    END;
    /
```

This produces the following output:

```
Veva
Eli
Chris
Steven
FALSE
```

Those two collections certainly aren't identical. Well, what a handy little package! He enthusiastically tells the team at their weekly status meeting that he has a present for them and invites them to use stringcoll_utils. Not an hour goes by before Lizbeth asks Delaware to visit her cubicle. "What's this all about?" she asks (with a clear subtext of "Gee, I guess your code is not to be trusted").

```
DECLARE
    customer_names    stringcoll_utils.string_tt;
    excuse_titles     stringcoll_utils.string_tt;
BEGIN
    FOR rec IN (SELECT * FROM mfe_customers)
    LOOP
        customer_names (rec.id) := rec.last_name;
    END LOOP;

    stringcoll_utils.show (customer_names);
END;
/
```

This produces the following output:

```
FEUERSTEIN
DECLARE
*
ERROR at line 1:
ORA-01403: no data found
ORA-06512: at "MFE_TEMP.STRINGCOLL_UTILS", line 8
```

"No data found? But we're not doing any queries in this code, none at all!" Delaware scratches his head, puzzled. Then he asks to see the data in the authors table. "Why should that matter?" is the response. It's a sensible response. Delaware runs a query and sees:

```
ID        LAST_NAME
--------  -----------------------
7869      FEUERSTEIN
8709      RUSSELL
....
```

Embarrassment soon propels Delaware to the heart of the difficulty: the mfe_customer.id values are not sequential—but his loops assume that the collection has every element defined between the low and the high index values! "Let me get right back to you, Lizbeth," Delaware says, and hurries back to his desk.

Solution: Write "full collection scans" so that there is no assumption about how the collection is filled.

A collection in PL/SQL is like a single-dimensional array. A collection differs from an array, however, in that two of the three types of collections (nested tables and associative arrays—formerly known as index-by tables) can be sparse, which means that the defined rows in the collection need not be sequentially or densely defined. You can, in other words, assign a value to row 10 and a value to row 10,000, and no rows will exist between those two.

Lizbeth used the customer ID as the index value, which allowed her to very conveniently emulate the primary key within the collection to look up a customer last name. Unfortunately for her, and for Delaware, his code assumed—through his use of the FOR loop in the show procedure and his incremental indexing by 1 in the eq function—that there were no gaps in the collection.

What they have both discovered is that when you scan a collection with a FOR loop, PL/SQL will check every index value from low to high, regardless of whether or not it is defined in the collection. The FOR loop is entirely ignorant of the fact that you are iterating through a collection. As soon as the FOR loop tries to access an undefined row, the Oracle database raises a NO_DATA_FOUND exception (yes, the database recycles the same exception for a different purpose—definitely not a best practice!).

When Delaware is looking at the code, he realizes that he is assuming that if an element exists at index N of the first collection, it must also exist at index N of the second collection.

With his reputation on the line, Delaware quickly changes his package to rely on built-in collection methods (FIRST, LAST, NEXT), as shown below, to do the scanning:

```
PACKAGE BODY stringcoll_utils
IS
   PROCEDURE show (list_in IN string_tt)
   IS
      l_index PLS_INTEGER := list_in.FIRST;
   BEGIN
      WHILE (l_index is NOT NULL)
      LOOP
         DBMS_OUTPUT.PUT_LINE (list_in (l_index));
         l_index := list_in.NEXT (l_index);
      END LOOP;
   END show;

   FUNCTION eq (list1_in IN string_tt, list2_in IN string_tt)
      RETURN BOOLEAN
```

```
    IS
        l_are_equal   BOOLEAN      := list1_in.COUNT = list2_in.COUNT;
        l_index       PLS_INTEGER := list1_in.FIRST;
        c_last1       CONSTANT PLS_INTEGER := list1_in.LAST;
    BEGIN
        WHILE ( l_are_equal AND l_index <= c_last1 )
        LOOP
            l_are_equal := list1_in (l_index) = list2_in (l_index);
            l_index := list1_in.NEXT (l_index);
        END LOOP;

        RETURN l_are_equal;
    EXCEPTION WHEN NO_DATA_FOUND THEN RETURN FALSE;
    END eq;
END stringcoll_utils;
```

By avoiding the FOR loop, Delaware no longer makes any assumptions about the contents of the collection. The code is a bit more complicated and verbose, but it is much less likely to raise exceptions.

Here are the guidelines you should follow to figure out how best to loop through the contents of collections:

- If your collection might be sparse, use FIRST and NEXT to move from the lowest to the highest index values. Use LAST and PRIOR to move from the highest to the lowest index values.
- If your collection was populated with a BULK COLLECT query, then it will *always* be either empty or sequentially filled. So in this case, you can use a FOR loop like this to iterate safely through the elements:

      FOR index_variable IN 1 .. collection_name.COUNT

  FOR loop code is so much simpler to write and maintain that you should use it whenever possible. It is a completely safe option with BULK COLLECT.
- For a minor variation on this theme, when you are working with FORALL (which is kind of like a loop) in Oracle Database 10g Release 2 and above, you can use the INDICES OF clause to automatically skip over undefined index values in the collection.

Best Practices for Branching Logic

There is a single, but important, best practice that governs the use of branching in PL/SQL programs via the following statements:

GOTO
> Allows you to "go to" a specified label in your program.

CONTINUE
> New in Oracle Database 11g. This statement lets you terminate the current iteration of a loop and move on to the next iteration.

Maze-like programs are never a good thing.

Use GOTO and CONTINUE only when structured code is not an option.

Both of these statements allow you to perform unstructured branchings of execution in your program. The overall best practice guiding the use of these statements is simple: avoid using them whenever possible.

Generally, you might consider using either GOTO or CONTINUE when you need to modify the complex logic of an existing program and are deeply fearful of the ripple effect of your changes. In such a situation, you want to make a "surgical strike," and then escape as cleanly as possible, leaving the existing logic as unchanged as possible.

If you decide that you do need to use either of these statements, the most important thing you can do is to clearly document your use of (and justification for) that statement. Here is an example:

```
PROCEDURE someone_elses_mess
/*
|| Author: Long Gone Consultant
|| Maintained by: Sad Employee
||
|| Modification History
|| When    Who    What
|| --------------------------------------------
|| 11/2000 Sad E. Fixed bug in logic. Used GOTO to bypass Gordian
||                 Knot (a big mess) of code left by L.C.
*/
IS
BEGIN
   IF ... THEN
      IF ... THEN
         FOR index IN 1 .. my _collection.COUNT
         LOOP
               ... some logic here

   /* 11/2000 Bypass with GOTO when new condition is met. */
   IF new_condition THEN
   GOTO emergency_bailout
   END IF;

   ... more logic here

         END LOOP;
         ... lots more code
      END IF;
      -- 11/2000 GOTO Target
   << emergency_bailout >>
   NULL;
   END IF;
END;
```

Here is an example of using the new CONTINUE statement to shortcut execution of a loop iteration, but not leave the loop (as would happen with an EXIT statement):

```
BEGIN
   FOR indx IN 1 .. my_collection.COUNT
   LOOP
      ... some logic here

   /* 11/2000 Skip rest of iteration when condition is met. */
   CONTINUE WHEN new_condition;

   ... more logic here

   END LOOP;
END;
```

Resources

Check out *Code Complete,* by Steve McConnell (Microsoft Press)—specifically, Chapter 16, "Unusual Control Structures"—for an in-depth discussion of the GOTO statement and recommendations for when it can justifiably be used.

CHAPTER 6

Doing the Right Thing When Stuff Goes Wrong

"Stop being so negative, Steven!", "Why do you always assume the worst?", "You're such a 'glass half empty' person, Steven."

Ah, the grief I get when I try to convince people of all that is wrong with the world! Can't you just enjoy life, they plead, instead of complaining about it? Sure, I can and I do. But I'll bet each of you knows a person like me: a congenital whiner, always finding problems, always taking the fun out of it for everyone else. (Oh, by the way, there is a web site for such folks at *www.despair.com*.)

Well, I suggest that in the world of programming, the whiners are correct, and should be highly prized resources on any development team! (Hire me, please!) You see, almost every programmer thinks he (gender choice is deliberate) is the cat's meow, the finest coder who ever lived. He can do no wrong; he writes really cool code; he is so, so clever; and he needs to write nary a comment in his code. As a result, that amazing code contains no errors and always acts exactly as expected. So why should such a remarkable person (like you, like me?) deal with the negative? That's someone else's problem.

Even if we accept that such a person actually exists (ha!), I would still argue that Super Programmer needs to pay lots of attention to error management. After all, those fickle, kinda dumb users might still use his program incorrectly, causing that pristine work of logic to fail.

No doubt about it: whether you are the perfect programmer or just a normal, everyday coder, you need to anticipate problems and handle them in your code. Otherwise, your applications will fail in unpredictable ways, and you will communicate those failures to users in confusingly disparate manners.

The best practices in this chapter will help you prepare for and deal with errors. I've divided these into three main sections:

Best Practices for Understanding Error Handling
> Presents "big picture" best practices for error management—understanding the various types of errors and how they are detected and reported.

Best Practices for Nitty-Gritty, Everyday Exception Programming
> Presents best practices for such everyday operations as naming exceptions and coding exception handlers.

Best Practices for Coding Defensively
> Presents best practices for assertion routines that will help protect you from those who might use your programs carelessly or in ignorance.

Best Practices for Understanding Error Handling

The best practices in this category deal with understanding error handling at a high level.

Ignorance is bad exception management.

Study how error raising, handling, and logging work in PL/SQL.

Problem: Know it alls don't know the most important thing: they're wrong!

Delaware (you *knew* this was about Delaware, didn't you?) likes to write his code in packages. And he likes to use lots of named constants to hide values and make it easier to understand his code. All good ideas! Here is an example of such a package:

```
PACKAGE pet_excuses_pkg
IS
   c_classic   CONSTANT VARCHAR2 (17) := 'Dog ate homework.';

   PROCEDURE analyze_pet_excuses;

   ... lots of other program headers ...
END pet_excuses_pkg;

PACKAGE BODY pet_excuses_pkg
IS
   PROCEDURE analyze_pet_excuses IS
   BEGIN
      ...
   EXCEPTION
      WHEN OTHERS
      THEN
         error_pkg.powerful_error_logging;
   END;

   ... lots of other program bodies ...
```

```
   PROCEDURE critical_init_logic
   IS
   BEGIN
      ... lots of important set-up logic ...
   END critical_init_logic;
BEGIN
   critical_init_logic;
EXCEPTION
   WHEN OTHERS
   THEN
      error_pkg.powerful_error_logging;
END pet_excuses_pkg;
```

Everything works fine in *pet_excuses_pkg*. In particular, all that critical initialization logic is run. Just to make sure, though, Delaware has added an exception section to trap and log any errors that occur in the code of the package.

Now Delaware needs to add another constant to the package, and he is in a big hurry, so he performs a quick copy and paste:

```
PACKAGE pet_excuses_pkg
IS
   c_classic   CONSTANT VARCHAR2 (17) := 'Dog ate homework.';
   c_classic2  CONSTANT VARCHAR2 (17) := 'Karl Rove deleted my emails.';

   ... everything else, spec and body, the same ...
END pet_excuses_pkg;
```

The code compiles without error, but when he runs the pet_excuses_pkg.analyze_pet_excuses (which he didn't change one bit), he now gets a VALUE_ERROR exception. What the heck? He looks at his package and confirms that he performs powerful error logging on any exception via WHEN OTHERS. How could an exception come out unhandled, and what is causing it?

Even worse, he runs the pet_excuses_pkg.analyze_pet_excuses program again, and now it *sort of* works. He doesn't get a VALUE_ERROR exception. Instead, the error indicates that none of the critical code in his critical_init_logic procedure ever ran. How can this be? It is part of the initialization section of the package!

"There must be something wrong with my installation of the Oracle database," mutters Delaware, because what he sees so directly challenges his understanding (his bedrock certainty) of how PL/SQL works. So, he backs up all of his code and data, installs the latest version of the database, imports everything, and runs smack into the same problem. "$%^&#ing buggy Oracle!" growls Delaware.

Lizbeth wanders by at just that moment, and pokes her head into Delaware's cubicle. Astonished to find that Delaware has lost six hours of time when they are already behind on the project, Lizbeth inquires as to the source of his frustration. After receiving an explanation, she nods wearily and says:

> I ran into that last week. Irritating isn't it? Look at your second constant. The string is longer, but you forgot to change the declaration. So it is failing, and your initialization code never even runs. But—and this is what really got me—Oracle still marks the package as initialized!

Delaware fights back a sob, manages not to punch his monitor, and barely finds the courtesy to thank Lizbeth for her information.

Solution: Take some time to familiarize yourself with how PL/SQL exception management works and what PL/SQL offers to help you get the job done.

Delaware thought he knew it all, and had all bases covered. What he didn't realize is that when an exception is raised in the process of declaring a package-level constant (or variable), the initialization section is not run. Furthermore, the exception section at the bottom of a package can only handle possible errors raised *in* the initialization section of that package, not in any of the programs defined in the package. Consequently, it does not trap the VALUE_ERROR exception. Finally, yes, it is true: even if the initialization section never runs, the Oracle database still marks the package as initialized! If you run into a problem in which the first call to your code does not work, yet subsequent calls do, then it's likely that there's a problem in the code executed by the PL/SQL runtime engine to initialize your package (either in the declaration or initialization section).

And since Delaware is a Super Programmer, he can't ask for help, can't appear to know less than anyone. So he loses almost a full day hanging his head against the wall. Poor Delaware!

Before getting into specific best practices, you should be sure to understand how exception handling works. Many of us *think* that we know all the rules and all that PL/SQL has to offer, but the reality is that there are some very unintuitive aspects to Oracle's error management in PL/SQL. Furthermore, in just about every new release of the database, Oracle adds some new twists and features.

I cannot do justice in this book to all these nuances, but I offer the following list of key reminders regarding the basic functionality and capabilities of error management in PL/SQL:

Execution section
> An exception section may possibly handle only those errors raised in the execution section of the block. Errors raised in the declaration and exception sections will not be handled within that block's exception section. This is the rule that made Delaware's life a living hell for a day. See Figure 6-1 for a visual depiction of these rules.

Propagation
> You can control the propagation of an exception (how far up the execution call stack the exception goes unhandled) by placing the code that raises an exception inside a nested anonymous block with its own exception section.

SQLERRM
> Don't use SQLERRM to retrieve the message associated with the last SQL error. Instead, call the DBMS_UTILITY.FORMAT_ERROR_STACK function. SQLERRM may truncate the error message, but the DBMS_UTILITY function will not.

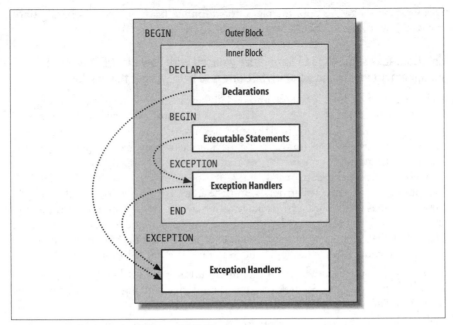

Figure 6-1. Exception handling in PL/SQL

SAVE EXCEPTIONS and SQL%BULK_EXCEPTIONS

Use SAVE EXCEPTIONS with FORALL to continue past exceptions in a bulk bind operation. Then iterate through SQL%BULK_EXCEPTIONS afterward to recover from or log errors. You should use this clause in just about every production usage of FORALL. Otherwise, you will not be able to manage errors effectively. See Chapter 9 for more information about FORALL.

DBMS_UTILITY.FORMAT_BACK_TRACE

Starting with Oracle Database 10g Release 2, use DBMS_UTILITY.FORMAT_BACK_TRACE to obtain the line number on which the most recent exception was raised. This is a critical piece of information, long missing in PL/SQL. You should call this function in every exception handler WHEN clause.

DBMS_ERRLOG

Starting with Oracle Database 10g Release 2, use DBMS_ERRLOG to continue past DML errors without raising an exception. Similar to SAVE EXCEPTIONS, the LOG ERROR clause for individual DML statements will cause error information to be written to the specified error table and no exception will be raised. After executing your SQL statements, you check the contents of the error table to see whether there were any problems.

AFTERSERVERERROR

This trigger allows you to define exception-handling logic for an entire Oracle database instance. This trigger fires only when an exception escapes unhandled from the outermost PL/SQL block. In addition, the trigger will not fire for certain exceptions, including ORA-00600 and ORA-01403.

Resources

You will find these resources helpful in explaining error handling:

- To gain a thorough understanding of PL/SQL error management, I suggest that you read Chapter 6, "Exception Handlers," of *Oracle PL/SQL Programming*.
- The *Oracle PL/SQL Developer's Workbook* contains a whole chapter of problems and solutions on error management features in PL/SQL.

I have included many of the quizzes from the Workbook on this book's web site. The filenames of all these quizzes start with "excquiz."

> I am sure that many readers will be asking: why doesn't the PL/SQL compiler warn us about assignments of default values that are too large for the variable? Oracle Corporation did add compile-time warnings in Oracle Database 10g, but this particular warning has not yet been implemented. Third-party tools like Toad's CodeXpert and PL/SQL Developer *do*, however, perform their own analysis, and such tools would have warned Delaware of his problem at the time his package was compiled.

All exceptions are not created equal.

Distinguish between deliberate, unfortunate, and unexpected errors.

An exception is an exception is an exception? Not really. Some exceptions, for example, indicate that the database is having very severe, low-level problems (such as ORA-00600). Other exceptions, like NO_DATA_FOUND, happen so routinely that we don't even really necessarily think of them as *errors*, but more as a conditional branching of logic ("If the row doesn't exist, then do this..."). Do these distinctions really matter? I think so, and Bryn Llewellyn, PL/SQL Product Manager as of the writing of this book, once taught me a very useful way to categorize exceptions:

Deliberate
> The code architecture itself deliberately relies upon an exception in the way it works. This means you must (well, *should*) anticipate and code for this exception. An example is UTL_FILE.GET_LINE.

Unfortunate
> This is an error, but one that is to be expected and one that may not even indicate that a problem has occurred. An example is a SELECT INTO statement that raises NO_DATA_FOUND.

Unexpected
> This is a "hard" error indicating a problem in the application. An example is a SELECT INTO statement that is supposed to return a row for a given primary key, but instead raises TOO_MANY_ROWS.

Let's take a closer, but brief, look at some examples that will drive home the exception categories. Then I will talk about how knowing about these categories can and should be useful to you.

Deliberate exceptions

We PL/SQL developers use UTL_FILE.GET_LINE to read the contents of a file, one line at a time. When GET_LINE reads past the end of a file, it raises NO_DATA_FOUND. That's just the way it works. So, if I want to read everything from a file and "do stuff," my program might look like this:

```
PROCEDURE read_file_and_do_stuff (
    dir_in IN VARCHAR2, file_in IN VARCHAR2
)
IS
    l_file   UTL_FILE.file_type;
    l_line   VARCHAR2 (32767);
BEGIN
    l_file := UTL_FILE.fopen (dir_in, file_in, 'R', max_linesize => 32767);

    LOOP
        UTL_FILE.get_line (l_file, l_line);
        do_stuff;
    END LOOP;
EXCEPTION
    WHEN NO_DATA_FOUND
    THEN
        UTL_FILE.fclose (l_file);
        more_stuff_here;
END;
```

You may notice something a bit strange about my loop; it has no EXIT statement. Also, I am running more application logic (more_stuff_here) in the exception section. I can rewrite my loop as follows:

```
LOOP
    BEGIN
        UTL_FILE.get_line (l_file, l_line);
        do_stuff;
    EXCEPTION
        WHEN NO_DATA_FOUND
        THEN
            EXIT;
    END;

    UTL_FILE.flcose (l_file);
    more_stuff_here;
END LOOP;
```

Now I have an EXIT statement in my loop, but that sure is some awkward code.

This is the kind of thing you need to do when you work with code that deliberately raises an exception as a part of its architecture. You'll find more in the next few sections about what I think you should about this.

Unfortunate and unexpected exceptions

I will cover these together because the two examples (NO_DATA_FOUND and TOO_MANY_ROWS) are tightly linked together. Suppose I need to write a function to return the full name of an employee (LAST,FIRST) for a particular primary key value.

I could write it most simply as follows:

```
FUNCTION fullname (
    employee_id_in IN employees.employee_id%TYPE
)
    RETURN VARCHAR2
IS
    retval   VARCHAR2 (32767);
BEGIN
    SELECT last_name || ',' || first_name
      INTO retval
      FROM employee
     WHERE employee_id = employee_id_in;

    RETURN retval;
END fullname;
```

If I call this program with an employee ID that is not in the table, the database will raise the NO_DATA_FOUND exception. If I call this program with an employee ID that is found in more than one row in the table, the database will raise the TOO_MANY_ROWS exception.

One query, two different exceptions—should you treat them the same way? Perhaps not. Do these two exceptions truly reflect similar kinds of problems?

NO_DATA_FOUND
> With this exception I didn't find a match. That *could* be a serious problem, but is not necessarily the case. Perhaps I actually expect that most of the time I will not get a match, and therefore will simply insert a new employee. It is, shall we say, *unfortunate* that the exception was raised, but in this case it is not even an error.

TOO_MANY_ROWS
> With this exception we have a serious problem on our hands: something has gone wrong with our primary key constraint. I can't think of a circumstance in which this would be considered OK or simply "unfortunate." No, it is time to set off the alarms, stop the program, and call attention to this very unexpected, "hard" error.

How to benefit from this categorization

I hope you agree that this characterization sounds useful. I suggest that when you are about to build a new application, you decide as much as possible the standard approach that you (and everyone else on the team) will take for each type of exception. Then, as you encounter (need to handle or write in anticipation of) an exception, decide into which category it falls, and then apply the already-decided-upon approach. In this way, you will write your code in a more consistent and productive manner.

Here are my guidelines for dealing with the three types of exceptions:

Deliberate
> You will need to write code in anticipation of this exception. The critical best practice in this case is to *avoid putting application logic in the exception section*. The exception section should contain only the code needed to deal with the *error:* log the error data, re-raise the exception, etc. Programmers don't expect application-specific logic there, which means that it will be much harder to understand and maintain.

Unfortunate
> If there are circumstances in which a user of the code that raises this exception would not interpret the situation as an *error*, then don't propagate this exception out unhandled. Instead, return a value or status flag that indicates that the exception was raised. You then leave it up to the user of the program to decide if that program should terminate with an error. Better yet, why not let the caller of your program tell it whether to raise an exception, and if not, what value should be passed to indicate that the exception occurred?

Unexpected
> Now we are down to the hard stuff. All unexpected errors should be logged, with a record of as much of the application context as possible to help explain why it occurred. The program should then terminate with an unhandled exception, usually the same one that was raised within the program (which can be done with the RAISE; statement), forcing the calling program to stop and deal with the error.

The following sections demonstrate how to apply these guidelines.

Problem: Application logic in the exception is hard to find and maintain.

You saw an example of this problem earlier, as a consequence of the deliberate NO_DATA_FOUND exception raised by the UTL_FILE.GET_LINE procedure. When using this program, I must create an exception handler for NO_DATA_FOUND in which I close the file and then process the data read from the file.

Solution: Avoid application logic in the exception section.

Jasper needs to write a program that will read in the contents of a file and then execute it as a DDL statement. He's used DBMS_SQL before, so he knows that he can take all the text of the DDL statement, put it into an array, and then call the PARSE function to parse and execute the statement. He's new to UTL_FILE, but he understands the basics. His first pass at writing the program looks like the read_file_and_do_stuff procedure shown earlier, namely:

```
PROCEDURE exec_ddl_from_file (
   dir_in IN VARCHAR2
 , file_in IN VARCHAR2
 )
```

```
IS
   l_file    UTL_FILE.file_type;
   l_lines   DBMS_SQL.varchar2a;
BEGIN
   l_file := UTL_FILE.fopen (dir_in, file_in, 'R');

   LOOP
      UTL_FILE.get_line (l_file, l_lines (l_lines.COUNT + 1));
   END LOOP;
```

He reads all the lines of the file into the l_lines array. He knows that UTL_FILE.GET_LINE raises the NO_DATA_FOUND exception, so he then adds an exception section:

```
EXCEPTION
   WHEN NO_DATA_FOUND
   THEN
      UTL_FILE.fclose (l_file);

      DECLARE
         l_cur    PLS_INTEGER;
         l_exec   PLS_INTEGER;
      BEGIN
         l_cur := DBMS_SQL.open_cursor;
         DBMS_SQL.parse (l_cur
                        , l_lines
                        , l_lines.FIRST
                        , l_lines.LAST
                        , TRUE
                        , DBMS_SQL.native
                        );
         l_exec := DBMS_SQL.EXECUTE (l_cur);
         DBMS_SQL.close_cursor (l_cur);
      END;
```

In other words, Jasper closes the file, then uses DBMS_SQL to parse and execute the DDL statement. It all makes so much sense, but also seems like a weirdly unbalanced program. The execution section consists of 4 lines of code, but the exception has 16 lines of code, none of it doing anything even remotely like handling an exception!

That's just too strange for Jasper, so he decides to do some *refactoring*, some internal restructuring of the code. His objective is to have only exception-handling code in the exception section and avoid what appears to be an infinite loop. Here is the end result, with an explanation of the most important changes in the table that follows:

```
1  PROCEDURE exec_ddl_from_file (
2     dir_in IN VARCHAR2, file_in IN VARCHAR2
3  )
4  IS
5     l_file    UTL_FILE.file_type;
6     l_eof     BOOLEAN;
7     l_lines   DBMS_SQL.varchar2a;
8
```

```
 9      PROCEDURE get_next_line (
10         line_out OUT VARCHAR2, eof_out OUT BOOLEAN
11      )
12      IS
13      BEGIN
14         UTL_FILE.get_line (l_file, line_out);
15         eof_out := FALSE;
16      EXCEPTION
17         WHEN NO_DATA_FOUND
18         THEN
19            line_out := NULL;
20            eof_out := TRUE;
21      END get_next_line;
22
23      PROCEDURE exec_ddl_statement (lines_in IN DBMS_SQL.varchar2a)
24      IS
25         l_cur    PLS_INTEGER;
26         l_exec   PLS_INTEGER;
27      BEGIN
28         l_cur := DBMS_SQL.open_cursor;
29         DBMS_SQL.parse (l_cur, l_lines
30                         , l_lines.FIRST, l_lines.LAST
31                         , TRUE, DBMS_SQL.native
32                         );
33         l_exec := DBMS_SQL.EXECUTE (l_cur);
34         DBMS_SQL.close_cursor (l_cur);
35      END exec_ddl_statement;
36   BEGIN
37      l_file := UTL_FILE.fopen (dir_in, file_in, 'R');
38
39      LOOP
40         get_next_line (l_lines (l_lines.COUNT + 1), l_eof);
41         EXIT WHEN l_eof;
42      END LOOP;
43
44      UTL_FILE.fclose (l_file);
45      exec_ddl_statement (l_lines);
46   EXCEPTION
47      -- Handle common UTL_FILE and DBMS_SQL errors here!
48      WHEN OTHERS
49      THEN
50         log_errors;
END exec_ddl_from_file;
```

Line(s)	Significance
9–21	The get_next_line procedure hides UTL_FILE.GET_LINE and converts the NO_DATA_FOUND exception to a Boolean flag. He can then exit the loop based on this flag value.
23–25	All the DBMS_SQL processing is placed in a separate, local procedure, so that it can be easily called as needed in the main body of exec_ddl_from_file.
39–42	The loop reads a line from the file and then exits when the end-of-file flag is TRUE. Now that loop isn't nearly so scary.

Line(s)	Significance
44–45	He closes the file and executes the DDL statement. Now it all happens in the execution section. The mysterious fog has cleared.
47–50	He doesn't need an exception section to trap and handle NO_DATA_FOUND, but he still should include an exception section to handle any problems that arise from reading the file or executing the DDL statement.

Jasper has applied my guideline by removing all application logic from the exception section. I hope that you will agree that the resulting program is much easier to understand.

Problem: Unhandled unfortunate exceptions make your code less flexible and more difficult to reuse.

You saw an example of this problem earlier, where the fullname function allowed the NO_DATA_FOUND exception to escape unhandled. I might fully expect no match to be found most of the time, and want to use that fact to go to a different branch of logic. I do not want to be forced into the exception section.

Solution: Transform the exception to a status indicator that can be interpreted by the user of that code.

Let's go back to that "full name" lookup function and apply our guidelines to its exceptions. If I pass an employee ID that has no match in the table, I don't want to necessarily allow the exception to escape unhandled. Also, as I suggested earlier, why not let the caller of your program tell it whether to raise an exception, and if not, what value should be returned to indicate that the exception occurred?

With these ideas in mind, I will change the fullname function to this:

```
1   FUNCTION fullname (
2      employee_id_in IN employees.employee_id%TYPE
3    , raise_if_ndf_in IN BOOLEAN := FALSE
4    , ndf_value_in IN fullname_t := NULL
5   )
6      RETURN VARCHAR2
7   IS
8      retval    VARCHAR2 (32767);
9   BEGIN
10      SELECT last_name || ',' || first_name
11        INTO retval
12        FROM employee
13       WHERE employee_id = employee_id_in;
14
15      RETURN retval;
16   EXCEPTION
17      WHEN NO_DATA_FOUND
18      THEN
19         IF raise_if_ndf_in
```

```
20      THEN
21          RAISE;
22      ELSE
23          RETURN ndf_value_in;
24      END IF;
25 END fullname;
```

I have added two additional parameters to the function:

raise_if_ndf_in
> If the user passes TRUE, he wants NO_DATA_FOUND to be treated as a "hard" error; that is, the exception should be raised and propagated out of the function unhandled.

ndf_value_in
> If the user passes FALSE for the previous parameter, he wants this value to be passed back as the indicator that NO_DATA_FOUND has been raised.

The exception-handling code in lines 17–24 implements precisely this logic. With my function implemented in this fashion, the caller of fullname can decide on a case-by-case basis how NO_DATA_FOUND should be treated (unfortunate or unexpected).

Problem: Unhandled unexpected errors cause a loss of information about the cause of the error.

You saw an example of this problem earlier, where the fullname function allowed the TOO_MANY_ROWS exception to escape unhandled. This error usually indicates a very serious data integrity issue, so I will want to log all relevant information from the block in which the error was raised. I can't do that if the exception propagates out unhandled to the enclosing block.

Solution: Handle those unexpected, "hard" errors and then re-raise the exception.

Because the fullname function is executing an implicit query (SELECT INTO), we also need to decide what to do about TOO_MANY_ROWS. We *could* do nothing, and simply let the error propagate out of the program unhandled.

We might, however, want to trap the exception and log the error, along with any application context information that will help us reconstruct the situation and figure out what went wrong. If I were using the Quest Error Manager error-management framework, I would write something like this:

```
EXCEPTION
    WHEN TOO_MANY_ROWS
    THEN
        q$error_manager.raise_error (
            error_code_in => SQLCODE,
            name1_in => 'EMPLOYEE_ID',
            value1_in => employee_id_in
        );
```

The raise_error procedure allows me to pass up to five name-value pairs as I log the error. The q$error_manager package also takes care of re-raising the exception and stopping the calling program.

In conclusion...

To wrap up this rather lengthy best practice ("All exceptions are not created equal"), let's summarize as follows:

- Understand the various types or categories of errors you will encounter as you write your program. I categorize the three types as deliberate, unfortunate, and unexpected
- Decide on the standard ways that you will write code to respond to these different errors.
- Write up all of this in a clear, short document so everyone on the team can easily get up to speed on this standard.
- Build or rely on templates and prebuilt components to implement as much of this code as possible.

On this final point, you can easily create a template, i.e., for a function that executes an implicit query and will need to deal with both NO_DATA_FOUND (unfortunate) and TOO_MANY_ROWS (unexpected). See the file *select into template.sql* (available on the book's web site) for an example of such a template.

One error management approach for all.

Use error-management standards to avoid confusion and conflicts.

General Problem: Chaos reigns!

If each programmer does things her own way, you end up with very uneven management of errors. Some people write errors out to a log table, others to a file. Some people use -20,000 for all user-defined exceptions. Other programmers use numbers that they "pick out of a hat" between -20,999 and -20,000. When this happens, end users can easily become very confused by the inconsistent way that information is reported to them.

In the following sections, I will go through some typical poor error-management scenarios, then offer a "one size fits all" solution that will help you do things right—when stuff starts going wrong.

Specific Problem 1: Get word back to the users.

Lizbeth is working on trigger logic. The business rule she needs to implement is that you have to be at least 15 years old to request a flimsy excuse on the company's web site.

On both update and insert actions on the mfe_customer table, Lizbeth must check the birth date of the customer and ensure that it is at least 15 years in the past. If not, she must stop the transaction from continuing and then let the user know what is wrong. "All right," Lizbeth says to herself determinedly:

> I need to put this code into a trigger and I need to raise an exception to stop the transaction. That much is clear. But how should I raise the trigger? Since the error information has to bubble all the way back "up" to the user running a Java app, I think I need to use RAISE_APPLICATION_ERROR. But that means I need to pick an error number within the range –20,999 and –20,000. Hmmmm.

Her gaze wanders over the walls of her cubicle. What number should she use? Her eyes catch on the address of the restaurant at which she is meeting her girlfriend that evening: 763 Albion Way. Problem solved—and here's the code she writes:

```
CREATE OR REPLACE TRIGGER no_babies_allowed_tr
  BEFORE INSERT OR UPDATE ON mfe_customer FOR EACH ROW
BEGIN
  IF :NEW.date_of_birth > ADD_MONTHS (SYSDATE, -1 * 15 * 12)
  THEN
    RAISE_APPLICATION_ERROR (
            -20763, 'A customer must be at least 15 years old!');
  END IF;
END no_babies_allowed_tr;
```

So what's the problem? This code "gets the job done," but in a rather clumsy way: Lizbeth has hardcoded the error number and the error message. She has also exposed the business rule (at least 15 years old) and implemented it in a clever way. All of these factors make this code hard to maintain and hard to understand.

And let's reflect for a moment on all that Lizbeth had to know or puzzle out in order to write this code. That's bad for productivity and bad for maintainability.

Specific Problem 2: How do I log my error? Let me count the ways…

Jasper is told to write a program to bill customers for all the flimsy excuses they have ordered. The document explains that if no customer is found for the customer ID provided, Jasper should log this fact, but then allow the calling program to continue. It is not, in other words, a big deal. If any other error occurs, then Jasper should log the error information and then re-raise the exception out of the program to the calling program or environment.

Being new to the project, Jasper is not familiar with the error-handling standards, so he checks in with Delaware, who somewhat dismissively points him to the errlog table with a seemingly clear instruction: "Write the error information to the error log table."

And so Jasper writes the following exception section:

```
EXCEPTION
  WHEN NO_DATA_FOUND THEN
    v_err := SQLCODE;
    v_msg := 'No customer for id ' || TO_CHAR (l_customer_id);
    v_prog := 'bill_customer'';
```

```
          INSERT INTO errlog VALUES (v_err, v_msg, v_prog, SYSDATE, USER);
       WHEN OTHERS THEN
          v_err := SQLCODE;
          v_msg := SQLERRM;
          v_prog := 'bill_customer';
          INSERT INTO errlog VALUES (v_err, v_msg, v_prog, SYSDATE, USER);
          RAISE;
    END;
```

Now, it would seem at first glance as though Jasper is doing something reasonable: he gathers up all the relevant information and places it in the errlog table. There are, however, some serious shortcomings with this exception section. Jasper does the following:

Executes the insert explicitly within each section

If he ever needs to change the table (e.g., to add another column), then each of these inserts must be modified. For example, when MFE upgrades to Oracle Database 10g, they will surely want to call the FORMAT_ERROR_BACKTRACE function of the DBMS_UTILITY package. This function will reveal the line number on which the error was raised, which is usually very important information.

Does not commit those inserts

In fact, Jasper *can't* commit his inserts here, because by doing that, he will also commit his outstanding transaction, which seems to have a bit of a problem. Yet, if the program (or user) executes a rollback, this log information will also be lost. An autonomous transaction would solve this problem, but you can't make a WHEN clause an autonomous transaction; that only applies to procedures and functions.

Writes a large volume of code

It takes Jasper a fair amount of time, effort, and—soon—debugging to ensure that all of this stuff works correctly. That is very frustrating to Jasper, because he needs and wants to focus on his high-level application logic. This exception section is nothing more than an irritating distraction: something he knows he should do, but would rather not have to deal with.

General Solution: One component, under source control, for all to use.

There is a way to avoid this kind of chaos: all developers should rely on a single component (which will usually consist of a central package or two, plus one or more supporting tables) that does most of the work for those developers. Rather than spend lots of time writing very dubious, custom exception-management code, you simply invoke the appropriate *service* in the component. The component knows about how to log errors, how to communicate them back to users, and how to re-raise exceptions. The burden of following the standard or even figuring it all out for yourself evaporates. You spend the absolute minimum amount of time dealing with errors, and you get back to your priority: implementing user requirements.

In the two sections that follow, I rewrite the problematic code assuming the availability of a freeware utility called the Quest Error Manager (represented so ably by the q$error_manager package). See the "Resources" section, later in this chapter, for information on how to obtain this utility.

Specific Solution 1: No more RAISE_APPLICATION_ERROR.

In this rewrite, Lizbeth will take care of two glaring problems:

- Rather than hardcode the implementation of the "is too young?" rule (the call to ADD_MONTHS), she takes a moment out of her busy schedule to add a new function (must_be_old_enough) to the mfe_rules package. She places in this function all the logic related to this rule, including the minimum valid age. Then she calls the function in the trigger.

- Rather than call RAISE_APPLICATION_ERROR directly, Lizbeth first defines a new error in the Quest Error Manager repository; the error name is "CUSTOMER_TOO_YOUNG". Then inside the trigger, she calls the error manager raise_error procedure and passes to it the *name* of the error and two name-value pairs (customer ID and date of birth). All of this information is then automatically stored in the error tables and passed back to the frontend for display to the user.

Here is the rewritten code:

```
CREATE OR REPLACE TRIGGER no_babies_allowed_tr
   BEFORE INSERT OR UPDATE ON mfe_customer FOR EACH ROW
BEGIN
   IF mfe_rules.must_be_old_enough (:NEW.date_of_birth)
   THEN
      q$error_manager.raise_error (
         error_name_in => 'CUSTOMER_TOO_YOUNG'
       , name1_in => 'CUSTOMER_ID'
       , value1_in =>  :NEW.customer_id
       , name2_in => 'DATE_OF_BIRTH;
       , value12_in =>  :NEW.date_of_birth);
   END IF;
END no_babies_allowed_tr;
```

A quick glance at this code gives us the feeling that there is actually more hardcoding than in the original version. Take a closer look. The hardcoding is now used only to specify the application-specific values that make up the *context* in which the error occurred (information that was not saved before at all). The error message and, more importantly, the formula for "too young" have now been hidden away, making the code more maintainable.

Specific Solution 2: Use declarative error handler routines.

Wouldn't it be nice if the error-handling standards consisted of more than "use that error log table"? With the Quest Error Manager (or another similar generic error-management framework) available, developers don't even have to *think* about the way that errors are logged. Logging could use a table or a file; it doesn't matter to the developers because they can stay focused on high-level application logic.

So, if Jasper uses the Quest Error Manager here, he can rely on standard errors that have already been defined in the repository, and stay well above the fray. The rewritten exception section might look like this:

```
EXCEPTION
    WHEN NO_DATA_FOUND THEN
        q$error_manager.register_error (
            error_name_in -> 'NO_SUCH_CUSTOMER'
            , name1_in => 'CUSTOMER_ID'
            , value1_in =>  l_customer_id);
    WHEN OTHERS THEN
        q$error_manager.raise_error (
            error_name_in => 'UNANTICIPATED-ERROR'
            , name1_in -> 'CUSTOMER_ID'
            , value1_in =>  l_customer_id);
END;
```

In the NO_DATA_FOUND handler, Jasper uses the register_error procedure to log the fact that the error occurred. This program will not, however, re-raise the exception. For OTHERS, he calls the raise_error program, which logs the error and then raises the exception again.

 In both of these cases I demonstrate the use of q$error_manager with error *names*. You can also use these same programs with error *codes* (that is, integer values).

Resources

The Quest Error Manager described for this best practice is available from Quest's ToadWorld portal at *www.ToadWorld.com*. You can link to this site from the book's web site as well.

Best Practices for Nitty-Gritty, Everyday Exception Programming

The best practices we've discussed up to this point are all "big picture" recommendations, which I certainly hope you will apply to your applications. Of course, beyond that, you will be writing error-related code on a day-to-day basis. You will want to consider the more specific best practices described in the following sections for those moments.

Your code makes me feel dumb.

Use the EXCEPTION_INIT pragma to name exceptions and make your code more accessible.

Problem: A little bit of laziness and a slight dose of advanced features can ruin a good program.

Jasper is excited. He attended a class on PL/SQL advanced features last week and learned about the FORALL statement. The instructor said that using this statement could improve the performance of multirow inserts by an order of magnitude or more. Right away, Jasper could think of a program in which such an improvement was desperately needed, and he vowed to try it when he returned from class.

So there he is, and into the program he goes. He converts his cursor FOR loop with an embedded insert into a BULK COLLECT query followed by a FORALL for the insert. The program *does* work a whole lot faster.

And to demonstrate what a good programmer he is, Jasper also makes sure to include an exception section for the program. The instructor had mentioned that when building production-quality code, you should always add a SAVE EXCEPTIONS clause to your FORALL statement. That way, if the Oracle database encounters an error during one of the inserts, it won't stop the whole FORALL process. It will save the error information and continue to the end of the array. And then Oracle will raise the ORA-24381 error, after which Jasper can check the contents of the SQL%BULK_EXCEPTIONS pseudocollection for all the errors.

So Jasper writes this exception section:

```
PROCEDURE insert_lots_of_rows
IS
...
EXCEPTION
   WHEN OTHERS
   THEN
      IF SQLCODE = -24381
      THEN
         FOR l_err_index IN 1 .. SQL%BULK_EXCEPTIONS.COUNT LOOP
         ...
```

And he feels justifiably proud of himself for making that extra effort, not just assuming that everything will go all right.

So imagine his disappointment when he shows his program to Lizbeth, and she reacts a bit angrily to his exception section: "What is that weird number −24381? How am I supposed to know what that means? Are you showing off how much you know to make me feel bad?"

Solution: Avoid writing "clever" code that shows just how much you know and how smart you are.

Jasper's problem was that he got a little bit lazy at the end of his development work on that program. Now, on the one hand, I think it's good—important, even—for programmers to be lazy. We should always be looking for ways to cut down on the code we have to write. On the other hand, you have to be very careful about *where* and *when* you are lazy.

Jasper wrote a hardcoded value into his exception section, "SQLCODE = –24381", and it made perfect sense to him, because he had just come back from a class and was familiar with such details. Lizbeth, however, hadn't attended the same class and wasn't very familiar with the FORALL statement. So when she looked at the code, it raised questions for her: "What does that number mean? Why is it here?" These are not *good* kinds of questions; they are questions that reveal her discomfort with the code. It made her feel that she was not smart enough. Certainly, Lizbeth is not going to feel comfortable making changes to such code.

We often encounter code like this, because many times programmers like to show off how "smart" they are by writing dense, complex programs. "Look at how much I can do in five lines of code!" they say to us. And we are supposed to be impressed?

I am most impressed by people who write code that I can easily understand—code that answers rather than raises questions. I deeply appreciate code that is so straightforward, so *non-clever*, that I feel perfectly at home when I open the file, and believe that I will be able to modify the program without being terrified about the side effects of my changes.

In this particular scenario, the solution is for Jasper to make a little more of an effort, and give a name to the –24381 exception. That name will then explain the code more clearly. You give names to exceptions that are otherwise identified only by an error number with the EXCEPTION_INIT pragma.

Properly chastened, Jasper goes back to insert_lots_of_rows, adds a declaration, and then changes the exception section:

```
PROCEDURE insert_lots_of_rows
IS
   errors_in_forall EXCEPTION
   PRAGMA EXCEPTION_INIT (errors_in_forall, -24381);
   ... other declarations
EXCEPTION
   WHEN errors_in_forall
   THEN
      FOR l_err_index IN 1 .. SQL%BULK_EXCEPTIONS.COUNT LOOP
      ...
```

I hope you will agree with me that this code is now much more welcoming and easier to understand.

You might also consider placing such error definitions in a package specification, so they can be shared. The way that errors_in_forall is defined in the previous example precludes it from being used in any other program. I could create a package like this:

```
PACKAGE oracle_exceptions
IS
    errors_in_forall EXCEPTION
    PRAGMA EXCEPTION_INIT (errors_in_forall, -24381);
    ...more of the same...
END;
```

And then my insert_lots_of_rows would look like this:

```
PROCEDURE insert_lots_of_rows
IS
    ... other declarations
EXCEPTION
    WHEN oracle_exceptions.errors_in_forall
    THEN
        FOR l_err_index IN 1 .. SQL%BULK_EXCEPTIONS.COUNT LOOP
        ...
```

See Chapter 8 for more information about packages.

To summarize the advice in this best practice, avoid referencing exceptions by their error numbers. If Oracle Corporation has not taken the time to give the exception a name, do it yourself!

Avoid programmer apathy.

Never use WHEN OTHERS THEN NULL.

Problem: The "I don't care" exception handler can cover up problems too indiscriminately.

Delaware needs to execute a series of DML statements. He wants to make sure he gets as much of the work done as possible. In other words, even if one of his DML statements raises an exception, he wants to execute all of the remaining statements. Here's the code he writes:

```
PROCEDURE do_it_all
IS
BEGIN
    BEGIN
        INSERT INTO table1 VALUES (...);
    EXCEPTION
        WHEN OTHERS THEN NULL;
    END;

    BEGIN
        UPDATE table2 VALUES (...);
    EXCEPTION
        WHEN OTHERS THEN NULL;
    END;
```

```
... and more of the same

    COMMIT;
END do_it_all;
```

It's just what the doctor ordered, and it works well enough in Delaware's basic tests. But when the code rolls out to production, and this code encounters the full range of possible data variations, many errors occur. Unfortunately, it takes a long time for anyone to notice that there are errors, since no exceptions are raised. And when the fact that errors are occurring *is* noticed, there is no way to see *what* is going wrong, because Delaware's code has deliberately ignored them.

Solution: Add value in WHEN OTHERS: log information and re-raise some exception or other!

The circumstances under which you will want to simply continue past an error are rare enough. But entirely *ignoring* that error (i.e., not logging any information or raising any exception) borders on pure negligence on the part of a developer. Here are a few guidelines to keep in mind:

- Only use WHEN OTHERS when you do not know of a specific exception that needs to be handled.
- Only use WHEN OTHERS when you need to trap an exception you cannot predict.
- If you are going to continue past the exception (that is, not re-raise an exception), then *at least* write some information out to a log to indicate that an exception did occur. This suggestion is valid for both WHEN OTHERS and any WHEN clause that itself raises an exception.
- Never, ever code the "I don't care" handler: WHEN OTHERS THEN NULL.

By the way, if you do need to continue past an exception that occurs in a DML statement, you might also consider using one of the following techniques:

- Use the FORALL statement to execute multiple DML statements in bulk, and include the SAVE EXCEPTIONS clause.
- Starting with Oracle Database 10g Release 2, you can use the DBMS_ERRLOG built-in package to specify that exceptions be written out to a predefined error table, rather than raising the exception. This will be much more efficient than trapping the exception and continuing.

Best Practices for Coding Defensively

In one important respect, writing software is similar to driving a car. You can be the best driver in the world, but if the other driver is awful, you can still have a big problem on your hands. So you drive *defensively*; you stay alert to the possibility that another driver might make a poor decision or be careless. You protect yourself as best you can.

It's the same with software. You believe that you are a fine programmer (and I have no reason to doubt that!), and that your programs work well. But have you guarded your programs against people who might use them carelessly or in ignorance? Probably not.

This section shows how you can use assertion routines to make sure that a person running your program does not violate any assumptions of that program.

 Assertion routines are also discussed as part of the Design by Contract paradigm in Chapter 1 in the section "Contracts work for the real world; why not software, too?".

You weren't supposed to do that with my program!

Use assertion routines to verify all assumptions made in your program.

Problem: Delaware expects everyone to be a know-it-all like him.

Delaware attended a course on collections—array-like structures in PL/SQL. He is now very excited about what he can do with collections—particularly using some of the most interesting features, like string indexing of collections.

Sunita asks him to build a utility to keep track of alternative names of flimsy excuses suggested by users. If a user tries one name, the *myflimsyexcuse.com* web site should be able to tell him, "No, you already tried that one. Think of another!" These tried-and-discarded alternatives are not stored in a database table; they are relevant only in this one session.

Those characteristics immediately get Delaware thinking about package-level variables, which persist for an entire session. He first constructs the specification of his excuse_tracker package as follows:

```
PACKAGE excuse_tracker
IS
   SUBTYPE excuse_excuse_t IS VARCHAR2 (32767);

   PROCEDURE clear_used_list;

   FUNCTION excuse_in_use (excuse_in IN excuse_excuse_t)
      RETURN BOOLEAN;

   PROCEDURE mark_as_used (excuse_in IN excuse_excuse_t);
END excuse_tracker;
```

Now that he has defined the public API (what the package needs to be able to do), he shifts focus to the package body. Relying on a string-indexed collection of Booleans, he can quickly construct his utility:

```
CREATE OR REPLACE PACKAGE BODY excuse_tracker
IS
   TYPE used_aat IS TABLE OF BOOLEAN INDEX BY excuse_excuse_t;
   g_excuses_used   used_aat;

   PROCEDURE clear_used_list
   IS
```

```
BEGIN
   g_excuses_used.DELETE;
END clear_used_list;

FUNCTION excuse_in_use (excuse_in IN excuse_excuse_t) RETURN BOOLEAN
IS
BEGIN
   RETURN g_excuses_used.EXISTS (excuse_in);
END excuse_in_use;

PROCEDURE mark_as_used (excuse_in IN excuse_excuse_t)
IS
BEGIN
   g_excuses_used (excuse_in) := TRUE;
END mark_as_used;
END excuse_tracker;
```

What could be simpler? What could be easier to use? To mark an alternative
name for a flimsy excuse as used, the programmer needs to do nothing more than
this:

```
excuse_tracker.mark_as_used ('My tummy was making loud noises.');
```

and then later on in the program, one can check whether that excuse has already
been used:

```
IF excuse_tracker.string_is_used ('My tummy was making loud noises.')
   THEN ...
```

Delaware spreads the word of his utility to the team, and the very next week,
Jasper realizes that this package will keep track of all kinds of strings, not just
excuses. And that is just what he needs in *his* part of the application. So he writes
the following program:

```
PROCEDURE mark_names_used (names list_in in DBMS_SQL.VARCHAR2A)
/* Note: VARCHAR2A is a collection type of strings
        defined in the DBMS_SQL package. */
IS
BEGIN
   /* Mark all names in list as used. */
   FOR l_index IN names_list_in.FIRST .. names_list_in.LAST
   LOOP
      excuse_tracker.mark_as_used (names_list_in (l_index));
   END LOOP;
END mark_names_used;
```

He then writes a program that builds the list of names and passes it to mark_
names_used; here is a very simplified version of that program:

```
DECLARE
   l_names    DBMS_SQL.varchar2a;
BEGIN
   l_names (1) := 'abc;';
   l_names (2) := my_package.name_from_somewhere_else();
   mark_names_used (l_names);

   ... and then lots more code
```

```
EXCEPTION
   WHEN OTHERS
   THEN
      DBMS_OUTPUT.put_line (DBMS_UTILITY.format_error_stack);
END;
```

Unfortunately, when he runs this block, he sees the following error:

```
ORA-06502: PL/SQL: numeric or value error: NULL index table key value
```

Not having worked with collections much himself, Jasper is stumped and frustrated. What is an "index table key value"? Why is this happening? Is there something wrong with Jasper's code? Is it a bug in the excuse_tracker package? Delaware's a smart guy, so Jasper figures it must be in his own code. He is embarrassed to ask Delaware about this, and he soon just gives up on using excuse_tracker.

Solution: Assume nothing! Make all assumptions explicit, and then validate them.

Jasper didn't do anything wrong...well, not directly, anyway. It turns out that the "name from somewhere else" function happened to return a NULL value. When he passed that NULL value to excuse_tracker, it tried to use it as an index value in the collection. NULLs can *never* be used in this way, however, so the Oracle database raised an exception.

So, yes, Jasper should know that. And he should make sure that all of his names are not NULL and...but wait a minute. Do these "shoulds" really fall on Jasper's shoulders? I think not. Instead, Delaware, the maker of the generic utility, should have stepped back from his code and asked himself:

- What am I assuming about the way this code will be used?
- What could go wrong when someone calls my programs?
- What errors can I anticipate and thus build in some additional checking for?

Delaware should have realized that someone unfamiliar with collections might pass in a NULL value and think that was perfectly fine. In fact, it *could* be a perfectly fine value that he or she wants to track. Well, with Delaware's implementation, that just isn't allowed.

Here's what Delaware should have done:

- Add an assertion program to his package as follows:
    ```
    PACKAGE BODY excuse_tracker
    IS
       PROCEDURE assert (expr_in IN BOOLEAN, text_in IN VARCHAR2)
       IS
       BEGIN
          IF NOT expr_in OR expr_in IS NULL
          THEN
             RAISE_APPLICATION_ERROR (-20000
                  , 'ASSERTION FAILURE! ' || text_in);
          END IF;
       END assert;
    ```
    This is a very simple program; you pass it a Boolean condition that you want to assert is *true*. If it evaluates to FALSE or to NULL, then the assertion routine

raises an exception, stopping the program, and passes back as the error message the text provided in the call to the assertion program.

- Call the assertion routine in each of the two main programs:

```
FUNCTION excuse_in_use (excuse_in IN excuse_excuse_t) RETURN BOOLEAN
IS
BEGIN
    assert (excuse_in IS NOT NULL
            , 'You must provide a non-NULL string to check in use!' );
    RETURN g_excuses_used.EXISTS (excuse_in);
END excuse_in_use;

PROCEDURE mark_as_used (excuse_in IN excuse_excuse_t)
IS
BEGIN
    assert (excuse_in IS NOT NULL
            , 'You must provide a non-NULL string to mark as used!' );
    g_excuses_used (excuse_in) := TRUE;
END mark_as_used;
```

If Delaware had done this, then when Jasper ran his program, he would have seen this error message:

```
ORA-20000: ASSERTION FAILURE! You must provide a non-NULL string to mark as
used!
```

Now the mystery is gone; the user (Jasper) is told explicitly the cause of the problem and implicitly how to fix it. Jasper can go back through his code and figure out where the NULL is coming from.

Let's summarize this best practice:

Every time you write a program, you make certain assumptions
Some assumptions can be embedded so deeply in the architecture of the application that you don't even realize you have made them.

A user of your program doesn't necessarily know about those assumptions
If you don't "code defensively" and make sure that your assumptions aren't violated, your programs can break down in unpredictable ways.

Use assertion routines to make it as easy as possible to validate assumptions in a declarative fashion
These routines, standardized for an entire application, take care of all the housekeeping: what to do when a condition fails, how to report the problem, and whether and how to stop the program from continuing.

Resources

The *assert.pkg* file, available on the book's web site, contains a generic assertion package that you can use to test any of the following conditions:

- Is it NULL or is it NOT NULL?
- Is the expression TRUE or FALSE?
- Does the date fall within a specified range?

The excuse_tracker package, and its much more sophisticated cousin, string_tracker, may also be found on the book's web site.

CHAPTER 7
Break Your Addiction to SQL

While working on the second edition of this book, I've been traveling to countries in Latin America and Europe, doing lots of presentations on best practices for PL/SQL. And in every one of these presentations, I've asked the attendees the following question:

> How many of you have any guidelines for how, when, and where you should write SQL in your PL/SQL code? For example, a piece of paper with a few dos and don'ts?

And in seminar after seminar, I am shocked at the number of hands that are raised. Or should I say, not raised? In a group of 100, perhaps 2 or 3 will raise their hands. In a group of 50 or 60, most commonly not a single person raises her hand.

I think I know why—and you probably do, too, since you should be asking yourself the same question and thinking about why you too are saying, "No, no standards for SQL."

PL/SQL developers (and their managers) take SQL completely for granted—they don't really give it a second thought, when it is written inside a PL/SQL program. The reason for this is that Oracle Corporation has made it so easy to write SQL statements inside PL/SQL. There is no need for JDBC, ODBC, or any other intermediate layer of code. Just write the SQL you need! Right there! Over and over again!

Well, I think that this casual, thoughtless approach to writing SQL is one of the biggest problems and challenges we face in our PL/SQL code. Consider the impact of SQL statements in both the writing and the managing of our code base:

- They are the cause of most of the performance problems in our code. Most optimization takes place, and must take place, in the SQL layer.
- Many, if not most, of the runtime errors in an application relate to problems with data being put into or taken from underlying database tables.
- Since the business model is constantly changing, the schema objects needed to implement that model must also change, causing a ripple effect of impact on application code.

The bottom line should be clear to everyone: the SQL statements in an application are the source of most of our "pain" as we develop and ready our application for production, and then maintain that application in the following years.

We really *must* stop taking SQL for granted. But to do this, we have to change our thinking about SQL—in essence, to break our addiction to writing SQL all over our applications—and I aim to help you do that through "shock therapy" (without the electricity).

This chapter offers a number of very specific recommendations and best practices for writing SQL within PL/SQL programs. But I am going to start off this chapter by first convincing you of a simple but astonishing fact:

> SQL is bad!

In the remainder of the chapter, I'll describe best practices in four categories:

General SQL Best Practices
> Presents fundamental best practices that apply to all of the SQL statements included in your PL/SQL programs.

Best Practices for Querying Data from PL/SQL
> Presents best practices aimed at retrieving information from the Oracle database.

Best Practices for Changing Data from PL/SQL
> Presents best practices for including DML statements (INSERT, UPDATE, DELETE) in your PL/SQL programs.

Best Practices for Dynamic SQL
> Presents best practices oriented specifically to the use of native dynamic SQL (NDS) and the built-in DBMS_SQL package. Dynamic SQL is more complex than static SQL and requires special handling.

SQL Is Bad!

Bad? SQL? How can it be bad? It is a fantastically useful way of specifying the sets of data you want to change or retrieve, without having to write programs to get that data. Yes, sure, that is true. SQL in and of itself is an elegant and powerful language. But SQL in PL/SQL? Bad, bad, bad!

Now, to prove this statement to you, I am going to rely on the power of symbolic logic. For most human beings, using logic to make an argument would not be terribly compelling. Software developers, however, have a very strong belief in and respect for logic. We use it each and every day to build (and fix) our software. Without logic, programming would be impossible and computers could not exist.

To prove to you that SQL is bad, I will take you step by step through a logical argument in the following sections.

Step 1. Hardcoding is bad.

I hope that everyone will readily agree with this first statement. It is drilled into our heads from the earliest days of learning how to write code. Let's take a moment, however, to clarify what this means.

Hardcoding occurs when you write something in your code that is, or is likely to be, repeated in other places in your code and/or changed at some point in the future. In other words, when you hardcode, you are saying to yourself and in your code: "This logic or value is never going to change, so I can stick it here, and here, and here, and everything will be fine, forever and ever."

Right.

Here is a classic example of hardcoding:

```
PROCEDURE give_raise (employee_in IN mfe_employees%ROWTYPE)
IS
BEGIN
   CASE employee_in.job_code
      WHEN 'CEO' THEN update_salary (employee_in.id, 1000000);
      WHEN 'PROGRAMMER' THEN update_salary (employee_in.id, 100);
   END CASE;
END give_raise;
```

In addition to the unjust hardcoded salary amounts, I have used literal values inside my program to identify particular job codes. Today, my program works correctly (that is, it works according to the requirements written by the CEO of My Flimsy Excuse), but only because "CEO" and "PROGRAMMER" are *at this time* the values used for the job codes. However, if those values are ever changed in the employees table, my program will fail.

There are, of course, many other types of hardcoding, often much more subtle than that shown in give_raise above. Consider this block of code:

```
1   DECLARE
2      l_id      mfe_employees.id%TYPE;
3      l_salary mfe_employees.salary%TYPE;
4
5      CURSOR emps_in_dept_cur IS
6         SELECT employee_id, salary FROM mfe_employees;
7   BEGIN
8      OPEN emps_in_dept_cur;
9      FETCH emps_in_dept_cur INTO l_id, l_salary;
10     ....
```

Can you identify the line with hardcoding? It is line 9. I have hardcoded the number of elements (2) that I fetch from the cursor. If I change my query to return a third value, this block will not compile. I will have to go down to line 9 and add a third variable. Wouldn't it be nice if I could set up my FETCH statement so that when I change my cursor SELECT list, my FETCH statement will automatically adapt to that change, and my code will compile without error? I can certainly do that, by using a record whose type is anchored to the cursor itself, as shown in the following example (line 5):

```
1  DECLARE
2     CURSOR emps_in_dept_cur IS
3        SELECT employee_id, salary FROM mfe_employees;
4
5     l_one_emp     emps_in_dept_cur%ROWTYPE;
6  BEGIN
7     OPEN emps_in_dept_cur;
8     FETCH emps_in_dept_cur INTO l_one_emp;
9     ....
```

I hope you will agree with me so far: hardcoding is bad, and there are many different ways that hardcoding can appear in our code. Now let's turn our attention back to SQL statements.

Step 2: Every SQL statement you write is a hardcoding.

Does that statement shock you? I expect that it does. Every SQL statement a hardcoding? You are probably ready to acknowledge that SQL statements can have hardcoded values inside them. But the entire SQL statement is hardcoding? Every single one?

Yes, that is my claim. And now I will prove it to you.

Think about the SQL statements that you write—inserts into tables with foreign keys, queries that join together multiple tables and views, updates against tables with check constraints—what do all these statements have in common? They contain information about the relationships among the various database objects. Those relationships are part of the massive entity-relationship diagram (ERD) that represents the business requirements implemented by our code.

Every SQL statement freezes in time a small portion of that overall ERD. That is, when I write a three-way join, I am actually saying something like this:

> I need to obtain information about an employee (mfe_employees table), the department in which she is located (mfe_departments table), and the name of her physical location (mfe_locations table). *At this point in time*, the way I will do that is by joining those three tables together with specific WHERE clauses.

So I write that query and stick it in my code. In fact, several of us write and/or copy that same three-way join into a half-dozen different programs. But two months later, the data model changes. For reasons far too complicated to explain in this short book, we decide to move the mfe_locations.name column into a new table, mfe_location_names. Suddenly, all those three-way joins are outdated: frozen in time, but the time has come and gone.

How is this static, frozen implementation of a portion of my data model any different from the hardcoding of the literal value "PRESIDENT" or the hardcoding of the number of items in my SELECT list within a FETCH statement? I don't see a difference. I don't see how we can avoid concluding that every SQL statement is a hardcoding of some part of my ERD. Do you?

Step 3. Draw the logical conclusion.

As I said earlier, we programmers are great believers in symbolic logic. It lies at the very heart of everything we do as software developers. Without logic, we couldn't write code. Without logic, we couldn't debug code. And *with* symbolic logic, I will now draw the only logical conclusion from the previous two steps, restated below in the form of a proof.

Statement	Symbolic representation
Hardcoding is bad.	HC = B
SQL is hardcoding.	SQL = HC
Therefore…SQL is bad.	SQL = B

I suppose you now expect me to say something like, "Oh, I'm just kidding around with you," but I'm not. I have just proven to you that every SQL statement we write has a fundamental problem, one that affects our ability to maintain, optimize, and enhance our applications.

Of course, just because something is "bad" doesn't mean that it isn't necessary. We *do* need to write SQL statements in our applications, and PL/SQL is the best place to put all the SQL in that application. Yet it's absolutely critical that PL/SQL developers and their managers shift their thinking about SQL. You should not take SQL for granted. You should not confuse "easy to write" with "unworthy of attention and care." I hope you find the recommendations in this chapter helpful in establishing a new perspective on SQL and a much improved way of writing SQL statements in your code.

General SQL Best Practices

The best practices in this section apply to all types of SQL statements you may write inside your PL/SQL programs.

The best way to avoid problematic code is to not write it.

Hide your SQL statements behind a programmatic interface.

Problem: PL/SQL developers are addicted to SQL!

> *Addiction*: The state of being enslaved to a habit or practice…to such an extent that its cessation causes severe trauma.
>
> —*dictionary.com*

Addition Indicator 1: Delaware spends half a day coming up with a complex five-way join to return all the data needed for a very common operation. He proudly announces his success in an email that includes the text of the query.

He uses the five-way in several places in his code. Simultaneously, Lizbeth and Jasper find a number of situations where they need the same data. Everyone is very happy. Well, they are happy until a few months go by, and the users decide they need some additional information from that query, and the five-way join changes to a six-way join.

Suddenly, everyone is frantically trying to remember where exactly they put those five-way joins. The Oracle database's dependency tracking information doesn't help all that much, so the team is left searching through program source code. In the meantime, Delaware fixes the "original" query, enhancing it to join six tables, and then sends out that bigger, fatter query to everyone so they can paste it over whatever occurrences of the five-way version they can find.

So they do that, and then a week later, users are complaining about performance, and it turns out that the big, complicated WHERE clause in the six-way join has a problem. So Delaware sorts it out and sends out another email and....

Some people never learn.

Addiction Indicator 2: Jasper needs to insert a row into the mfe_customer table. That table has 10 mandatory (not nullable) columns, six foreign keys, one primary key, six check constraints, and three unique indexes. Some part of Jasper realizes that after he writes the insert, he really should add an exception section with WHEN clauses for at least these errors:

- DUP_VAL_ON_INDEX
- ORA-01400: Column value cannot be NULL.
- ORA-02290: Check constraint violated
- ORA-02291: Integrity constraint violated—parent key not found

Who has time for that? Instead, Jasper engages in the time-honored tradition of Programming by Prayer: "I hope and pray to whatever God or gods I believe in or anyone else believes in that these errors will not occur!" Further, he rationalizes to himself: "These errors *won't* occur because we've got constraints defined. Simply can't happen." Uh-huh. The application rolls out and the errors come rolling in.

Delaware and Jasper are addicted to SQL, and they don't even realize it.

PL/SQL developers generally cannot even conceive of writing application code without writing SQL statements. And since it is so easy to do that within PL/SQL, they write their SQL without a moment's hesitation, firmly believing that they are doing nothing more than using PL/SQL as it was intended.

What they are really doing, however, is compromising their ability to tune, enhance, and maintain their code base.

Solution: Never repeat a SQL statement; instead, implement SQL behind procedures and functions.

It is ironic that one of the most wonderful features of PL/SQL—its tight syntactic integration with SQL—also leads to some of the worst practices by PL/SQL developers, as we saw in the previous section. Fortunately, it isn't all that difficult to repair the situation, once developers acknowledge that there is a problem.

The key principle to follow is that the same logical SQL statement should never be repeated. Repetition is at the core of the problems we've discussed. The best way to avoid repeating SQL is to avoid *writing* SQL. Yet we need to query data and we need to write data. Something, somewhere, needs to execute SQL, which leads us directly to the best way to avoid writing it:

> Hide all of your SQL statements behind subprogram interfaces, and then call those subprograms as needed.

Let's look at some specific applications of this general rule.

 Chris Rimmer, one of this book's technical reviewers, offers this additional advice for hiding SQL: "I find that an excellent way to avoid this kind of hardcoding is to use a view to encapsulate join logic. The problem with having join logic in PL/SQL packages is that you may have a SQL statement that requires several of these rules in it. The Oracle database doesn't (yet!) allow us to combine several cursors into one. But it does allow us to combine several views into one."

Never hardcode or expose a query in your application-level code. When you are writing application-level code, you are responding more or less directly to user requirements. This is very high-level logic, and to be productive, you want to stay at that high level as much as possible. SQL statements are intimately connected with user requirements, and SQL certainly offers a high level of abstraction when it comes to asking for and changing data in the database. Still, the internal "details" of that SQL statement (which tables to reference, how to construct a WHERE clause, etc.) are often well below the abstraction of a user requirement. The more time you spend writing SQL, the less time you spend implementing your real requirements.

Consider the five-way join that Delaware built so proudly. Multiple copies of that query led to reduced productivity and performance. Now imagine if Delaware had taken another approach: he gets the query working and then puts it inside a function. The function returns a collection of records based on the query:

```
PACKAGE complex_queries
IS
    CURSOR big_join_cur IS
    .... all the SQL stuff right here ....;

    TYPE big_join_aat IS TABLE OF five_way_join_cur%ROWTYPE
        INDEX BY PLS_INTEGER;

    FUNCTION big_join (...parameter list...) RETURN five_way_join_aat;
END complex_queries;
```

Now instead of emailing everyone the contents of the cursor, he lets everyone know that they can simply call complex_queries.big_join, get back the collection of records, and process the data from there. So everyone calls the function, and life goes on. Then weeks later, when they discover the need to change the query to a six-way join or they realize that performance is awful and the big, fat query needs a tune-up, Delaware can change only the implementation of the cursor. The application code that calls the function doesn't have to change at all! In other words:

> By hiding your query behind a function, you make it possible to change your implementation without having to change application code (or at least you minimize the impact on application code).

In this example, Delaware was retrieving multiple rows of data, so he used a collection as the function return type. If you are returning multiple rows of data back to a non-PL/SQL host environment, you might want to return a cursor variable instead. If you are returning a single row of data, your function should return a record. In all cases, however, the key principle is the same: the SQL is not written directly in the application code.

And let's face it: if you don't write it, you can't repeat it!

Encapsulate INSERT, UPDATE, and DELETE statements behind procedure calls. As important as it is to encapsulate queries, hiding DML operations is even more critical, since these statements usually are involved in more performance problems and more runtime errors. Of course, DML statements are usually (not always) simpler in structure than queries. An insert is an insert is an insert...so why bother with encapsulation? The most compelling case I can offer has to do with error handling.

We all write inserts, and just about every table we work with has constraints: a primary key, multiple foreign keys, check constraints, etc. Every single one of these constraints could be violated with your DML statements. And we generally deal with this reality in one of several inadequate ways:

Denial
> You simply deny the possibility (likelihood) of an error's occurring with rationalizations like "It's *never* going to raise DUP_VAL_ON_INDEX—we check for uniqueness on the frontend!"

Unhandled exception
> "So what if an exception is raised? It will stop the insert, that's the main thing. I'll let the exception bubble up, and the users will call Support."

WHEN OTHERS
> "OK, I will trap the error and log whatever information I can find about the situation. There. Satisfied?"

So why do I call these inadequate?

Denial

Never say "never!" We should not depend on frontend coders to catch everything. Sure, the insert won't succeed, so bad data won't get into the database. Still, if you want to stop the problem from recurring, you need to trap and log that error.

Unhandled exception

This has the same basic drawback as denial. If you don't handle the exception, you can't log it, which will make it harder to fix the source of the problem.

WHEN OTHERS

Good, now you are trapping the exception! The problem with WHEN OTHERS, however, is that you have to write lots of code in that one section to log different information, depending on the error. And even if you *do* take the time to write a WHEN OTHERS for the insert at hand, are you going to do that for *every* insert that you write? Probably not. Who has time for that?

The bottom line is that if you want to avoid denial and write solid error management for your DML, the only realistic way to make that happen is to write (or generate) that DML statement *just once* inside a procedure, and put all the error logic in that single program. Then, whenever anyone performs the DML through the procedure, they get the full benefit of all that error management logic!

The path to an effective programmatic interface for your SQL. Have I made a convincing case? I hope you will agree that we should avoid writing SQL whenever possible; and when we do write it, we should make sure we are not repeating SQL statements that have already been written.

The best way to avoid repetition is to hide those pesky SQL statements behind procedures and functions. I can almost hear you thinking:

Fine, I'm willing to entertain this notion. But we write lots and lots of SQL. Are you saying that we now have to write hundreds of additional programs? Who has time for that? And think about all the bugs we would be placing in our applications. Your advice doesn't sound very practical at all.

Well, if I were really proposing to you that you write all those subprograms yourself, I would have to agree with you—it's impractical, to say the least. Instead, I propose the following:

Generate as much of this code as you can, and hand-code only that which you cannot generate.

And when you write your custom SQL statements, you need to decide where to put them so that they are easy to find and use.

Let's first take a look at SQL generation, and then I will return to the challenge of organizing the *remaining* SQL that we still have to write ourselves.

There are many paths to SQL generation. For example, if you have built Oracle Forms applications, you have relied heavily on generated SQL within those base table blocks. In the Java world, a utility called Hibernate generates SQL for use within Java classes, as part of its overall management of interaction between Java and the database. Oracle Designer has long offered the ability to generate table APIs or TAPIs (table application programmatic interfaces) that handle many of the most common SQL operations on tables and views.

Oracle Designer is not, however, used by most PL/SQL shops, nor is Oracle Forms. I personally don't use either of these tools, but I really like table APIs, so I have written my own SQL generator (actually, two of them). The first, PL/Generator, is still available, but has been largely superseded by a very powerful, free tool from Quest: the Quest CodeGen Utility.

CodeGen is a generic code generator (I like to think of it as a *design pattern factory*); you can use to generate all kinds of PL/SQL code, as well as any other type of code (Java, HTML, Delphi, C#, etc.). But one thing it does really well "out of the box" is to generate a set of packages for a table or view that automatically covers almost all of the common SQL operations you will ever need to write. This book is not the appropriate place for an extensive training on CodeGen, but you can get lots more information (and the software, too) at *www.qcgu.net/*. For now, I'll just describe the overall architecture of CodeGen's table APIs, and leave it to you to explore further.

CodeGen generates the following code for your tables:

Change package
> This package encapsulates insert, delete, and update operations. The default name for this package is `table_name_cp`.

Query package
> This package encapsulates query operations. The default name for this package is `table_name_qp`.

Types package
> This package predefines a number of standard types, including collection, record, and cursor variable types. The default name for this package is `table_name_tp`.

In all cases, CodeGen "mines" the data dictionary for information about your tables that would imply the need for certain kinds of code. For example, if it finds a foreign key, it assumes that you probably will want to retrieve all the rows for a given foreign key, deletes all rows for that foreign key, and so on.

With these packages generated and compiled into your development schema, you will have an enormous, well-organized, very consistently named, and highly optimized toolbox of code to draw from as you build your application.

Let's look at an example from the world of My Flimsy Excuse. Suppose that Lizbeth needs to write a procedure to retrieve all the flimsy excuses ever used by a customer, and then analyze how successful specific excuses were for the customer (this will require multiple passes against the data). Without a table API in place, she might write code like this:

```
PROCEDURE analyze_excuse_use (customer_id_in IN mfe_customers.id%TYPE)
IS
   TYPE excuses_aat IS TABLE of mfe_excuses%ROWTYPE
      INDEX BY PLS_INTEGER;
```

```
      l_excuses excuses_aat;
      l_index PLS_INTEGER;
   BEGIN
      FOR excuse_rec
       IN (SELECT * FROM mfe_excuses
            WHERE customer_id = customer_id_in)
      LOOP
         l_excuses (l_excuses.COUNT + 1) := excuse_rec;
      END LOOP;

      FOR l_index IN 1 .. l_excuses.COUNT
      LOOP
         do_the_analysis (l_excuses (l_index));
      END LOOP;

      .... and then other passes through the data ....
   END analyze_excuse_use;
```

Using the CodeGen packages, this procedure would look like this (boldface indicates usages of the table API packages):

```
   PROCEDURE analyze_excuse_use (customer_id_in IN mfe_customers_tp.id_t)
   IS
      l_excuses mfe_customers_tp.mfe_customers_tc;
      l_index PLS_INTEGER;
   BEGIN
      l_excuses := mfe_customers_qp.ar_fk_excuses_by_customer (customer_id_in);

      FOR l_index IN 1 .. l_excuses.COUNT
      LOOP
         do_the_analysis (l_excuses (l_index));
      END LOOP;

      .... and then other passes through the data ....
   END analyze_excuse_use;
```

In other words, with a predefined API, I do not have to declare my collection type—it's already there for me in the types package. And I don't have to write the query; I just call the function. Even better, I don't have to wonder about the best way to write the query. This function automatically takes advantage of BULK COLLECT to maximize performance.

Of course, it is not possible to generate all of the SQL statements you will need in an application. Some of it will have to be handwritten. So do you just abandon the idea of encapsulation and put those custom (and usually the most complex) statements wherever you need them? Absolutely not! You adhere to the core principle: never repeat a SQL statement.

Here's what I did as I built the backend of Quest Code Tester for Oracle:

- For each table for which I needed to write custom SQL, I created an "XP" package. That doesn't stand for "Extreme Programming." Instead, it means "eXtra stuff"—the custom logic.

- In this XP package, I put all the custom logic and business rules and so forth related to this table.

- I also created other "eXtra stuff" packages for business entities—that is, higher-level constructs that are based on (and involve relationships among) multiple tables.

The result is a highly organized repository of backend code that provides virtually all of my SQL needs. And if I run across a new requirement (e.g., a new six-way join or any other variation of an update), I simply write it in my XP package and test it thoroughly. Then it's available for me, right now, and for all of us, later on.

You may write PL/SQL code, but SQL always takes precedence.

Qualify PL/SQL variables with their scope names when referenced inside SQL statements.

Problem: Global search-and-replace to the rescue!

Sunita asks Delaware to make a change to the delete_usages procedure. This program scans through excuse usage in the last year and removes any usage of excuses that are no longer active.

The header of the program looks like this:

```
PROCEDURE delete_usages (
    excuse_id_maybe_not_used IN mfe_excuses.excuse_id%TYPE)
```

Delaware absolutely *hates* that parameter name and does a global search-and-replace, as shown in Figure 7-1. Now, he's quite happy. He proceeds to make his change, tests a thing or two, and moves the program into production. The next day, users are screaming bloody murder: "Where did my excuses go? Why is everything cleared out?"

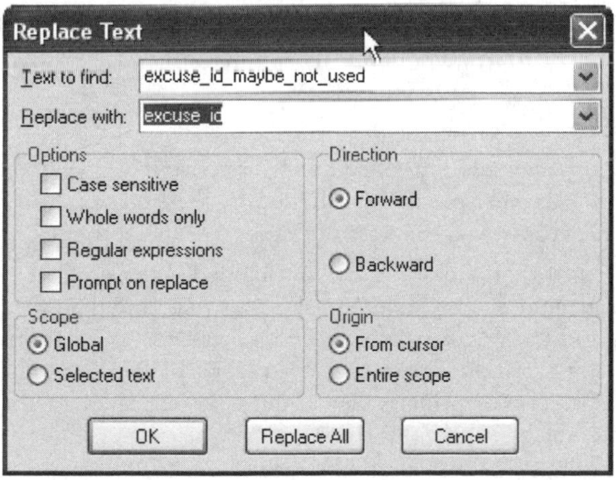

Figure 7-1. Global search-and-replace

The team very quickly concludes that there might just be a problem in the newly changed delete_usages procedure. Delaware, heart pounding at the possible loss of production data, opens up the program and scans through the code for DELETE statements. He then comes across this horrifying line:

```
DELETE FROM mfe_excuses WHERE excuse_id = excuse_id;
```

And that, dear reader, is one heck of a WHERE clause. A howl of agony erupts from Delaware's very soul. Everyone cringes. "He did it again," mutters Lizbeth.

Solution: Always check after global search-and-replace, and qualify all variable references.

Delaware was a very naughty boy. He used global search-and-replace, which is a very risky proposition in a program. He then compounded his sin by not taking the time to review every replacement to make sure his code still made sense. As a result, the DELETE statement that used to work:

```
DELETE FROM mfe_excuses WHERE excuse_id = excuse_id_maybe_not_used;
```

turned into an unconditional DELETE that removed all the rows. Bummer, as they say.

Notice that you *may* declare a variable that has the same name as a table, a column, or a view. The PL/SQL compiler won't get confused, but you might, and your SQL statements inside PL/SQL might not work as intended. So you should always make sure that there is no ambiguity between SQL and PL/SQL identifiers.

Certainly, in this particular instance, Delaware could have avoided all the heartache by making sure that the parameter name was different from the column name. This objective is normally achieved by adding prefixes or suffixes to the "root" argument name ("excuse id") to make clear that it is an argument. For example, I always append a suffix that shows the argument mode (_in, _out, or _io). I would have changed the silly argument name as follows:

```
PROCEDURE delete_usages (excuse_id_in IN mfe_excuses.excuse_id%TYPE)
```

and the DELETE statement would have been OK:

```
DELETE FROM mfe_excuses
  WHERE excuse_id = excuse_id_in;
```

Sadly, this is not really a foolproof solution. Suppose that a year goes by and the users ask to track another piece of information: "the excuse that is *in* the current excuse." In other words, you can nest an excuse within another excuse.

"OK," says the DBA. "I will add a column named 'excuse_id_in' and make it a foreign key to the mfe_excuse table." So she does that, and then the backend code is recompiled and the delete_usages procedure has no compilation errors. But it certainly will not work as expected. Now the DELETE statement deletes only those rows in which the primary key (excuse_id) is equal to the "in" excuse (excuse_id_in), which is likely never going to be true.

Bottom line: just because the name of your variable or argument is not currently used as a column name in your program, that does *not* mean that it couldn't become a column name later in the life of that program.

To avoid the confusion and bugs that can arise from such a development, you should qualify all references to PL/SQL variables inside SQL statements with their scope name (usually the name of the procedure or function in which the SQL statement is placed). Taking this approach with delete_usages, I would have the following:

```
PROCEDURE delete_usages (excuse_id_in IN mfe_excuses.excuse_id%TYPE) IS
BEGIN
   ...some logic, then:

   DELETE FROM mfe_excuses
    WHERE excuse_id = delete_usages.excuse_id_in;
```

Since tables, views, and PL/SQL program names all share the same namespace, it will be difficult to run into a naming conflict with this approach (but not impossible, since I could name my *packaged procedure* "mfe_excuses").

When one transaction is not enough.

Use autonomous transactions to isolate the effect of COMMITs and ROLLBACKs.

Problem: Your error log entries have disappeared!

Jasper is very pleased with himself. He has created his first generic utility: an error logging mechanism. Here it is:

```
PROCEDURE log_error (code IN PLS_INTEGER, msg IN VARCHAR2)
IS
BEGIN
   INSERT INTO error_log (errcode, errtext, created_on, created_by)
               VALUES (code, msg, SYSDATE, USER);
END log_error;
```

Now he can easily and quickly write information to his error log whenever needed. He writes the following program, using the logger program:

```
PROCEDURE make_changes

BEGIN
   perform_first_change ();
   perform_second_change ();
EXCEPTION
   WHEN OTHERS THEN
      log_error (SQLCODE, DBMS_UTILITY.FORMAT_ERROR_STACK);
      RAISE;
END;
```

When Jasper runs make_changes, the Oracle database raises an exception:

```
BEGIN
*
ERROR at line 1:
ORA-01403: no data found
ORA-06512: at "HR.MAKE_CHANGES", line 21
ORA-06512: at line 2
```

"Oh, goody!" says Jasper, rubbing his hands together in anticipation. "Now let's look at the log!" Unfortunately, when he queries from the log table, he gets unwelcome news:

```
SELECT * FROM error_log;
no rows selected
```

What went wrong? Where did the error log information go?

Solution: Save your log information separately from your business transaction logic.

When an unhandled exception propagates out of the PL/SQL runtime engine back to the host environment, that host environment usually (but not always) performs a full rollback in your session. That is certainly how SQL*Plus works. So in the above scenario, Jasper's program *did* write a row out to the error log, but then that row was rolled back.

Jasper *could* put a commit inside his error log procedure, but doing so would then also save any outstanding changes in the session. This is very undesirable because it is likely that there was some sort of problem with the business transaction (raising an exception). Ideally, Jasper could save just his error log, without also saving the other changes in the session.

Well, way back in Oracle8*i*, Oracle implemented this ideal and called it the *autonomous transaction*. To make a PL/SQL block (procedure, function, trigger, non-nested anonymous block) an autonomous transaction, simply include the following statement in the declaration section of the block:

```
PRAGMA AUTONOMOUS_TRANSACTION;
```

Then if you execute at least one DML statement in your program, you will need to execute a COMMIT; or ROLLBACK; statement in every exit path from the program. In other words, your autonomous transaction block must be a self-contained transaction. You cannot leave without either committing or rolling back any changes made in that program.

Here is a rewrite of log_error as an autonomous transaction:

```
PROCEDURE log_error (code IN PLS_INTEGER, msg IN VARCHAR2)
IS
   PRAGMA AUTONOMOUS_TRANSACTION;
BEGIN
   INSERT INTO error_log (errcode, errtext, created_on, created_by)
                VALUES  (code, msg, SYSDATE, USER);
   COMMIT;
EXCEPTION
   WHEN OTHERS THEN ROLLBACK;
END log_error;
```

With this implementation, I can now see the log information, even with an unhandled exception:

```
BEGIN
*
ERROR at line 1:
ORA-01403: no data found
ORA-06512: at "HR.MAKE_CHANGES", line 21
ORA-06512: at line 2

SELECT * FROM error_log
/
```

ERRCODE	ERRTEXT	CREATED_O	CREATED_BY
100	ORA-01403: no data found	01-JUN-07	HR

Autonomous transactions can come in very handy, but remember that each one of these programs operates in its own transaction "space." They do not share locks with the session from which the program was called. So if you start to throw PRAGMA AUTONOMOUS_TRANSACTION statements into lots of programs, you may suddenly encounter deadlocks. If this happens, look for code in which you have assumed that you could make a change to a row that was modified by another program in your application.

I don't always want to save my changes.

Don't hardcode COMMITs and ROLLBACKs in your code.

Problem: Is everything Lizbeth does in her programs some kind of hardcoding?

Everyone knows what hardcoding is: you put a literal value directly in your code instead of "hiding it" behind a variable, constant, or function name—as in:

```
IF l_employee.salary > 10000000 THEN
    must_be_ceo ();
END IF;
```

And we all know that this is a bad thing to do. Even if it doesn't seem as though that literal value could ever change, we know that it will, and then we will have to track down every occurrence of the number, and change each one. So that's the easy part of hardcoding. The hard part is recognizing all the different kinds of hardcoding that can appear in your code. For example, I suggest to you that every time you write COMMIT; or ROLLBACK; in your code, you have hardcoded the *transaction boundary*. That is, once you commit, you cannot undo your changes. And once you roll back, those changes are gone. Lost forever....

"Well, duh!" you are likely thinking. "That's the whole point of those statements. Now you are just being silly."

Not at all. This is one of those situations that seems so clear at first glance, but upon closer inspection is quite a bit more complicated. Let's follow along with Lizbeth as she tests one of her programs, and get a better understanding of this dynamic.

Lizbeth has created a program to adjust the popularity ratings of excuses, partitioned by gender. The specifications for this program call for a commit, so she writes the following:

```
PROCEDURE adjust_ratings (gender_in IN VARCHAR2)
IS
BEGIN
    .... execute many queries and DML statements ....
    COMMIT;
END adjust_ratings;
```

It is then time to test her program. She must write the code to set up the various tables on which the program depends (and to which it writes). Some of these tables have hundreds of thousands of rows of data, so it is not at all practical to load them from scratch each time. In fact, what really makes the most sense is to be able to run her program, look at the changes to the tables, and then (assuming that something is still wrong) issue a rollback after running adjust_ratings to return the state of the data back to its starting point.

No problem! Lizbeth just goes into her code and makes this change:

```
PROCEDURE adjust_ratings (gender_in IN VARCHAR2)
IS
BEGIN
    .... execute many queries and DML statements ....
    -- Don't commit while testing COMMIT;
END adjust_ratings;
```

Now she can run her tests, roll back, and run some more tests, without having to go through an elaborate, time-consuming setup process. And when she has fully tested the program and is sure it works, she changes the program back to its original state:

```
PROCEDURE adjust_ratings (gender_in IN VARCHAR2)
IS
BEGIN
    .... execute many queries and DML statements ....
    COMMIT;
END adjust_ratings;
```

Let's recap those steps:

1. Write the program.
2. Modify the program for testing.
3. Test the program until you are sure it works.
4. Then change the program.

What's wrong with this picture? You are not supposed to change your code *after* you finish testing! Sure, it's not a big deal to comment the COMMIT; statement out and then back in again, but what if there are dozens of such statements in your code? How will you make sure that you have changed them all?

Do you see now what I mean when I claim that the COMMIT; statement is also hardcoding? Just as a SQL statement hardcodes a part of our schema, COMMIT; hardcodes the transaction boundary. This situation seems so unambiguous at first, but once we look at the requirements for testing our code, that inflexible transaction boundary becomes an obstacle. Sometimes we want the commit to take place, but other times, we'd really rather it didn't.

Solution: Call your own program to do the commit (or rollback), and make it more flexible.

The solution to this problem is simple:

> Never call COMMIT; or ROLLBACK; directly in your code. Instead, call a program that will do the commit for you, and design that program so you can dynamically turn commits/rollbacks on and off, without changing the application code.

I have already built such a program (the my_commit.perform_commit procedure), which you can download and use (see the "Resources" section, later in this chapter). Let's see how it works. To take advantage of my commit, Lizbeth would change her procedure as follows:

```
PROCEDURE adjust_ratings (gender_in IN VARCHAR2)
IS
BEGIN
    .... execute many queries and DML statements ....
    my_commit.perform_commit ();
END adjust_ratings;
```

By default, committing is enabled, and perform_commit will do the commit; here is the implementation of this utility:

```
PROCEDURE perform_commit (context_in IN VARCHAR2 := NULL)
IS
BEGIN
    trace_action ('perform_commit', context_in);

    IF committing ()
    THEN
        COMMIT;
    END IF;
END;
```

It contains a built-in tracing facility that you can turn on to "watch" commits. But the main thing is the conditional statement that commits only when the package setting is enabled.

So when Lizbeth tests her code, she can disable saving and then run the program:

```
SQL> EXEC my_commit.turn_off
SQL> EXEC adjust_ratings ('MALE')
```

And after she has finished analyzing the results, she can simply roll back and test again.

Resources

You can download the my_commit package from this book's web site. Use these files:

my_commit.pks
> Package specification.

my_commit.pkb
> Package body.

Q##MY_COMMIT.qut
> Export file for the Quest Code Tester test definition that you can use to verify the behavior of the perform_commit procedure.

Best Practices for Querying Data from PL/SQL

Querying data is so fast and easy inside the Oracle database and PL/SQL that it can be very challenging for developers to pay attention to how they write these queries. The best practices described in this section highlight areas of special concern; you should most definitely pay attention to these areas when you write your code.

It's always better to fetch items into a single basket.

Fetch into cursor records, never into a hardcoded list of variables.

Problem: A change in one place affects many others—never a good idea.

Lizbeth creates a package to store a complicated three-way join and make it easier to reuse that join:

```
PACKAGE serial_package
AS
    PRAGMA SERIALLY_REUSABLE;

    CURSOR bewildering_cur
    IS
        SELECT E.excuse_id,  E.last_name, H.last_excuse_id
          FROM mfe_excuses E, mfe_customers C, mfe_history H
          WHERE .... big complex expression ... ;
END serial_package;
```

 When you add a SERIALLY_REUSABLE pragma to your package, you are telling the Oracle database that you do *not* want package-level data to persist in your session. Instead, after each use of the package in a block, the package is set back to an uninitialized state. In the context of this package, the pragma means that the cursor will be closed, even if you don't explicitly run the CLOSE statement. If you would like to see the impact of this statement, run the *serial_package.sql* script available on the book's web site.

Jasper then uses this package as follows:

```
PROCEDURE use_three_way_join
IS
    l_id          mfe_excuses.excuse_id%TYPE;
    l_lname       mfe_customers.last_name%TYPE;
    l_last_id     mfe_history.last_excuse_id%TYPE;
BEGIN
    OPEN serial_package.bewildering_cur;

    FETCH serial_package.bewildering_cur
     INTO l_id, l_lname, l_last_id;
    ....
END use_three_way_join;
```

After tiring out his fingers with those declarations, he finishes writing his program and tests it. It looks great, so off it goes to production. Months later, requirements change, and Lizbeth needs to add another column to the SELECT list of the three-way join: E.first_name (the first name of a customer). So she does so.

And then, even though Jasper's program doesn't need the first name, his program will *not* compile. His FETCH statement has the wrong number of elements in it. In fact, this is yet *another* example of hardcoding! Now Jasper and others must go and change their programs to reflect the new SELECT list, even though he doesn't use the new values. This is a very poor use of developer time.

Solution: Skip all those declarations and replace them with a single record.

This is one of those best practices that actually involves writing *less* code! The rule is simple:

> Whenever you fetch data from a cursor, you should fetch into a record whose structure is derived directly from that cursor with the %ROWTYPE attribute.

Let's apply this advice to Jasper's procedure:

```
PROCEDURE use_three_way_join
IS
    l_one_row  serial_package.bewildering_cur%ROWTYPE;
BEGIN
    OPEN serial_package.bewildering_cur;

    FETCH serial_package.bewildering_cur INTO l_one_row;
    ....
END use_three_way_join;
```

Gone are the multiple declarations: now a single record declaration replaces them all. And gone is the fetch into a list of values: instead, Jasper fetches into a record.

When Lizbeth upgrades the cursor and adds new columns in the SELECT list, the use_three_way_join procedure will be marked invalid. When it is next compiled, however, the structure of the l_one_row record will automatically adapt to the new SELECT list. And if Jasper's code does not need to use any of the new columns, his code will not need to be modified.

So always fetch into records—life will be easier and better!

Answer the question being asked; that is, be a good listener.

Use COUNT only when the actual number of occurrences is needed.

Problem: Delaware is not a good listener.

Sunita drops by Delaware's cubicle on her way to a status meeting. She compliments him on his new three-piece suit with elegant green vest and then gets down to business: "I need you to write a function that tells us if there is at least one excuse requested by a customer within the specified time frame."

Eager to please a manager who recognizes a smart dresser, Delaware gets right to work, and minutes later comes up with the following function:

```
FUNCTION excuse_used_between (
    customer_id_in IN mfe_customers.ID%TYPE, start_in IN DATE, end_in IN DATE
)
    RETURN BOOLEAN
IS
    l_count    PLS_INTEGER;
BEGIN
    SELECT COUNT (*) INTO l_count
      FROM mfe_excuses
     WHERE customer_id = customer_id_in
       AND used_on BETWEEN start_in AND end_in;

    RETURN l_count > 0;
END excuse_used_between;
```

He tests it, and it works just fine. An hour later, Sunita comes out of her meeting, and Delaware shows her his fine work. She looks over the code quickly and a frown passes over her face. "A frown?" thinks Delaware. "But it's *perfect*."

"Delaware, thanks for moving so quickly on this, but I am curious about something," says Sunita, "We only need to know if there are *any* excuses used, correct?"

"Yep."

"So then, why are you coming up with the total count of excuses used?"

Groan. Lower head to desk. Pat on head from Sunita. "That's OK, Delaware. Just make sure your code answers the right question."

Solution: Use COUNT only when you need to know "How many rows?"

Delaware was asked to determine whether there was *at least one* excuse used by the customer. And he got to that answer, but he did so by asking (via SQL) the question: "How *many* excuses were used?"

So who cares? He got the right answer, and that's all that matters, right?

Not really. Sure, we can treat the program as a black box, ignore the implementation, and only determine whether or not it meets user requirements. In fact, we *must* do that—when we *test* the program for correctness.

Once we have established correctness, however, it's important to think about maintainability and performance. The program shown above is challenging to maintain, precisely because the code that Delaware wrote is misleading. The code says "I need to know many rows were found," but that is not what the program header asks. That kind of disconnect causes confusion and makes it easy to introduce bugs.

From a performance standpoint, this implementation is even more troubling. The customer must wait for the function to get the full count of rows, which is totally unnecessary and could take much more time than an approach that simply verifies "at least one row."

Well, Delaware may often be in too much of a hurry, but he's no dummy. As soon as Sunita asked her question, he saw the problem. So he quickly revamps the function as follows:

```
FUNCTION excuse_used_between (
    customer_id_in IN mfe_customers.ID%TYPE, start_in IN DATE, end_in IN DATE
)
    RETURN BOOLEAN
IS
    l_dummy        PLS_INTEGER;
    l_any_used     BOOLEAN;

    CURSOR any_used_cur
    IS
        SELECT 1 dummy_value FROM mfe_excuses
         WHERE customer_id = customer_id_in
           AND used_on BETWEEN start_in AND end_in;
BEGIN
    OPEN any_used_cur;

    FETCH any_used_cur INTO l_dummy;

    l_any_used := any_used_cur%FOUND;

    CLOSE any_used_cur;

    RETURN l_any_used;
END excuse_used_between;
```

In this version, Delaware moves the query to an explicit cursor, and fetches only a single, dummy value—because the data being returned is irrelevant. The question is only: was at least one row found? In the execution section, he opens the cursor and fetches the first row. At that point, he has all the information he needs, so he checks whether a row was found, closes the cursor, and returns the Boolean value. Now the code reflects more clearly its purpose and it doesn't waste cycles coming up with the total.

In conclusion, don't use the COUNT function to answer either of the following questions:

- Is there at least one row matching certain criteria?
- Is there more than one row matching certain criteria?

Use COUNT only when you need to answer the question, "How *many* rows match a certain criteria?"

Your code makes my head spin.

Don't use a cursor FOR loop to fetch just one row.

Problem: Jasper chooses the wrong time to be lazy.

Jasper writes a function to return all the information about a customer from the customer ID. It looks like this:

```
FUNCTION one_customer (customer_id_in IN mfe_customers.ID%TYPE)
   RETURN mfe_customers%ROWTYPE
IS
BEGIN
   FOR record_from_cursor IN (SELECT * FROM mfe_customers
                              WHERE id = customer_id_in)
   LOOP
      RETURN record_from_cursor;
   END LOOP;
END one_customer;
```

And isn't Jasper delighted with himself! He has figured out a way to avoid declaring any local variables and has kept his code down to an absolute minimum, primarily by relying on the cursor FOR loop. His query will identify just one row, so the loop body executes only once, which is good, because as soon as it runs, it takes the currently selected record and returns it to the calling program.

Writing lean code is a fine thing, but in this case Jasper chose the wrong priorities. He got lazy with the cursor FOR loop and ended up with a program full of issues.

Solution: Use the cursor FOR loop only when fetching multiple rows.

First, let's list the problems with Jasper's function:

An error may occur
> If the customer ID is not found in the table, the Oracle database will raise the error *ORA-06503: PL/SQL: Function returned without value*. Personally, I consider such an error an embarrassment. "What? You can't even ensure that the function actually returns *something*?"

The program is hard to maintain
> There is a disconnect between what the program header says it wants and what the body of the program implies with its approach. Specifically, the header says "Get me one row," while the body—a cursor FOR loop—says "for each row identified by this cursor, do something."

A function's body should clearly reflect the purpose of the program, and it should not be misleading or confusing. Furthermore, it should *always* return a value unless an exception is raised. The following code offers a much better implementation of one_customer:

```
FUNCTION one_customer (customer_id_in IN mfe_customers.id%TYPE)
   RETURN mfe_customers%ROWTYPE
IS
   l_one_customer    mfe_customers%ROWTYPE;
BEGIN
   SELECT * INTO l_one_customer
     FROM mfe_customers
    WHERE id = customer_id_in;

   RETURN l_one_customer;
EXCEPTION
   WHEN NO_DATA_FOUND THEN RETURN l_one_customer;
END one_customer;
```

True, Jasper has to write some more code, but now it will not raise ORA-06503, and it clearly reflects the intention of the program stated in the header.

Best Practices for Changing Data from PL/SQL

With PL/SQL, you can not only query information from the underlying Oracle database, but also change data in tables with the INSERT, UPDATE, and DELETE operations. The best practices described in this section provide some DML-specific recommendations.

Assume the worst!

Don't forget exception handlers for your DML statements.

Problem: Jasper knows what he's supposed to do. He just can't bring himself to do it.

In his latest program, Jasper must perform several different DML statements, including an insert into the mfe_customer table. This table has a primary key, a few unique indexes, and a number of foreign keys. It's a critical and complicated table. So Jasper writes the INSERT statement, and then stares at it. He hears the tick of the clock on the wall. He is reminded of how they are weeks behind schedule on the project. And so he says to himself:

> By the time we get to the INSERT, we must have already made sure that the unique values are unique and that the foreign key values exist as primary keys in the other tables. Surely, that was done. So now I don't have to worry about any of those errors being raised. That could never happen.

In other words, he decides to be optimistic, hopeful...and probably very foolish.

Solution: Make sure that any errors that can be anticipated are logged and communicated to the user.

It's certainly lots easier to avoid writing exception handlers for all of your DML statements. They can take a lot of time, especially if your development team has not standardized on a single, reusable component that you can call to get the job done.

That kind of optimistic thinking, however, is bound to cause lots of problems sooner or later. Sure, you could argue that if the DML statement raises an exception, that error will be propagated to the enclosing block, stopping the process. It's not as though you are completely *ignoring* the possibility. Yet if you do not trap the exception within the current block or context, it is usually very difficult to extract from that block the application-specific information that is so critical for understanding why the problem occurred in the first place.

The best way to ensure solid error handling for your DML operations is to use a table API, as I recommended at the beginning of this chapter. (See the section "The path to an effective programmatic interface for your SQL.") These predefined programs will have within them all the error handling that is needed (either because it is generated or because it was handcoded—in either case, written once and, we assume, following best practices). So you just call the program, instead of writing the DML statement, and you are done.

If, however, you are not using a table API and are handcoding your DML operations wherever you want and need them, please take the time to:

- Add an exception section.
- Trap any errors that you can anticipate might occur.
- Save any relevant application information to your error log.
- Communicate back to the user in his own terms (that is, not necessarily the "raw" Oracle error message) any information that will help resolve the issue or report it to Oracle Support.

Things only get more complicated over time.

List columns explicitly in your INSERT statements.

Problem: It's hard to think about what a table will be like in the future.

Yes, Jasper is writing an INSERT statement yet again. He is adding information to the mfe_options table, which helps users track their preferences in various aspects of their use of excuses. Here is the structure of the table:

```
CREATE TABLE mfe_options (
     category VARCHAR2(100)
   , name VARCHAR2(100)
   , value VARCHAR2(4000)
);
```

To give you a sense of the data, here is part of the setup script for that table:

```
BEGIN
    INSERT INTO mfe_options (category, name, value)
        VALUES ('WELCOME_SCREEN', 'COLOR', 'GREEN');
    INSERT INTO mfe_options (category, name, value)
        VALUES ('WELCOME_SCREEN', 'COLOR', 'BLUE');
    INSERT INTO mfe_options (category, name, value)
        VALUES ('WELCOME_SCREEN', 'ALWAYS_SHOW', 'NO');
    INSERT INTO mfe_options (category, name, value)
        VALUES ('WELCOME_SCREEN', 'ALWAYS_SHOW', 'YES');
END;
```

Now Jasper needs to insert a row into this table based on data provided by the administrator for the account, so he writes this code:

```
PROCEDURE add_option (
    category_in IN VARCHAR2, name_in IN VARCHAR2, value_in IN VARCHAR2)
IS
BEGIN
    INSERT INTO mfe_options VALUES (category_in, name_in, value_in);
END add_option;
```

It works just fine—until the users decide that they want to be able to keep track of the default value within each category. So Delaware changes the table as follows:

```
ALTER TABLE mfe_options ADD is_default VARCHAR2(1) DEFAULT 'N';
```

And suddenly, even though the add_option does not do anything with default values, it will not compile.

Solution: Always explicitly list the columns that are part of the INSERT statement.

Jasper made the mistake of assuming that the structure of the mfe_options table would never change. He expressed that assumption in his code by leaving off the list of columns between the table name and the VALUES keyword. He should have written the procedure as follows:

```
PROCEDURE add_option (
    category_in IN VARCHAR2, name_in IN VARCHAR2, value_in IN VARCHAR2)
IS
BEGIN
    INSERT INTO mfe_options (category, name, value)
        VALUES (category_in, name_in, value_in);
END add_option;
```

Because the new column has a default value (and is also nullable), Jasper doesn't *have* to include it when he does an insert. And since he now states explicitly which columns should be assigned values on insert, the add_option procedure will recompile without errors after he adds the is_default column.

As you write your code, you need to keep in mind that *everything is likely to change*, and usually that change will make your code more complicated, as well as blow up previously hidden "software mines"—little points of hardcoding and assumptions that are now violated. In essence, areas of your code that are insufficiently flexible will break when changes stress that code.

Adding the explicit list of columns to your INSERT statement will make your code more flexible over time, and it will also more clearly self-document the intent of the insert.

Timing is everything in the world of cursors.

Reference cursor attributes immediately after executing the SQL operation.

Problem: I check the contents of the SQL%ROWCOUNT too late in the game.

I have had the good fortune to have published 10 books with O'Reilly Media on the subject of PL/SQL. Let's suppose that all of my titles contain the word "PL/SQL" (and that all O'Reilly books with PL/SQL in the title were authored or coauthored by yours truly).

We've gotten some complaints about the thickness of some of the books. I surely never intended that, simply by picking up one of my texts, a dear reader might be threatened with bodily injury. So we have decided to reduce the font size, which should cut the page count in half. We now need to update the top-secret O'Reilly book database (implemented, of course, in the proprietary database technology known as Oracle), so of course Tim O'Reilly comes to me, the worldwide expert on PL/SQL, to get the job done. (Note that I am making this up!) And I produce this program:

```
DECLARE
    PROCEDURE show_max_count
    IS
        l_total_pages PLS_INTEGER;
    BEGIN
        SELECT MAX (page_count) INTO l_total_pages
          FROM oreilly_catalog
          WHERE type = 'BOOK' AND title LIKE '%PL/SQL%';
        DBMS_OUTPUT.PUT_LINE ('Biggest page count is now: ' || l_total_pages);
    END;
BEGIN
    UPDATE book SET page_count = page_count / 2
     WHERE title LIKE '%PL/SQL%'
       AND status = 'IN PRINT';

    show_max_count;

    DBMS_OUTPUT.PUT_LINE ('Pages adjusted in ' || SQL%ROWCOUNT || ' books.');
END;
```

When I run this program, I see the following output:

```
Biggest page count is now: 498
Pages adjusted in 1 books.
```

One book? Has O'Reilly done the unthinkable and changed all but one of my books to "out of print?" Horrors!

Fortunately, that is not the case....

Solution: Remember that SQL% attributes always refer to the most recently executed implicit cursor in your session.

My intention in this program is to display the number of books that have been updated. Between my UPDATE and my reference to SQL%ROWCOUNT, however, I call a procedure (show_max_count) that executes an implicit SELECT MAX. The reference to SQL%ROWCOUNT will, therefore, reflect the outcome of the SELECT rather than the UPDATE.

Because the SELECT uses a group function (MAX), only one row is returned—hence, the confusing message.

INSERT, UPDATE, and DELETE statements are all executed as *implicit cursors* in PL/SQL. In other words, you don't *explicitly* declare, open, and process these kinds of statements. You simply issue the INSERT, UPDATE, or DELETE statement, and the underlying Oracle SQL engine takes care of the cursor management.

You can obtain information about the results of the implicit operation most recently executed in your session by checking any of the cursor attributes listed in the following table.

Attribute	Returns
SQL%ROWCOUNT	Number of rows affected by the DML statement
SQL%ISOPEN	Always FALSE, since the cursor is opened and then closed implicitly
SQL%FOUND	TRUE if the statement affects at least one row
SQL%NOTFOUND	FALSE if the statement affects at least one row

There is only one set of SQL% attributes in a session; they always reflect the last implicit operation performed. You should, therefore, keep to an absolute minimum the code that falls between the DML operation and the attribute reference. Otherwise, the value returned by the attribute might not correspond to the desired SQL statement, resulting in bugs that are hard to resolve.

And while we are talking about DML-related cursor attributes, here's another tip to keep in mind:

> Check SQL%ROWCOUNT when updating or removing data that "should" be there.

The SQL%ROWCOUNT cursor attribute returns the numbers of rows affected by the most recent implicit query, INSERT, UPDATE, or DELETE statement executed in your session. Check this value to verify that the action completed properly. (Note that updates and deletes don't raise an exception if no rows are affected.)

Going back to O'Reilly's fictitious book database, suppose that someone doing the data entry on my books spelled my name incorrectly when he entered my books into the repository. Now he needs to fix it and he wants to make sure he got all 10 (actually, 11, since I also coauthored a book on MySQL!). So, in addition to executing the UPDATE statement, I will need to check the value of the appropriate cursor attribute.

```
BEGIN
   UPDATE book
      SET author = 'FEUERSTEIN, STEVEN'
    WHERE author = 'FEVERSTEIN, STEPHEN';

   IF SQL%ROWCOUNT < 11
   THEN
      ROLLBACK;
      DBMS_OUTPUT.PUT_LINE ('Find the rest of Steven''s books, rapido!');
   END IF;
END;
```

Alternatively, you can avoid referencing the SQL% attributes whenever possible, and instead rely on the RETURNING clause to retrieve at least some of the information you might need. For example, I can change the previous block of code to:

```
DECLARE
   l_count_modified PLS_INTEGER;
BEGIN
   UPDATE book
      SET author = 'FEUERSTEIN, STEVEN'
    WHERE author = 'FEVERSTEIN, STEPHEN'
    RETURNING l_count_modified;

   IF l_count_modified < 11
   THEN
      ROLLBACK;
      DBMS_OUTPUT.PUT_LINE ('Find the rest of Steven''s books, rapido!');
   END IF;
END;
```

Best Practices for Dynamic SQL

Dynamic means that the SQL statement or PL/SQL block that you execute is constructed, parsed, and compiled at *runtime*, not at the time the code is compiled (this is referred to as *static code*). Dynamic SQL offers a tremendous amount of flexibility—but also complexity.

The PL/SQL language offers two implementations of dynamic SQL:

Native dynamic SQL (NDS)
   Native statements in the PL/SQL language (EXECUTE IMMEDIATE and OPEN-FOR) used to execute dynamic SQL statements.

DBMS_SQL built-in package
   A large and complex API to the low-level steps required to construct and execute SQL statements dynamically.

In general, you will find it much easier to write and maintain dynamic SQL programs with NDS rather than DBMS_SQL. In Oracle Database 10g and earlier, however, consider using DBMS_SQL in any of these situations:

Dynamic SQL method 4

At the time you write your program, you don't know either the number of elements in your SELECT list or how many variables will need to be bound. NDS is not well suited to this challenge. This is the most complicated kind of dynamic SQL, requiring the most (and the most flexible) code.

Describe columns

You need to get information about the values being returned by your dynamic SELECT. The DBMS_SQL.DESCRIBE_COLUMNS procedure will provide you with this information.

Very large SQL statement

If your statement has more than 32K characters, you will need to use the collection overloading of DBMS_SQL.PARSE to parse that statement. This scenario often arises when you are generating SQL statements for tables with lots of columns.

The Four Methods of Dynamic SQL

It is helpful to recognize four different types or *methods* of dynamic SQL. Here is a very quick summary; see *Oracle PL/SQL Programming* for more details.

Method 1

DDL statements (e.g., CREATE TABLE) or DML statements (INSERT, UPDATE, DELETE) that contain no placeholders for bind variables.

Method 2

DML statements that contain at least one placeholder, but the number of placeholders is known at the time you compile your code.

Method 3

Queries that contain a fixed number of elements in the SELECT list. That is, I am fetching 1, 6, or 13 columns, and that fact is fixed at compile time.

Method 4

At the time you write your program, you don't know either the number of elements in your SELECT list or how many variables will need to be bound. Native dynamic SQL is not well suited to this challenge.

In Oracle Database 11*g*, PL/SQL offers a variety of new features to allow for interoperability between native dynamic SQL and DBMS_SQL. You will now be able to blend the best of each of these features into an optimal solution. Here is a brief summary of these features; check the Oracle documentation for more details:

EXECUTE IMMEDIATE and OPEN-FOR (NDS)
> Now accept a CLOB argument, allowing dynamic SQL statements larger than 32K.

DBMS_SQL.TO_REFCURSOR
> Converts a DBMS_SQL cursor handle to a cursor variable, based on the predefined weak SYS_REFCURSOR type. You can start with DBMS_SQL and then manipulate the data identified by that dynamic statement with standard cursor variable functionality.

DBMS_SQL.TO_CURSOR
> Converts a cursor variable to a DBMS_SQL cursor handle. You can start with native dynamic SQL and then shift over to DBMS_SQL to take advantage of DESCRIBE_COLUMNS or some other DBMS_SQL-specific functionality.

Make it easy to untangle and debug your dynamic SQL statements.

Always parse a string variable; do not EXECUTE IMMEDIATE a literal.

Problem: There's something wrong with Lizbeth's dynamic SQL, but she can't figure it out.

Lizbeth sits at her desk, angry with herself. It is Saturday at 3:00 P.M. The sun is shining. But for some reason, she decided that morning that she really wanted to build a new program that would essentially do a "SELECT * FROM my_table" inside PL/SQL. In other words, she would supply the name of the table, and the program would display the data in the table.

So here she sits, five hours later, unable to figure out why her program isn't working.

Why did Lizbeth decide to do this? She'd just read about dynamic SQL and especially dynamic SQL method 4, and she wanted to try her hand at implementing a method 4 program. She got all excited about it, and couldn't wait. She came to the office early and, in a burst of energy and inspiration, wrote the implementation of a program with this header:

```
PROCEDURE intab (
   table_in IN VARCHAR2
 , where_in IN VARCHAR2 DEFAULT NULL
 , colname_like_in IN VARCHAR2 := '%'
 )
```

In other words, she provided the name of the table, an optional WHERE clause, and an optional filter to identify a subset of columns to display. Then she expected the program to display the data on the screen using DBMS_OUTPUT. But depending on the inputs she provides, she gets errors like this:

```
ORA-00903: invalid table name
ORA-00933: SQL command not properly ended
```

and it is really hard for her to get at the source of the problem. The SQL statement is very generic, and is parsed as follows:

```
DBMS_SQL.parse (g_cursor
                ,    'SELECT' || l_select_list
                || ' FROM ' || table_in
                ||        ' ' || l_where_clause
                , DBMS_SQL.native
                );
```

That's about as generic as you can get, and it makes it impossible for her to see what might be wrong.

Solution: Make sure your exception section can display the string that failed to parse.

It's very admirable of Lizbeth to use part of her weekend to extend her knowledge of and expertise in PL/SQL. If only she'd read this book first! Then she would have realized that her mistake is how she embeds the generic SQL statement she constructs directly inside the call to DBMS_SQL.PARSE.

Because she builds the query inside the parse call, when and if it fails, she cannot easily see that string. And let's face it: when you are working with dynamic SQL, your complicated, built-on-the-fly statement is bound to have errors (if only while you are writing—and debugging—the code that constructs it). So, you need to anticipate that reality and code for it.

Here's what Lizbeth should have done:

1. Define a local variable to hold the dynamic SQL string:

   ```
   l_query_string VARCHAR2(32767);
   ```

2. Construct the query and assign it to the variable:

   ```
   l_query_string := 'SELECT ' || l_select_list || ...
   ```

3. Parse that variable instead of the literal string:

   ```
   DBMS_SQL.parse (g_cursor, l_query_string, DBMS_SQL.native);
   ```

4. In the exception section of the program, log or display this string, along with other critical information:

   ```
   EXCEPTION
      WHEN OTHERS
      THEN
         DBMS_OUTPUT.PUT_LINE (
            'Dynamic Query Error: ' || DBMS_UTILITY.FORMAT_ERROR_STACK);
         /* Note: backtrace is only available in Oracle Database 10g and
            above. */
   ```

```
            DBMS_OUTPUT.PUT_LINE (
                'Error backtrace: ' || DBMS_UTILITY.FORMAT_ERROR_BACKTRACE );
            DBMS_OUTPUT.PUT_LINE (l_query_string);
        END;
```

With these steps taken, when Lizbeth's SQL statement fails, she can immediately look over the way it was put together. Usually the problem is nothing worse than a missing comma or a misplaced single quote. That's easy enough to fix—if you can see the SQL statement.

This same piece of advice applies to EXECUTE IMMEDIATE. Always use this statement as follows:

```
        EXECUTE IMMEDIATE variable_or_constant;
```

Never pass a literal string directly to EXECUTE IMMEDIATE.

Give the RDBMS a break.

Avoid concatenation of variable values into dynamic SQL strings.

Problem: You have lots of dynamic SQL updates, with different values each time.

Jasper is very happy to be at My Flimsy Excuse. His previous job was at WarMart, a wide-reaching chain of humongous stores devoted to retailing for the military-industrial complex. This company, whose growth was fueled by the massive increases in the U.S. military budget post–September 11, has so many employees that the company's DBA has decided to break up the single employees table into distinct tables, one for each location in which a store is located (a rather dubious database design choice!).

So Jasper one day finds himself writing a program to adjust salaries for cashiers by a specified percentage (he had rather dim expectations of that percentage being a positive number). Here is his implementation:

```
        PROCEDURE adjust_salary (adjust_percent_in IN NUMBER, job_in IN VARCHAR2)
        IS
        BEGIN
            FOR loc_rec IN (SELECT city FROM wm_offices)
            LOOP
                EXECUTE IMMEDIATE    'UPDATE wm_emp_'
                                || loc_rec.city
                                || ' SET salary = salary * (1+('
                                || TO_CHAR (adjust_percent_in)
                                || '/100)) WHERE job = '
                                || job_in;
            END LOOP;
        END adjust_salary;
```

Looks good—on paper. But when this program is run in production for a large number of combinations of adjustment percentage and job categories, the DBA raises a big fuss. It turns out that the SGA cursor cache is filling up with thousands of variations of the above UPDATE statement, pushing other preparsed cursors out of the cache, thus causing extra parsing and slowing down the entire instance of Oracle.

Solution: Bind, don't concatenate, to optimize performance and simplify dynamic string construction.

In writing the code he did, Jasper caused instance-wide performance issues—and also made his life more difficult than necessary. The problem was that he concatenated the values for adjustment percent and job title directly into the dynamic update string. As a result, with each change in these values (and there were many), the SQL statement is changed, and so requires another parse—and a distinct place in the cursor cache.

He could have avoided these extra actions and overhead by *binding* values into his dynamic SQL string. Consider the following rewrite of adjust_salary:

```
1   PROCEDURE adjust_salary (
2       adjust_percent_in IN NUMBER, job_in IN VARCHAR2
3   )
4   IS
5       l_dml VARCHAR2 (32767);
6   BEGIN
7       FOR loc_rec IN (SELECT city FROM wm_offices)
8       LOOP
9           l_dml :=
10                  'UPDATE wm_emp_'
11              || loc_rec.city
12              || ' SET salary = salary * (1+(:percentage_change/100))
13                      WHERE job = :job_category';
14
15          EXECUTE IMMEDIATE l_dml USING adjust_percent_in, job_in;
16      END LOOP;
17  END adjust_salary;
```

In this version, Jasper follows the first best practice recommendation in this section: assign the dynamic SQL string to a variable. And in this string, notice that he has replaced the concatenations of percentage and job with *placeholders* (:percentage_change and :job_category) that say, in effect, "a value must be inserted here when you execute the string."

Then on line 15, Jasper adds the USING clause to EXECUTE IMMEDIATE. He includes the correct number of values, and then the Oracle database does the rest: first, it parses the "generic" version of the update, with the placeholders. The parse phase determines that the update is syntactically correct. Next, the placeholders are replaced with the actual bind values from the USING clause. Finally, the statement is executed.

With this approach, even as the adjustment percentage or job category changes, the SQL statement that is parsed does not change. So the SQL engine reduces the amount of work it does parsing. What's more, only a single cursor is cached in the SGA, which means less swapping inside the cache.

Finally, when you use bind variables, you greatly simplify the task of writing the dynamic SQL string. You don't have to write all that concatenating code *and* you don't have to perform datatype conversions. The USING clause automatically performs native binding of the appropriate types.

 You can bind only *variable values*. You can't bind in the names of tables or columns, nor can you bind in parts of a SQL statement structure, such as the entire WHERE clause. In these cases, you must use concatenation.

So you think you know what users might do with your code?

Do not allow malicious injection of code into your dynamic statements.

Problem: So many teenagers, so many ways to enter data at the web site.

Jasper builds a web page that allows the user to specify the WHERE clause of a query against the relevant tables. Of course, the users don't realize that they are changing the WHERE clause. They don't know anything about WHERE clauses. They simply click on checkboxes and type values into fields—but changing the WHERE clause is the net effect.

When a visitor to the web page presses the Submit button, Jasper calls the following program, which declares a record of the appropriate type, selects the single row of data for that WHERE clause criterion, and then passes that record to another program for processing.

```
PROCEDURE process_data (
    table_in IN VARCHAR2, where_in IN VARCHAR2
)
IS
    l_block varchar2(32767) :=
        'DECLARE l_row ' || table_in || '%ROWTYPE;' ||
        'BEGIN' ||
        '   SELECT * INTO l_row ' ||
        '     FROM ' || table_in || ' WHERE ' || where_in || ';' ||
        '   user_query_pkg.internal_process_data (l_row); ' ||
        'END;';
BEGIN
    EXECUTE IMMEDIATE l_block;
END process_data;
```

Jasper tests this program, both separately as a backend routine and through the web page. It seems to work pretty well, so the enhanced application is rolled out to production. A few weeks later, the DBA notices some really strange stuff going on in an application schema: tables are being created that violate naming conventions; jobs are being queued up for execution in the early hours of the morning.

An alarm is raised. Security has been violated! The proper authorities are notified, and after a few months of investigation, they find and arrest the culprit: a fourteen-year-old boy who has made a habit of visiting various sites and probing for weaknesses. He found a big one in the process_data procedure and exploited it mercilessly.

So what weakness did this boy find in this program?

First, he selected "Excuses" as the table from which he would query (this translated to mfe_excuses). Then he tried various strings for the qualifier without success until he entered "id = 100". That didn't raise an error, so then he typed the following:

```
id = 100; EXECUTE IMMEDIATE 'CREATE PROCEDURE backdoor (str VARCHAR2) IS
BEGIN
EXECUTE IMMEDIATE str; END;';
```

and to his delight (or so we can assume, anyway), this string did not cause an error either! At this point, he had created a "backdoor" procedure in the MFE environment that he could use to easily execute commands, such as:

```
id = 100; backdoor ('drop table mfe_excuses');
```

This is definitely not what Jasper had in mind, in fact, he doesn't even really see how this can be possible.

Solution: Avoid concatenation of SQL text, rely on bind variables, and secure your schemas.

How was it possible for this teenager (a boy with *way* too much time on his hands) to *inject* malicious code into Jasper's program? At first glance, Jasper's dynamic PL/SQL block looks "tight":

```
'DECLARE l_row ' || table_in || '%ROWTYPE;' ||
'BEGIN' ||
'   SELECT * INTO l_row ' ||
'      FROM ' || table_in || ' WHERE ' || where_in || ';' ||
'   user_query_pkg.internal_process_data (l_row); ' ||
'END;';
```

You supply the table name, and it is stuffed right into the FROM clause. You supply a WHERE clause, and that comes *after* the WHERE keyword and before the semicolon. There's no room for games or manipulation there, right? Wrong. All this teenager had to do was put a ";" inside his WHERE clause string. That "early" semicolon terminates the query and then allows him to initiate his own, new command.

How rude! And also how inevitable, in this world of 24/7 access, where every web site is an invitation to crack. That's why it is extremely important that developers who write dynamic SQL (and, in particular, dynamic PL/SQL blocks) pay careful attention to the issue of SQL injection.

You can minimize the risk of SQL injection as follows:

Don't allow user schemas to create new objects, like tables and programs
They should only be able to run existing programs and modify existing tables.

Avoid concatenation of entire chunks of SQL syntax
That gives the malicious cracker more opportunities to subvert your program.

Rely whenever possible on bind variables, instead of concatenation
You cannot inject code through a placeholder. You can only substitute that placeholder with a value of the appropriate type.

It's rude to drop someone else's objects.

Apply the invoker rights method to stored code that executes dynamic SQL.

Problem: A seemingly handy utility goes badly wrong.

Delaware is tired of writing queries against user_objects to generate commands to drop multiple objects, or even clean out an entire schema. He decides to take advantage of dynamic SQL inside PL/SQL to build himself a handy utility. This is what he comes up with:

```
PROCEDURE drop_whatever (
    nm IN VARCHAR2 DEFAULT '%', typ IN VARCHAR2 DEFAULT '%')
IS
    dropstr   VARCHAR2 (32767);

    CURSOR object_cur IS
        SELECT object_name, object_type
          FROM user_objects
         WHERE object_name LIKE UPPER (nm) AND object_type LIKE UPPER (typ);
BEGIN
    FOR objrec IN object_cur
    LOOP
        dropstr := 'DROP ' || objrec.object_type || ' ' || objrec.object_name;
        BEGIN
            EXECUTE IMMEDIATE dropstr;
            DBMS_OUTPUT.put_line (dropstr || ' - SUCCESSFUL!');
        EXCEPTION
            WHEN OTHERS THEN
                DBMS_OUTPUT.put_line (dropstr || ' - FAILURE!');
        END;
    END LOOP;
END drop_whatever;
```

With drop_whatever installed in his schema, Delaware can drop all tables that start with "TEMP" as follows:

```
SQL> EXEC drop_whatever ('TEMP%', 'TABLE')
```

And he can clean out all the packages in his schema by typing nothing more than this:

```
SQL> EXEC drop_whatever ('%', 'PACKAGE')
```

"Wow, dynamic DDL is fun!" mutters Delaware to himself. He is, in fact, so excited that he makes sure everyone can use his program:

```
SQL> GRANT EXECUTE ON drop_whatever TO PUBLIC;
```

Then he sends a note to everyone on the team, inviting them to put drop_whatever to use.

An hour later, Delaware logs onto his schema and gets a very rude surprise: all of his tables are gone! A chill run downs his spine. He had just spent hours setting up several tables for a complex test. Sweat breaks out on his upper lip. His suit feels tight. And at that same moment, he gets a call from Lizbeth: "Delaware, I just tried to use drop_whatever to get rid of all the tables in my temp schema, but it didn't remove any of them. What did I do wrong?"

Solution: Make sure your dynamic SQL programs run under the invoker's authority.

Poor Delaware! He was trying to do the right thing by offering to share his program with everyone. Unfortunately, he forgot to *test* that program when run from a different schema. For that lapse, he will pay a severe penalty.

So how did Lizbeth manage to drop Delaware's tables instead of her own? The header of the drop_whatever procedure tells the story, by omission:

```
PROCEDURE drop_whatever (
   nm IN VARCHAR2 DEFAULT '%', typ IN VARCHAR2 DEFAULT '%')
```

The omission is that there is no AUTHID clause in the procedure header. And that means that Oracle used the default setting for AUTHID, which is:

```
PROCEDURE drop_whatever (
   nm IN VARCHAR2 DEFAULT '%', typ IN VARCHAR2 DEFAULT '%')
   AUTHID DEFINER
```

As a result, when this program is executed, it runs with the privileges of the schema in which the program is *defined*. So when Delaware runs the program from schema DELAWARE_DEV to drop tables, it drops tables in his schema. And when Lizbeth runs the program from schema LIZBETH_DEV to drop tables, it *still* drops tables in the DELAWARE_DEV schema!

Bad luck for Delaware.

What he should have done was use the following AUTHID clause:

```
PROCEDURE drop_whatever (
   nm IN VARCHAR2 DEFAULT '%', typ IN VARCHAR2 DEFAULT '%')
   AUTHID CURRENT_USER
```

With this setting, when Lizbeth runs the drop_whatever procedure, the query against user_objects will be resolved according to Lizbeth's privileges, which means that it will return (and she will drop) database objects defined in the LIZBETH_DEV schema.

The bottom line is that whenever you create a stored program (schema-level or within a package) that parses a dynamic SQL statement, you should define that program with the AUTHID CURRENT_USER setting. By doing so, you will minimize the possibility of a very unwelcome surprise.

Resources

You can find a complete implementation of the drop_whatever procedure, including the autonomous transaction statement and exception handling, in the *dropwhatever.sp* file on the book's web site.

CHAPTER 8

Playing with Blocks (of Code)

One of my greatest joys as a dad with a young child was to play blocks with my son, Eli. I very much enjoyed taking individual pieces of plastic or wood, and combining them together to create all sorts of structures. I think Eli did, too, but it is entirely possible that I was often the more excited of the two of us at making that tall, slim, stable tower (he was delighted more by knocking it down!).

What I have come to realize over the years is that writing software has many parallels to playing with blocks.

Applications are extremely complicated constructions, and this fact should come as no surprise. After all, an application is our attempt to capture a small slice of reality inside our virtual world of cyberspace, and the real world is incredibly complex (and always changing).

Furthermore, our brains can keep track of only so much information at once. And that's why languages like PL/SQL allow us to build named subprograms (procedures and functions), and even group those elements together into packages and object types. Rather than write big blobs of spaghetti code that go on and on for thousands of lines, we can create smaller units of logic, each with its own name. We can then combine these individual units to implement more and more of the application requirements.

This chapter offers advice on how to play most effectively with blocks of PL/SQL code. It is divided into four main sections:

Best Practices for Parameters
> Presents best practices for including, naming, and changing parameters for the subprograms you write in PL/SQL.

Best Practices for Procedures and Functions
> Presents best practices for dividing code into individual subprograms (procedures and functions).

Best Practices for Packages
> Takes a step back to present best practices for how the subprograms can and should be combined into packages.

Best Practices for Triggers
> Presents best practices for using triggers, which you can use to associate business rules with specific database objects.

Best Practices for Parameters

The header of a subprogram consists of its name, an optional parameter list, and a RETURN clause (if the subprogram is a function). While it is possible to define procedures and functions without any parameters, you will usually not do this. Instead, you should use the parameter list to clearly describe the values that the program needs to do its job, and the values that the program will *return* to the calling block of code.

> In a number of the best practices in this section, I will refer to *formal* parameters and *actual* parameters. "Formal parameter" refers to the parameter that is declared in the parameter list and manipulated inside the program. "Actual parameter" refers to the value, variable, or expression that is passed in to the program when it executed.

Once a program is in use, you can't change it willy-nilly.

Ensure backward compatibility as you add parameters.

Problem: Lizbeth's program needs to do more, and do it differently.

Lizbeth wrote a program several years ago to analyze how thoroughly a customer is taking advantage of My Flimsy Excuse's services. The header of the program looked like this:

```
FUNCTION usage_estimate (
    customer_id_in IN customer.id%type
  , frequency_check_in IN BOOLEAN
  , variety_check_in IN BOOLEAN
  ) RETURN PLS_INTEGER
```

The program was very popular and was used in dozens of different places in the MFE backend code. Then yesterday, Sunita informed Lizbeth that she needed to add another factor to the way that the usage estimate is computed: the time of day the excuse was requested (day or night time).

"That's easy!" said Lizbeth, and she changed the header of the program as follows:

```
FUNCTION usage_estimate (
    customer_id_in IN customer.id%type
  , frequency_check_in IN BOOLEAN
  , variety_check_in IN BOOLEAN
  , daytime_usage_in IN BOOLEAN
) RETURN PLS_INTEGER
```

Then she changed the algorithm in the function to take this into account. She tested the program and it worked very nicely. She then checked it in and went home for the evening, feeling well satisfied with her work.

When Lizbeth comes to work the next morning, however, some bad news awaits her: in the overnight build, several programs failed to compile even though they have not been changed. What went wrong? After a tense half-hour of analysis, the pattern becomes clear: every single one of those programs calls usage_estimate!

Solution: Make sure all new IN arguments have defaults, or add an overloading.

Lizbeth was so focused on improving her program to meet the new requirements that she forgot about the fact that her program was already being called, and that those invocations of usage_estimate knew nothing about the new daytime usage check.

To ensure that the code base is consistent and will compile, Lizbeth needs to do one of three things:

- Provide a default value for the new, trailing IN parameter.
- Go back to each existing invocation of usage_estimate and add the new parameter.
- Create a distinct overloading of usage_estimate that contains the new parameter, leaving the existing program header unchanged.

In the case of usage_estimate, the simplest solution is #1, for which the parameter list would look like this:

```
FUNCTION usage_estimate (
    customer_id_in IN customer.id%type
  , frequency_check_in IN BOOLEAN
  , variety_check_in IN BOOLEAN
  , daytime_usage_in IN BOOLEAN DEFAULT FALSE
) RETURN PLS_INTEGER
```

Now, any existing call to usage_estimate will continue to be valid, and with the default value of FALSE, will not be affected by the daytime usage analysis.

If, on the other hand, some of those existing calls to usage_estimate really *do* need to take the time of usage into account, then Lizbeth or someone else will need to go to each of those calls and add this parameter, with the appropriate value.

Finally, if the mode of the new parameter is IN OUT or OUT, Lizbeth cannot rely on default values to mask the new argument. The program is *returning* data where it did not do so before. This probably means a substantial change in functionality. In this case, Lizbeth will most likely want to create *another* version of the program, leaving the existing program unchanged.

The best way to do this is for Lizbeth to make sure that her subprogram is defined inside a package, and then add an overloading of that subprogram: a procedure or function with the same name, but with the new parameter list that contains the OUT or IN OUT argument. The PL/SQL runtime environment will automatically match the right invocation of the subprogram by the number and type of parameters.

As Lizbeth adds those overloadings, she should make sure that she doesn't end up copying and pasting the implementation of the original program into the new overloadings. Instead, she should have one "core" program that all the others call. The parameter list of this single location for all her logic would need to support all the parameter variations of the overloadings. Each overloading would then simply pass appropriate values for their usage.

For more information on overloading, read the upcoming section "'Easy to use code' is code that is used—and reused."

What the heck do those parameter values mean?

Use named notation to self-document subprogram calls and pass values more flexibly.

Problem: What seems obvious at the moment of writing is far less clear months or years later.

Delaware really likes his job with My Flimsy Excuse. Not only are the other developers on his team very pleasant and smart, but management at the company is down-to-earth and really committed to seeing everyone do well. This is very noticeable to him, because his previous position at Sunburn, Inc. made him cynical about corporate management. He'll never forget the time he discovered the business_as_usual procedure, buried deep within the Sunburn CEO's dashboard application, used to run the company.

The call to business_as_usual looked like this:

```
DECLARE
    l_ceo_salary        NUMBER;
    l_lobbying_dollars  NUMBER := 100000;
BEGIN
    business_as_usual (50000000
                    , l_lobbying_dollars
                    , SYSDATE + 20
                    , l_ceo_salary
                    );
```

It caught his eye mostly because he had no idea what was going on. What were those values for? It was very hard to tell from the call to this program. His curiosity piqued, he searched out the implementation of the program and found this:

```
PROCEDURE business_as_usual (
    advertising_budget_in    IN       NUMBER
  , contributions_inout      IN OUT   NUMBER
  , merge_and_purge_on_in    IN       DATE DEFAULT SYSDATE
  , obscene_ceo_bonus_out    OUT      NUMBER
  , cut_corners_in           IN       VARCHAR2 DEFAULT 'WHENEVER POSSIBLE'
)
```

And then he understood why the call to the program was made as obscure as possible. He decided to fix that problem by changing the way the values were passed to the program.

Solution: Use named notation to make everything clear.

Delaware changed the call to business_as_usual as follows:

```
business_as_usual
        (advertising_budget_in     => 50000000
      , contributions_inout        => 1_lobbying_dollars
      , merge_and_purge_on_in       => SYSDATE + 20
      , obscene_ceo_bonus_out       => 1_ceo_salary
      );
```

Now anyone looking at this code would understand exactly what was going on. Delaware certainly understood more than enough by this time, and he handed in his resignation the following day. Life was too short to work at a company like Sunburn, led by a person like "Chainsaw" Sal Burlap.

Before his departure from Sunburn, Delaware took advantage of a very nice feature in PL/SQL called *named notation*. With named notation, you specify in the parameter list the name of a formal parameter *along with* the actual parameter value by using this format:

formal_parameter => *actual_parameter*

The alternative to named notation, which most of us use most of the time, is called *positional notation*. With this approach, the actual parameter is associated *implicitly* with the formal parameter by position.

In addition to improving the readability of your code, named notation allows you to:

Change the order in which you supply actual parameters
    You might want to emphasize certain parameters in a given call to a program.

Use the default value of an IN argument regardless of the position in the parameter list
    With positional notation, you can avoid providing an actual parameter for any trailing (at the end of the parameter list) IN arguments that have default values. But if an IN OUT or OUT parameter appears in the list after your IN argument with a default, you *must* use named notation to "skip over" that inner IN argument.

I am tempted to recommend that you always use named notation. The advantages in readability are so great. But there are a few drawbacks to using named notation:

You need to know or look up the names of the parameters
> Then you have to type them! All of this takes time, and we rarely feel that we have the time for such "niceties." On the other hand, PL/SQL editors are getting better at generating program calls with named notation. If you have one that offers this feature, by all means take advantage of it.

With named notation, you are hardcoding the parameter names
> If, in the future, a programmer changes a parameter name, your program might fail to compile—even though there has been no change in actual functionality. This is certainly a concern, but because we tend to be wary about changing the interfaces to existing programs, our parameter names are not likely to change. Besides, you would face the same challenge if a programmer somehow changed the order of the parameters and you were using positional notation—and the resulting errors would be harder to find.

Where'd that data come from?

Functions should return data only through the RETURN clause.

Problem: Jasper returns data in a very confusing manner.

Jasper needs a program to retrieve several pieces of information about an excuse: the title, the author, and the word count. In just a few moments he builds the following function:

```
FUNCTION excuse_title (
    excuse_id_in IN mfe_excuse.isbn%TYPE
  , author_out OUT mfe_excuse.author%TYPE
  , word_count_out OUT mfe_excuse.word_count%TYPE)
RETURN mfe_excuse.title%TYPE
IS BEGIN
    ... implementation unimportant! ...
END excuse_title;
```

And then he puts this function to use as follows:

```
PROCEDURE process_excuse (excuse_id_in IN mfe_excuse.isbn%TYPE)
IS
    l_title mfe_excuse.title%TYPE;
    l_author mfe_excuse.author%TYPE;
    l_word_count mfe_excuse.word_count%TYPE;
BEGIN
    l_title := excuse_title (l_id, l_author, l_word_count);
    ...
```

Jasper is proud that he took the time to put this retrieval logic into its own program. Now it can be used in many places in the application. He shows everyone excuse_title at the weekly code review session. Imagine his dismay when Delaware snorts:

Humph. Well, Jasper, it's absolutely peachy keen that you wrote a reusable function. But that is not a program I would ever want to use. The name says you are giving me a title, and you are, but then you are also passing back all that other stuff. It's self-contradictory, and I have to declare a bunch of individual variables to use the darned thing!

Jasper pouts; he was so looking forward to a pat or two on the back. Sunita gives Delaware a dirty look and shakes her head. "Jasper," she says, drawing his attention away from Delaware's gloomy outlook, "Hiding the lookup was an excellent move. You just need to take a step or two further, and make sure there are no mixed messages. Let's redesign excuse_title together."

Solution: Return multiple values through a single, composite structure or with a procedure.

Here are the steps that Sunita takes to revamp the lookup function and make it more useful:

1. *Make sure the name of the program reflects what it does.* In this case, the program doesn't return just the title; it returns several pieces of information about an excuse. Let's call it the "excuse_info" function.

2. *Pass everything in the RETURN clause.* Rather than returning one value through the RETURN clause and another through the parameter list, let's pass everything back in the RETURN clause, using a composite structure—in this case, a record.

Here, then, is the new header of the program:

```
FUNCTION excuse_info (id_in IN mfe_excuse.id%TYPE)
   RETURN mfe_excuse%ROWTYPE
```

And here is the revised usage of this function:

```
PROCEDURE process_excuse (excuse_id_in IN mfe_excuse.isbn%TYPE)
IS
   l_excuse mfe_excuse%ROWTYPE;
BEGIN
   l_excuse := excuse_info (l_id);
```

Now the code is leaner and cleaner. Everything that is returned by the function is deposited into a single record. And if you are concerned about returning all the data in a table's row, when you need only a small subset of its columns, you can always create your own user-defined record, as shown here:

```
PACKAGE excuse_pkg
IS
   TYPE key_info IS RECORD (
      title mfe_excuse.title%TYPE
    , author mfe_excuse.author%TYPE
    , word_count mfe_excuse.word_count%TYPE
   );

   FUNCTION excuse_info (id_in IN mfe_excuse.id%TYPE)
      RETURN key_info;
END excuse_pkg;
```

To sum up: the whole point of a function is to return a value (whether it's a single, scalar value or a composite, such as a record or a collection). If you also return data back through the parameter list with OUT or IN OUT arguments, the purpose and usage of the function will be obscured.

If you need to return multiple pieces of information, take one of the following approaches:

Return a record or a collection of values
> Make sure to publish the structure of your record or collection (the TYPE statement) in a package specification so that developers can understand and use the function more easily.

Break up a single function into multiple functions, all returning scalar values
> With this approach, you can call the functions from within SQL statements.

Change a function into a procedure
> Unless you need to call a function to return this information, just change it to a procedure returning multiple pieces of information through the OUT arguments in the parameter list.

If you follow these guidelines, your subprograms will be more likely to be used and reused, because they will be defined in ways that make them easy to understand and apply in your own code.

Your function may also then be callable from within a SQL statement, which encourages even wider use of your program. Note, though, that there are restrictions on function calls from SQL. You may not call a function with an OUT argument from within SQL. You also may not call a function that returns a record (the datatypes of all parameters must be SQL-compatible).

Best Practices for Procedures and Functions

A *procedure* is a program that executes one or more statements. It is called as a standalone statement in the execution or exception section of a PL/SQL block. A *function* is a program that executes one or more statements and returns a value. Functions are always called within expressions and are never standalone PL/SQL statements. A function may be called in any part of a PL/SQL block. The vast majority of the code we write ends up in a procedure or a function, so best practices for writing these programs are especially important.

Write tiny chunks of code.

Limit execution section length to no more than 50 lines.

Sure, you're laughing out loud. Programs with no more than 50 lines of code? That's ridiculous! You write code for the real world, and the nuances of that world *cannot* be captured in 50 lines of code. Why, you're lucky if you can keep your programs under 1,000 lines of code!

OK, did you get all that out of your system? Have you calmed down? Good. So, yes, let's deal with reality. My suggestion is not that you can fit all the logic of your application into 50 lines of code (or less). I know you will need to write thousands of lines of code. That's what I do and certainly have done myself. Instead, this recommendation addresses how best to organize those thousands of lines of code.

Before starting my story of why and how this recommendation is so valuable, let me dispel the mystery surrounding that seemingly arbitrary number 50. Why 50? Because a chunk of code consisting of no more than 50 lines will fit on a single piece of paper and can be displayed on a monitor at a decent resolution. In other words, without turning pages, without paging up and down in a document, you will be able to see *all* the logic in that execution section. (And, no, if you live in Europe and use A4 paper, or have a really big monitor, you may not extend this number to 75 or 100 or whatever "fits"!)

Problem: Lengthy blobs of spaghetti code are unmanageable

I have, at times, found writing software to be very embarrassing. It's embarrassing to hand off an application to users, thinking I've tested it thoroughly, and then have them find a bug the first time they try to use it. And it's embarrassing (even if no one ever notices my embarrassment) when I write an execution section that is so long and torturous in structure that I find myself on line 746 typing "END LOOP;" and I suddenly realize that I've forgotten what loop it is that I am ending.

When the execution section of a program goes on and on for hundreds, even thousands, of lines, it is difficult to avoid the following problems:

Visualization
> You have a hard time understanding and visualizing the overall flow of the program. You cannot see the forest for the trees.

Confusion
> As hard as it is for the author of the program to understand what is going on, it is much harder (and even frightening) for another person to work with that program.

Reusability
> It is more difficult to reuse code in the application. For a program to be useful (and used) in a variety of circumstances, it needs to have a very narrow focus and no or few side effects.

Well, I imagine that you agree with me. No one really likes to go digging through enormous mounds of code, trying to figure out what is going wrong, or how to add an enhancement that doesn't break the program in a hundred unknown ways. So how do you avoid spaghetti code?

Solution: Use step-wise refinement and local subprograms to make code transparent in purpose and design.

We humans can handle only so much complexity at one time. If your manager stopped by your cubicle and told you "Build an order entry system, now," surely you wouldn't open up your editor and start typing:

```
PROCEDURE order_entry_system ...
```

It's much too big a task to take on all at once. Instead, you would break up that enormous challenge into major *subsystems*, like Reports, Order Management, Fulfillment, etc. Even those subsystems are much too big in scope, however, to deal with immediately. So, you would come up with a list of subtasks within each area. And you would do this until you finally reached a level of detail that you could sensibly begin implementing with your programming language.

This process of breaking things down, step by step, is known as *step-wise refinement* or *top-down design*. It applies not only to "big" jobs like building an order entry system, but also to "smaller" jobs, like an individual, but still complicated, program. And one critical technique for applying step-wise refinement to an individual program (and achieving the goal of no more than 50 lines in an execution section) is that of *local subprograms*. Let's take a look.

The folks at My Flimsy Excuse have a good problem: their web site has become very popular. People need more and more flimsy excuses with each passing day. There is, unfortunately, a downside to that success: increasing numbers of customers are calling to ask for help or complaining about their excuses (to which, unfortunately, MFE may not respond with, ahem, flimsy excuses).

It's time for MFE to professionalize its support organization (which will be given the name "No Excuses"), and Sunita's team is called upon to build the software to help No Excuses do a stellar job. Lizbeth is assigned the task of building a program to distribute unhandled customer calls out to members of No Excuses.

Not only have the support organization users written a 50-page document describing the functionality needed, but they have very thoughtfully provided a high-level summary of what the program is supposed to do:

> While there is at least one unhandled call, assign that call to a member of the No Excuses team who is underutilized (i.e., that person's queue of calls is lower than the average for the department). Notify the customer when the assignment has been made.

Lizbeth decides that with this summary alone, she has enough information to get started. She creates a new procedure in the ne_call_mgr package as follows:

```
PROCEDURE distribute_calls (
   department_id_in IN mfe_employees.department_id%TYPE)
IS
BEGIN
   WHILE ( calls_still_unhandled ( ) )
   LOOP
      FOR emp_rec IN emps_in_dept_cur (department_id_in)
      LOOP
```

```
      IF current_caseload (emp_rec.employee_id) <
            avg_caseload_for_dept (department_id_in)
      THEN
         assign_next_open_call_to (emp_rec.employee_id, l_case_id);
         notify_customer (l_case_id);
      END IF;
    END LOOP;
  END LOOP;
END distribute_calls;
```

Lizbeth stops at this point and shows the code to Sunita, asking her, "Can you tell what this program does?" And Sunita looks at it for a moment and replies:

> While there is still at least one unhandled call, then for each employee in the specified department, if his current case load is less than the average for his department, he is relatively underutilized. So assign the next open call to that employee and notify the customer.

"Excellent!" says Lizbeth, and returns to her program.

I hope that you will find yourself able to read this execution section as easily as Sunita did. The code "speaks" so clearly because it is composed of a series of calls to subprograms whose names describe the activity they perform. Why did Lizbeth do this?

She had looked ahead in the documentation and found that the users provided 17 pages of requirements on how to "assign the next open call" alone. It almost instantly overwhelmed her. So instead of getting lost in that jungle of details, she simply put a "placeholder" in her execution section: the invocation of assign_next_open_call_to. And she did the same thing for every other complicated part of that execution section's algorithm.

The result is an execution section of only 11 lines of code. Well, that's fewer than 50! But is Lizbeth done? Not at all. In fact, this execution section is really little more than pseudocode, since it cannot even compile.

Getting one's program to compile is very handy, to say the least. So Lizbeth now declares all necessary elements to achieve a successful compile. The declaration section soon looks like this:

```
 1  PROCEDURE distribute_calls (
        department_id_in IN mfe_employees.department_id%TYPE)
 2  IS
 3     l_case_id    mfe_cases.ID%TYPE;
 4
 5     CURSOR emps_in_dept_cur (
 6        department_id_in IN mfe_employees.department_id%TYPE) IS
 7        SELECT * FROM mfe_employees
 8         WHERE department_id = department_id_in;
 9
10     FUNCTION calls_still_unhandled RETURN BOOLEAN
11     IS
12     BEGIN
13        RETURN NULL;
```

```
14    END calls_still_unhandled;
15
16    FUNCTION current_caseload (employee_id_in IN mfe_employees.ID%TYPE)
17       RETURN PLS_INTEGER
18    IS
19    BEGIN
20       RETURN NULL;
21    END current_caseload;
22
23    FUNCTION avg_caseload_for_dept (employee_id_in IN
         mfe_employees.ID%TYPE)
24       RETURN PLS_INTEGER
25    IS
26    BEGIN
27       RETURN NULL;
28    END avg_caseload_for_dept;
29
30    PROCEDURE assign_next_open_call_to (
31       employee_id_in IN mfe_employees.ID%TYPE
32     , case_id_out OUT mfe_cases.ID%TYPE )
33    IS
34    BEGIN
35       NULL;
36    END assign_next_open_call_to;
37
38    PROCEDURE notify_customer (case_id_in IN mfe_cases.ID%TYPE)
39    IS
40    BEGIN
41       NULL;
42    END notify_customer;
43 BEGIN
44    WHILE (calls_still_unhandled ( ))
45    LOOP
46       FOR emp_rec IN emps_in_dept_cur (department_id_in)
47       LOOP
48          IF current_caseload (emp_rec.employee_id) <
49                avg_caseload_for_dept (department_id_in)
50          THEN
51             assign_next_open_call_to (emp_rec.employee_id, l_case_id);
52             notify_customer (l_case_id);
53          END IF;
54       END LOOP;
55    END LOOP;
56 END distribute_calls;
```

To achieve a clean compile, Lizbeth needed to declare a variable, a cursor, and a series of subprograms whose headers match those called in her execution section (lines 10 through 42). She did so, but with a trivial implementation, because she hasn't yet given any thought to what those programs will need to do. She focused, in other words, on the interface and high-level design, rather than on the low-level implementation.

Lizbeth did this by declaring procedures and functions directly *within* another procedure. These are called *local or nested subprograms*, and they can be defined in the declaration of *any* PL/SQL block (anonymous or named). Local subprograms offer a very handy way of *hiding the details* of a complicated program—and, in the process, keeping the execution section very short and readable. They are called "local" because they can be called only from within the execution section of the block in which they are defined (or any other local subprogram defined after it in the block's declaration section).

When Lizbeth successfully compiles the distribute_calls procedure shown above, she can be very confident that at *this* level of detail she has fully implemented user requirements without introducing any bugs. Take a look at lines 44 through 55. Where can bugs fit into such code? Those lines merely repeat the user requirements.

Of course, those requirements *do* get more detailed further on in the document; Lizbeth is by no means done. Now it is time to drill down another layer in the requirements. So she turns next to the first of the 17 pages describing how to "assign the next open call" to an underutilized employee, and repeats the same process in this local program:

1. Find or create a summary of what the program does.
2. Translate that summary into high-level PL/SQL code.
3. Put that code into the execution section of this local procedure.
4. Create the next layer of local subprograms, initially as stubs.
5. Make sure that the program compiles.

The result is an implementation of assign_next_open_call_to as follows:

```
PROCEDURE assign_next_open_call_to (
    employee_id_in IN mfe_employees.ID%TYPE
  , case_id_out OUT mfe_cases.ID%TYPE )
IS
    PROCEDURE find_next_open_call (case_out OUT NUMBER)
    IS
    BEGIN
       NULL;
    END find_next_open_call;

    PROCEDURE assign_to_employee (emp_id_in IN NUMBER, case_in IN NUMBER)
    IS
    BEGIN
       NULL;
    END assign_to_employee;
BEGIN
    find_next_open_call (case_out);
    assign_to_employee (emp_id_in, case_out);
END assign_next_open_call_to;
```

I'll bet you get the idea. Lizbeth repeats this process until the local subprogram is of such granularity of detail that it no longer makes sense to put a "placeholder" for that detail in her execution section. At this point, she finishes her implementation, still with a relatively small amount of code, and then moves on to the next local subprogram in distribute_calls.

And that, dear reader, is how you keep your execution sections to 50 lines or less!

Let's sum up the key benefits of "tiny chunks":

Your code is much more readable, and therefore maintainable
> In big blobs of code, you have to stare at the low-level details and infer the intention of the code. Liberal use of subprograms results in code that explicitly states its purpose.

You are much less likely to copy and paste or repeat logic in your programs
> Instead, those local subprograms become instantly available as reusable code.

You will write significantly fewer bugs
> By employing step-wise refinement and focusing on describing the logical flow of the user requirements, you will find that it is much more difficult to make mistakes, miss requirements, and get totally lost in the details of algorithmic complexity.

After you start following the "tiny chunks" guideline, you will become allergic to big blobs of code. You will start to get nervous as your execution section extends beyond 30 or 40 lines. At 100 lines, you will break out into a sweat and feel the craving for a local subprogram. Give into that craving and write much higher-quality code!

There's more to tiny chunks than just local subprograms.

Local subprograms are very handy for hiding details in that specific block of code. They cannot, however, be called from any *other* block of code. That's fine when the logic is too specific to be used anywhere else. Sometimes, though, the code we write today can and will be used elsewhere tomorrow. And if the logic is buried inside a local subprogram, it can be hard to find, extract, and generalize.

You can define a subprogram in any of the following places in your code (shown in increasing order of *visibility* within your code base):

Local subprogram
> Can be called only within the block in which it is defined.

Private package subprogram
> Defined in the package body only, this subprogram is *private* to the package and can be called only by other subprograms in that package.

Public package subprogram
> Declared in the package specification, this subprogram can be called by any program run from a schema that has EXECUTE authority on the package.

Schema-level procedure or function (not defined inside a package)
> Has the same visibility as a public package subprogram; can be called by any program run from a schema that has EXECUTE authority on *this* program.

Every time you create a new procedure or function, you must decide at which level or scope you wish to make this subprogram available. Here is the rule I used to make my decision:

Define the subprogram as close as possible to its usage(s).

Let's apply this rule to distribute_calls. Currently, all its subprograms are local. Suppose, however, that the following factors must also be taken into consideration:

- Functionality to determine caseload size per employee and average caseload of a department is needed in many other places in the application. Those certainly sound like useful and fairly generic functions.

- The process of notifying a customer of a change to his case is needed in several places in the ne_call_mgr package (which also contains distribute_calls). There are also different types of notification (e.g., case assigned, case closed, case reopened).

As Lizbeth is writing distribute_calls and creating stubs for current_caseload and avg_caseload_for_dept, she thinks to herself:

I need these here, but the information they retrieve is not specific to distribute_calls. In fact, now that I think of it, I remember reading a memo from Sunita last week proposing the creation of a new ne_analysis package that would include programs just like this!

It would be silly, therefore, to "bury" the implementation of these functions inside distribute_calls. Instead, Lizbeth stops her work on the new procedure, gets approval from Sunita to build ne_analysis, and soon produces this package specification (but not the body):

```
PACKAGE ne_analysis
IS
   FUNCTION current_caseload (employee_id_in IN mfe_employees.ID%TYPE)
      RETURN PLS_INTEGER;

   FUNCTION avg_caseload_for_dept (employee_id_in IN mfe_employees.ID%TYPE)
      RETURN PLS_INTEGER
END ne_analysis;
```

She compiles the package specification, and then returns to distribute_calls, removes the local subprogram stubs, and changes the execution section to:

```
BEGIN
   WHILE (calls_still_unhandled ())
   LOOP
      FOR emp_rec IN emps_in_dept_cur (department_id_in)
      LOOP
         IF ne_analysis.current_caseload (emp_rec.employee_id) <
               ne_analysis.avg_caseload_for_dept (department_id_in)
         THEN
            assign_next_open_call_to (emp_rec.employee_id, l_case_id);
            notify_customer (l_case_id);
```

```
      END IF;
   END LOOP;
  END LOOP;
 END distribute_calls;
```

She can now compile distribute_calls and make sure it all "holds together." Then she returns to ne_analysis, implements the package body, and fully tests her generic utilities. When she is satisfied that the two functions work as advertised, she is ready for the next step with distribute_calls: notify_customer.

Just last week, Lizbeth wrote a program named close_case, which changed the status of the case and also sent word to the customer via email that the case was closed. That made perfect sense then, but now she finds herself thinking about writing very similar logic for notify_customer. She is tempted to copy and paste; after all, the new program (notify_customer) is not exactly the same as close_case.

Fortunately, Lizbeth chooses the path of the righteous (reuse) and takes these steps:

1. Go back to close_case and isolate all the logic used to send the customer the email into its own subprogram within close_case. Call it notify_customer.

2. Compile the reorganized close_case (actually, the whole ne_call_mgr) package and run the regression test for close_case to ensure that no mistakes were made.

3. Now move notify_customer out of close_case and up to the package body level. It has the same header as the subprogram inside distribute_calls:

   ```
   PACKAGE BODY ne_call_mgr
   IS
       PROCEDURE notify_customer (case_id_in IN mfe_cases.ID%TYPE)
       IS
       BEGIN .... END notify_customer;
   ```

4. Ensure that the package still compiles and that tests of close_case are successful.

5. Examine the requirements for notification inside distribute_calls and compare them to the new package-level notify_customer program. Notice that the message that must be sent for a "case closed" is different from that of a "case assigned."

6. Change the header of notify_customer to accept the message, so that this procedure can be used in both places; change the implementation of notify_customer to pass the dynamic message, rather than the "case closed" message there from its former life inside close_case:

   ```
   PACKAGE BODY ne_call_mgr
   IS
       PROCEDURE notify_customer (
           case_id_in IN mfe_cases.ID%TYPE
         , message_in IN VARCHAR2)
       IS
       BEGIN .... END notify_customer;
   ```

7. Go back to close_case and change the call to notify_customer to pass the message.

8. Recompile the package and test close_case. Assuming that it passes, Lizbeth is now done with her reworking of close_case. Attention shifts back to distribute_calls.

9. Remove the stub local subprogram of notify_customer. It is now implemented by the package-level program. Change the call to notify_case in the execution section of distribute_calls to pass the appropriate message:

```
BEGIN
   WHILE (calls_still_unhandled ())
   LOOP
      FOR emp_rec IN emps_in_dept_cur (department_id_in)
      LOOP
         IF ne_analysis.current_caseload (emp_rec.employee_id) <
               ne_analysis.avg_caseload_for_dept (department_id_in)
         THEN
            assign_next_open_call_to (emp_rec.employee_id, l_case_id);
            notify_customer (l_case_id
            , 'Case has been assigned to '
            || emp_rec.employee_full_name);
         END IF;
      END LOOP;
   END LOOP;
END distribute_calls;
```

10. Continue with the implementation of distribute_calls.

Notice that the execution section of this procedure is the same length and has the same number of subprogram calls in it, but now two of those (current_caseload and avg_caseload_for_dept) are defined in another package, whereas a third (notify_customer) is defined in this same package, but at the package body level.

Lizbeth has now made the most of existing code, increased the total amount of reusable code (available for her and others to use), and minimized the custom code she has had to write. She heads home that evening well satisfied with her work on distributed calls.

Resources

It sure would be nice if you didn't have to do all that work of creating the local modules as stubs, writing the parameter lists, and so on. And might you not forget to implement one of those "null" stubs? After all, the code compiles! To help you create code following the "50 lines or less" guideline more quickly and easily, I have created the topdown package (available in the *topdown.zip* file on the book's web site). Using topdown, you place comments or program calls in your code that indicate where you want a local module. You then run *topdown.refactor* and it will automatically expand your comments into the desired code. Check it out—I think you will like it a lot, and it does (I believe) represent the first automated refactoring utility for PL/SQL developers!

Every program should be an island (of purpose).

Minimize side effects and maximize reuse by creating programs with narrowly defined purposes.

Problem: Delaware packs it all in and no one wants to use it.

MFE management has issued a directive: "We must make our web site smarter! Don't force the user to search through thousands of possible excuses. Whenever possible, recommend an appropriate excuse to the user."

Ever diligent, Sunita immediately asks Delaware to write a new function that will take in a variety of data points and return a recommendation for the best flimsy excuse for that customer. She will then have the rest of the team use this program to smarten up as much of their code as possible. While Delaware is building this function, he also decides to:

- Display the main information about the customer. That will be useful feedback on the correctness of the program.
- Update a new table that keeps track of all recommendations passed back to the customer. Management wants a record of just how smart they've gotten.

This is what the function looks like, minus the implementations of the local subprograms that contain the bulk of the logic:

```
FUNCTION recommended_excuse (
    customer_id_in IN mfe_customer.id%TYPE
  , who_its_for_in IN VARCHAR2 DEFAULT 'BOSS'
  , alibi_needed_in IN BOOLEAN DEFAULT FALSE
) RETURN mfe_excuse.id%TYPE
IS
    l_return mfe_excuse.id%TYPE;
    l_customer mfe_customer%ROWTYPE;

    FUNCTION one_customer ( ...
    FUNCTION internal_recommend_calc ( ...
    PROCEDURE display_customer_info ( ...
    PROCEDURE track_recommendation ( ...
BEGIN
    l_customer := one_customer (customer_id_in);
    l_return := internal_recommend_calc (l_customer
      , who_its_for_in, alibi_needed_in);
    display_customer_info (l_customer);
    track_recommendation (l_customer, l_return);
    RETURN l_return;
END recommended_excuse;
```

Delaware likes the function; after all, it does so many useful things, all nicely collected in one program. He tells the rest of the team about it, and assumes that they will be able to make good use of it (there are, after all, so many different places on the web site that could be so much smarter!).

Yet when he runs a query against ALL_DEPENDENCIES to find the database objects that are dependent on (that is, call) recommended_excuse, it tells him "no rows found." What the heck? Delaware seeks out Lizbeth and asks her why she hasn't used recommended_excuse. She says:

> Oh, I used it—sort of. I needed the recommendation, but it didn't make any sense to display the customer information and I couldn't immediately track the recommendation. The users haven't yet decided if they want to use it. So I just copied and pasted that "internal recommend calculator" function sitting inside your program, and I used that for my own recommendation program.

Lizbeth smiled. "Thanks for thinking through that algorithm, Delaware. It was tricky stuff!"

Solution: Write programs with very specific purposes and avoid hidden (a.k.a. global) dependencies.

When Delaware hears Lizbeth say that she copied his code, he wants to scream: "Noooooooo...." The whole point of his assignment was to provide a single recommendation function that *everyone* would use. Instead, his code is already spawning clones. It's no big deal now, but when the time comes to enhance or fix that tricky logic, how will they be able to make sure that *all* the clones are updated?

At first, Delaware is royally annoyed at Lizbeth. But then he thinks back over what she said and realizes that she has a point (and, after all, the user is never wrong). He *did* put an awful lot of really excellent functionality into that program... but what if the user of the program cannot or does not want to use that functionality?

Delaware goes back to the drawing board and soon announces that he has replaced the single function with a package containing two subprograms:

```
PACKAGE mfe_smarts
IS
    FUNCTION recommended_excuse (
        customer_id_in IN mfe_customer.id%TYPE
      , who_its_for_in IN VARCHAR2 DEFAULT 'BOSS'
      , alibi_needed_in IN BOOLEAN DEFAULT FALSE
    ) RETURN mfe_excuse.id%TYPE;

    PROCEDURE track_recommendation (
        customer_id_in IN mfe_customer.id%TYPE
      , recommended_excuse_id_in IN mfe_excuse.id%TYPE);

END mfe_smarts;
```

In addition, Delaware has removed the "display customer" code entirely. He now realizes that operation can and should be done outside of these programs. Lizbeth calls him immediately after receiving the email announcement, thanking him and letting him know that she has replaced her copy-and-paste job with a call to mfe_smarts.recommended_excuse. "That's just what I needed," she writes at the end of the note. "Thanks so much!"

Let's draw some general conclusions from Delaware's experience. If you want developers to reuse programs (a key ingredient of success in any application), then you should:

Make sure your programs are tightly focused on a particular area of functionality
> Each program needs, in other words, to serve a single purpose—and the name should clearly reflect that purpose. The more varied the feature set of a program, the less likely that it will meet the needs of others.

Limit the functionality of your programs
> If you find yourself saying "While I'm at it, why don't I...", stop and take a close look at what you are doing. Do you really need to add this functionality? Has someone, anyone, expressed a need for it? Don't write code just for the heck of it. That increased volume of code will only result in more complexity, more bugs, and less time to implement the critical functionality in your application.

Avoid side effects and hidden/global actions within your programs
> The track_recommendation activity not only diluted the focus of recommended_excuse; it inserted a row in the tracking table. This DML operation is a side effect. The fact that Delaware does this is not at all apparent in the header of the program or in its name. So people using the program might not even realize that the DML operation is executed—until they encounter unexpected behavior.

There are several specific consequences of putting DML inside a subprogram:

- The DML cannot be called inside a SQL query (unless it is an autonomous transaction).
- That insert becomes a part of the application transaction (again, unless the subprogram is an autonomous transaction).
- The performance profile of the program changes dramatically—it slows down.

So, do not add DML statements to a program without careful consideration; you certainly should not "hide" DML operations inside a program with another stated purpose.

Gifts should always come tightly wrapped.

Hide business rules and formulas inside functions.

Problem: Jasper actually thinks a rule will never change!

The powers that be in MFE decide that to use the services of the web site, you must be at least 15 years old. This information is posted on the web site; it is included in the text of the EULA (end user license agreement) that every customer must read and check; and it must be applied in many places in the application.

Fortunately, it is also a very easy rule to write in PL/SQL. So Jasper creates a trigger on the mfe_customer table to ensure that no one younger than 15 actually registers successfully. Here it is:

```
CREATE OR REPLACE TRIGGER are_you_too_young
    AFTER insert OR update
    ON mfe_customer FOR EACH ROW
BEGIN
    IF :new.date_of_birth >
            ADD_MONTHS (SYSDATE, -12 * 15)
    THEN
        RAISE_APPLICATION_ERROR (-20703
        , 'You must be at least 15 yrs old to use My Flimsy Excuse.');
    END IF;
END;
```

He tests the trigger and it works just fine. A few days later, Jasper build a batch-processing script that checks and loads more than 10,000 potential new MFE customers from a sister company. In this case, he needs to make sure that the customer is not too young, and if so, log that fact in the error table and then continue the rest of the data load:

```
1  FOR rec IN (SELECT * FROM omp_customer_data)
2  LOOP
3     IF ADD_MONTHS (SYSDATE, -160) > rec.date_of_birth
4     THEN
5        err.log ('Potential customer ' || rec.customer_id ||
6           ' is not 15 years old.');
7     ELSE
8        ...load the data
```

And so on from there. Jasper—and others on the team—apply this rule in numerous locations in the code.

Imagine his dismay, then, when he receives a memo from the CEO that says: "The minimum age for registration has been changed from 15 to 21 in order to comply with increasingly strict rules regarding the use of Internet resources by minors." Yikes! Now Jasper has to go find all those rules. What to look for? "ADD_MONTHS"? "date_of_birth"? "15"? The duplicate implementations of that rule have come back to bite Jasper in the behind.

Even worse, by writing the rule more than once, he has greatly increased the likelihood that he will introduce bugs into his code. In fact, take a close look at lines 3–6 in the last block of code. There are *three* bugs in those four lines:

- Jasper multiplied 12×15 incorrectly. The "−160" should be "−180."
- Jasper has used the wrong operator: ">" when he should have used "<" (compare this code to the previous, first implementation of the rule).
- The error message is wrong. It says that the person is "not 15" when it should say that the person is "not at least 15."

That's the sort of thing that happens when you write the "same" code over and over again.

Solution: Wrap or hide all business rules and formulas inside functions.

Jasper has a panic attack. What is he going to do? He decides to ask Lizbeth for advice. Lizbeth, having seen this sort of thing many times in the past (and learned her lesson a long time ago), knows exactly what to do:

> Before you change any of those now-obsolete rules, write a single function that implements the rule. Put it inside a special "customer rules" package, if there isn't one already. Test it thoroughly. Then go back to each place in which you coded the rule, and replace it with nothing more than a call to a function.

Jasper's eyes light up. That sounds so sensible, so straightforward. Why didn't *he* think of that? In fact, he suddenly thinks of something else: he needs to stop hard-coding error messages as well. So he writes these two functions:

```
PACKAGE BODY mfe_customer_rules
IS
    c_minimum_age CONSTANT NUMBER := 21;

    FUNCTION customer_old_enough (dob_in IN DATE) RETURN BOOLEAN
    IS
    BEGIN
        RETURN NVL (
            dob_in <= ADD_MONTHS (SYSDATE, -1 * 12 * c_minimum_age),
            FALSE
        );
    END customer_old_enough;

    FUNCTION customer_min_age_msg RETURN VARCHAR2
    IS
    BEGIN
        RETURN 'A My Flimsy Excuse customer must be at least ' ||
                TO_CHAR (c_minimum_age) ||
                ' years of age.';
    END customer_min_age_msg;
END mfe_customer_rules;
```

And then he uses Quest Code Tester to quickly build and run a test for the business rule function, mfe_customer_rules.customer_old_enough (check out *mfe_customer_rules.pkg* and *mfe_customer_rules.qut* on the book's web site). Satisfied that the program works, he goes back to the trigger and changes it to this:

```
CREATE OR REPLACE TRIGGER are_you_too_young
    AFTER insert OR update
    ON mfe_customer FOR EACH ROW
BEGIN
    IF NOT mfe_customer_rules.customer_old_enough (:NEW.date_of_birth)
    THEN
        RAISE_APPLICATION_ERROR (
            -20703, mfe_customer_rules.customer_min_age_msg () );
    END IF;
END;
```

He makes similar changes throughout the code base. The work goes more quickly than he expects. And when, a month later, the CEO announces that after consultation with lawyers, they are going to change the minimum age to 18, Jasper doesn't freak out. He just shrugs, shakes his head, changes the default value of the c_minimum_age constant, recompiles the customer rules package, reruns his tests, and washes his hands of the matter.

"Ah," he says to himself, "so this is my reward for doing things right!"

The recommendation to hide business rules and formulas is one of the most important best practices you will ever read—and, I hope, follow. Do you ever find yourself using the words "never" or "always" as you think about the code you are writing? If so, you are putting a bug in your program right *there*, unless your use of those words is in a sentence that reads like one of these:

> That's never going to stay the same.
>
> That's always going to be changing.

In other words, the one aspect of any software project that never changes is that *everything changes*. Business requirements, data structures, user interfaces: all of these things change, and change frequently. One of our most important tasks is to write code that adapts easily to these changes.

So, whenever you need to enforce a business rule or calculate a formula, put it inside a subprogram that hides the individual steps (which might change) and returns the results (if any).

One way in, one way out: multiple exits confuse me.

Limit functions to a single RETURN statement in the execution section.

Problem: Sunita tosses off "quick-and-dirty" code in a function lookup routine.

As part of the No Excuses customer support project, Sunita's team needs to convert single-letter abbreviations into status descriptions—for example, "O" converts to "OPEN," "C" to "CLOSED," etc. The team is really busy, so Sunita volunteers to write this one. There are three case statuses, and she quickly produces just the code that is needed:

```
FUNCTION status desc (cd_in IN VARCHAR2) RETURN VARCHAR2
IS
BEGIN
   IF cd_in = 'C'
   THEN
      RETURN 'CLOSED';
   ELSIF cd_in = 'O'
   THEN
      RETURN 'OPEN';
   ELSIF cd_in = 'I'
   THEN
      RETURN 'INACTIVE';
   END IF;
END status_desc;
```

She tries it out for those three values (the only values that can be present in the mfe_case table) and it works fine. She hands it off to Lizbeth for review and integration and gets back to the important job of managing her team. But, it sure feels good to have gotten her hands "dirty" by writing code.

Problem: Sure, the program works—but only if you assume a perfect world.

Lizbeth, being very busy herself, glances at Sunita's work, says to herself, "That's not how I would have done it," but figures that it will work and checks in the code. Several weeks later, when the team starts more robust testing, the following error starts popping out of the application:

```
ORA-06503: PL/SQL: Function returned without value
```

This is upsetting to Lizbeth. She takes –06503 errors as a personal affront. It is such a deep design flaw in a function. How could she have done such a thing? After a few minutes of analysis, Lizbeth tracks the problem back to status_desc. She shakes her head, relieved that it wasn't her code and also disappointed with herself, because she should have known this was going to happen. She takes a closer look at the program and is a bit shocked to realize that:

- The program assumes that *only* "C," "O," or "I" will be passed in to the function.
- The program requires that the characters be in uppercase.
- There is no ELSE clause in the IF statement.
- All the strings are hardcoded.
- This is an ideal structure for a CASE statement.

In short, this is a very quick-and-dirty implementation, pretty much what you'd expect when a manager steps in to "help"—in between status meetings and whatever else managers do.

Solution: Don't allow multiple exit points from the function.

Lizbeth is feeling pressured for time, so she decides to fix only the most critical bugs in the code (failure on passing in lowercase values and also the ORA-06503). She comes up with this:

```
FUNCTION status_desc (cd_in IN VARCHAR2) RETURN VARCHAR2
IS
   l_return   VARCHAR2 (32757);
BEGIN
   l_return :=
      CASE UPPER (cd_in)
         WHEN 'C' THEN 'CLOSED'
         WHEN 'O' THEN 'OPEN'
         WHEN 'I' THEN 'INACTIVE'
      END;
   RETURN l_return;
END status_desc;
```

Instead of executing a RETURN inside each IF clause, Lizbeth declares a single return variable. She uses a CASE expression to set the value of that return variable, and then the last line of the function returns the value. Now there is absolutely no way that the function can end its execution section without returning a value!

A good general rule to follow as you write your PL/SQL programs is "one way in and one way out." In other words, there should be just one way to enter or call a program (and there *is*; you don't have any choice in this matter). And there should be one way out, one exit path from a program (or loop, as well) on successful termination. By following this rule, you end up with code that is much easier to trace, debug, and maintain.

For a function, this means that you should think of the execution section as a funnel; all the lines of code narrow down to the last executable statement, which is nothing more than:

```
RETURN return value;
```

Note the following:

- You can, and should, still have RETURN statements in your exception handlers. Not every exception should be passed unhandled from your function. For more details, see the best practice in Chapter 6 titled "All exceptions are not created equal."
- It is possible (i.e., it is acceptable syntax) to use an "unqualified" RETURN statement in a procedure, as follows:

```
IF all_done
THEN
    RETURN;
END IF;
```

In this case, the procedure immediately terminates and returns control. You shouldn't do this, however, as it results in unstructured code that's hard to debug and maintain This recommendation also holds for the initialization section of a package.

The Oracle database's PL/SQL compile-time warnings can automatically analyze your functions and determine whether there are any sequences within the program that will result in the ORA-06530 error. To use this feature, enable the warning:

```
ALTER SESSION SET WARNINGS = 'ENABLE:5005'
/
```

Then recompile the program:

```
ALTER program_type program_name COMPILE
/
```

If the database reports a warning, then you have a problem, which you can then track down in your code.

Black or white programs don't know from NULL.

Never return NULL from Boolean functions.

Problem: Jasper gets really confused with a Boolean function returning a NULL.

Customers of My Flimsy Excuse have expressed a lot of interest in excuses involving pets, and the web developers want to start incorporating sounds that reinforce the kinds of excuses chosen. So Jasper is assigned the job of writing a function to determine whether a specified excuse is pet-related or not. For the sake of simplicity, that condition is specified as "Does the excuse title contain the word 'dog' or 'cat'?"

So Jasper writes the following function:

```
FUNCTION is_pet_excuse (title_in IN mfe_excuses.title%TYPE)
   RETURN BOOLEAN
IS
   c_title CONSTANT mfe_excuses.title%TYPE := UPPER (title_in);
BEGIN
   RETURN INSTR (c_title, 'DOG') > 0 OR INSTR (c_title, 'DOG') > 0;
END is_ pet_excuse;
```

"Gee, that was easy," Jasper says to himself, and he starts using the function immediately in his code:

```
IF NOT is_pet_excuse (l_title)
THEN
   just_do_the_usual;
ELSE /* Must be a cat or dog! */
   make_it_bark_or_meow;
END IF;
```

When the new web page goes into production, though, customers find that their excuses are barking at them, even when those excuses have nothing to do with pets. What is going on here?

Solution: Ensure that a Boolean function returns only TRUE or FALSE.

After some debugging and analysis, Jasper realizes that under some strange circumstances, the title being passed to is_pet_excuse is NULL. That shouldn't be happening, but it is. Unfortunately, what that means for is_pet_excuse is that the function *returns* a NULL value.

"Well," thinks Jasper, "I can take care of that," and he changes his code to the following:

```
IF NOT NVL (is_pet_excuse (l_title), TRUE)
THEN
   just_do_the_usual;
ELSE /* Must be a cat or dog! */
   make_it_bark_or_meow;
END IF;
```

The immediate fire has been put out, but Jasper doesn't like the change he made. It is very awkward, and who is going to remember to do this each time is_pet_excuse is called?

Thinking a bit more about it, Jasper identifies the source of his discomfort: his function is supposed to answer the question, "Is the excuse related to pets or not?" That is a very "black or white" question, and if the excuse title is NULL, then surely the excuse could not possibly be related to pets. So why is Jasper propagating Oracle's "three-value logic" for Booleans (TRUE, FALSE, and NULL) out to users of is_pet_excuse?

When you build your own Boolean functions, make sure they return only TRUE or FALSE. It might make sense to return a NULL for a non-Boolean function (indicating, for instance, that no data was found). When the function returns a Boolean, however, a user of that function expects a "black or white" answer and no gray.

Best Practices for Packages

Packages are the fundamental building blocks of any well-designed application built in the Oracle PL/SQL language (at least until Oracle improves the robustness of its object implementation). A package consists of a specification and a body, although in some cases a body is not required. The specification tells a user what she can do with the package: what programs can be called, what data structures and user-defined types can be referenced, and so on. The package body implements any programs in the package specification; it can also contain private (i.e., not shown in the specification) data structures and program units.

Where there is one program, there will soon be two.

Avoid schema-level programs; instead, group related code into packages.

Problem: It seemed that there would be only one program—now there are many.

Sunita asks Jasper to create a function to parse a delimited string into individual elements. Jasper loves these kinds of puzzles and throws together a solution in no time (available in the file string_to_list.sf):

```
FUNCTION string_to_list (string_in IN VARCHAR2
   , delim_in IN VARCHAR2 := ',')
   RETURN DBMS_SQL.varchar2a
IS
   l_item      VARCHAR2 (32767);
   l_startloc  PLS_INTEGER       := 1;
   l_nextloc   PLS_INTEGER;
   l_items     DBMS_SQL.varchar2a;
```

```
FUNCTION next_item (
   start_location_in IN PLS_INTEGER
 , end_location_in IN PLS_INTEGER
) RETURN VARCHAR2
IS
BEGIN
   RETURN CASE end_location_in
      /* Two consecutive delimiters, NULL item */
      WHEN start_location_in THEN NULL
      /* No more delimiters, get rest of string */
      WHEN 0 THEN SUBSTR (string_in, start_location_in)
      /* Extract next item between two delimiters. */
      ELSE SUBSTR (string_in
                  , start_location_in
                  , end_location_in - start_location_in
                  )
   END;
END next_item;
BEGIN
   IF string_in IS NOT NULL
   THEN
      LOOP
         l_nextloc := INSTR (string_in, delim_in, l_startloc);
         l_items (l_items.COUNT + 1) :=
            next_item (l_startloc, l_nextloc);

         IF l_nextloc = 0 THEN EXIT;
         ELSE
            l_startloc := l_nextloc + 1;
         END IF;
      END LOOP;
   END IF;

   RETURN l_items;
END string_to_list;
```

He even takes a few minutes to verify the correctness of this program with Quest Code Tester (string_to_list.qut). And then he notifies everyone on the team about his new program—and they use it.

Sunita is so impressed that she assigns Jasper the task of building some other string utilities they will need, including:

- Reverse a string.
- Return the string between a start and an end location (a variation on the built-in function SUBSTR).
- Take a collection of strings and return a comma-delimited list.

Jasper dives in with eagerness and soon has a handful of distinct, schema-level (a.k.a. "standalone," or not inside a package) string functions and procedures, as in:

```
FUNCTION reverse_string ...
```

He sends out another memo listing all of his programs, and Delaware writes back, saying: "That's a lot of stuff to remember, Jasper. Why don't you put it all in a package, so the programs are easier to find?" Jasper groans. If he does that, then he will have to go back to every call to string_to_list (and his other utilities) and add the package name and dot character. But he recognizes a good idea when he sees one.

Solution: Put in the dot from the start: package.subprogram.

Delaware *definitely* has the right idea. Jasper was having lots of fun building interesting little utilities, but he hadn't given any thought to how to make all that cool stuff accessible and findable. He started with a single string function, and didn't even realize that he would be doing anything else in this area. His assignment then evolved to create multiple utilities to help manipulate strings. Each program has a different name and a different purpose, but all of the programs relate to strings.

Unfortunately, by creating lots of individual, schema-level programs, Jasper makes it hard for other members of the team to view all of his string utilities and pick from them the specific program that they need. Instead, they have to look through all the functions and procedures shown in their schema browsers until they come to a program that seems to do the job.

In hindsight, it becomes clear to Jasper that he should have created a single package and put all the string utilities inside it. So he does just that, naming it "tb_strings" (toolbox for strings). Now, when a developer needs a string function, she knows to zoom down alphabetically to the "tb" packages (that's the standard naming convention for generic utilities). When she sees one called "tb_strings," she knows that if the function she is looking for exists, it must be in this package.

That's great, but the team still has a problem: everyone must now go back to all the existing calls to the original string_to_list function and change them to tb_strings.string_to_list.

Let's draw some general recommendations from this experience:

Avoid writing schema-level procedures and functions
> Always start with a package. Even if there is just one program in the package at the moment, it is very likely that there will be more in the future. So "put in the dot at the start," and you won't have to add it later.

Use packages to group together related functionality
> A package gives a name to a set of program elements: procedures, functions, user-defined types, variable and constant declarations, cursors, and so on. By creating a package for each distinct area of functionality, you create intuitive containers for that functionality. Programs will be easier to find, and therefore less likely to be reinvented in different places in your application.

Keep your packages small and narrowly focused
> It doesn't do much good to have just three packages, each of which has hundreds of programs. It will *still* be hard to find anything inside that bunch of code.

"Easy to use code" is code that is used—and reused.

Anticipate programmer needs and simplify call interfaces with overloading.

Problem: Some of Oracle's supplied packages are harder to use than they should be.

It's time to give Sunita's team a break and instead pick on Oracle Corporation. Now, let me be very clear about one thing: I *love* Oracle. Oracle in general and PL/SQL in particular have been very good to me. I write some books about PL/SQL and—voilà!—I can stop commuting to a consulting job and instead work from home and travel to various parts of the world to share my ideas on how best to write PL/SQL. Thank you, Larry!

So, whenever I criticize something that Oracle has done, please understand that it is done with the best of intentions: namely, to make PL/SQL even better (but never, ever, to get a cheap laugh—uh-huh).

Oracle installs hundreds of packages with every instance of the database. These supplied, or built-in, packages expose valuable functionality through easy to use interfaces, allowing us to do so many things not present natively in PL/SQL—for example, read and write files, display output to the screen, generate random numbers, and much more.

Because these packages are used by tens of thousands of developers and DBAs, it is very important for Oracle to implement the packages so that they are as easy to use and as helpful as possible. And for the most part, they meet this objective. There are some cases, however, in which more care could have been taken. In these cases, we end up writing more code than we should, or we struggle to get our jobs done where it should have been trivial. Let's look at two examples: the EXECUTE function in the DBMS_SQL built-in package and the PUT_LINE function in the DBMS_OUTPUT package.

DBMS_SQL.EXECUTE executes a SQL statement or PL/SQL block. It is a function that returns an integer value. If I execute a DML statement (INSERT, UPDATE, DELETE), then DBMS_SQL.EXECUTE returns the number of rows modified by the statement. For all other statements, however, the value returned by DBMS_SQL.EXECUTE is to be ignored.

Thus, if I am executing a DDL statement, such as "drop table XYZ," I must declare a local variable and use it in the call to DBMS_SQL.EXECUTE. I usually write such code as follows:

```
DECLARE
    l_cursor PLS_INTEGER := DBMS_SQL.OPEN_CURSOR ( );
    l_dummy PLS_INTEGER;
BEGIN
    DBMS_SQL.PARSE (l_cursor, 'DROP TABLE XYZ', DBMS_SQL.NATIVE);
    l_dummy := DBMS_SQL.EXECUTE (l_cursor);
END;
```

In other words, I have to declare a variable, l_dummy, in order to call DBMS_SQL.EXECUTE, but I don't use it; it is simply a "dummy" variable.

I don't know about you, but I really dislike writing code that is completely unnecessary—except that it is absolutely required in this case because of the way the developer designed the program I am using.

 The Oracle database does not currently require that you execute your DDL statement. Instead, the simple act of parsing that DDL statement will also lead to its execution and a commit. Oracle Corporation does not guarantee that this will always be the case and recommends that you always explicitly execute after parsing.

And then consider DBMS_OUTPUT.PUT_LINE. The purpose of this program is to display the value of the variable passed to it. I can display a string, number, or date as shown below:

```
BEGIN
    DBMS_OUTPUT.PUT_LINE (SYSDATE);
    DBMS_OUTPUT.PUT_LINE ('A');
    DBMS_OUTPUT.PUT_LINE (1);
END;
```

But if I want to display a Boolean, I must write code like this:

```
BEGIN
    IF my_boolean THEN DBMS_OUTPUT.PUT_LINE ('TRUE');
    ELSIF NOT my_boolean THEN DBMS_OUTPUT.PUT_LINE ('FALSE');
    ELSE DBMS_OUTPUT.PUT_LINE ('NULL');
END;
```

And if I want to display a CLOB value, I must write code like this:

```
CREATE OR REPLACE PROCEDURE display_clob (clob_in IN CLOB)
IS
    l_amount     PLS_INTEGER    := 255;
    l_position   PLS_INTEGER    := 1;
    l_buffer     VARCHAR2 (255);
BEGIN
    LOOP
        DBMS_LOB.READ (clob_in, l_amount, l_position, l_buffer);
        DBMS_OUTPUT.put_line (l_buffer);
        l_position := l_position + l_amount;
    END LOOP;
EXCEPTION
    WHEN NO_DATA_FOUND OR VALUE_ERROR
    THEN
        DBMS_OUTPUT.put_line ('** End of data');
END;
/
```

You can find this code in the *display_clob.sp* file on the book's web site.

That's a big pain in the seat of my pants! Now as a user of PL/SQL, I really don't understand why I have to do this. If DBMS_OUTPUT.PUT_LINE displays my data structure on the screen, then it seems to me that it should do that job for any valid PL/SQL datatype. It's very frustrating!

Solution: Create multiple programs with the same name (overloading) that anticipate user needs.

Overloading (also known as *static polymorphism* in the world of object-oriented languages) is the ability to declare two or more programs in the same scope with the same name. While you can do this in the declaration section of any PL/SQL block, it's most useful and common in package specifications.

The primary reason to overload programs in your package is to transfer the "need to know" about how to use your functionality from the user to the package itself. You anticipate the different ways that developers will want to use the packaged feature and then offer matching variations of the "same" program.

Let's see how I can apply this idea to DBMS_SQL.EXECUTE and DBMS_OUTPUT.PUT_LINE. In other words, if I could change those built-in packages, what would I do?

Here is the current, sole declaration of DBMS_SQL.EXECUTE (taken from the *dbmssql.sql* file in the *$ORACLE_HOME\Rdbms\Admin* directory):

```
PACKAGE SYS.DBMS_SQL AUTHID CURRENT_USER
IS
    FUNCTION execute(c IN INTEGER) RETURN INTEGER;
```

What I would do is add an overloading of this program, but in a procedure form:

```
PACKAGE SYS.DBMS_SQL AUTHID CURRENT_USER
IS
    FUNCTION execute(c IN INTEGER) RETURN INTEGER;
    PROCEDURE execute(c IN INTEGER);
```

With this overloading in place, I could continue to use the function version when executing a DML statement (since I want to see how many rows were modified). When I execute a DDL statement, however, I could use the procedure version and avoid declaring that dummy variable:

```
DECLARE
    l_cursor PLS_INTEGER := DBMS_SQL.OPEN_CURSOR ();
BEGIN
    DBMS_SQL.PARSE (l_cursor, 'DROP TABLE XYZ', DBMS_SQL.NATIVE);
    DBMS_SQL.EXECUTE (l_cursor);
END;
```

Overloading by program type (procedure and function) is unusual, but it can go a long way toward improving the ease of use of your packages.

Now on to DBMS_OUTPUT.PUT_LINE. The fundamental problem with this procedure is that *it is not overloaded at all*! There is just one declaration of PUT_LINE, accepting a single string as its sole argument. Thus, PUT_LINE can only display the values of data structures that can be implicitly or explicitly converted to VARCHAR2.

The solution is quite straightforward: add overloadings of PUT_LINE to the DBMS_OUTPUT package; each overloading is passed a different datatype, and then "does the right thing" with it—displays the string representation of that data.

Unfortunately, as far as I can tell, Oracle Corporation has no plans to do this with DBMS_OUTPUT. So I went ahead and did it myself in the "p" package (see the *p.pks* and *p.pkb* files on the book's web site). It contains numerous overloadings of the "l" procedure, so that I can, for instance, display the contents of a file by writing nothing more than this:

```
DECLARE
   l_file UTL_FILE.FILE_TYPE;
BEGIN
   l_file := UTL_FILE.FOPEN ('c:/temp', 'myfile.txt');
   p.l (l_file);
END;
```

I don't have to think about it. I just assume that my display procedure displays a file, and pass it the handle to the file. The package takes care of everything for me.

And that is the power of overloading!

> Yes, I know. "p.l" is a strange name for a procedure. But my rationale is that I wanted to define a substitute for DBMS_OUTPUT.PUT_LINE that would let me type the smallest number of characters possible to say "show me this." I like typing 3 characters instead of 20!

Best Practices for Triggers

Database triggers are a crucial part of any well-designed application. By placing logic in a trigger, you associate business rules closely with a specific database object, guaranteeing that these rules are always applied to any action taken against that object.

Uncertainty in trigger execution is a most unsettling emotion.

Consolidate "overlapping" DML triggers to control execution order, or use the FOLLOW syntax of Oracle Database 11g.

Problem: Seemingly random trigger behavior is driving Jasper nuts.

Sunita asks Jasper to add some new validation to the mfe_excuses table, to be run before the table is inserted or updated. Jasper notices that another ON INSERT OR UPDATE trigger (an extremely complicated one) already exists for this table.

Rather than edit that trigger and possibly introduce an error, Jasper creates a new trigger like this:

```
CREATE OR REPLACE TRIGGER mfe_excuses_bui_2
BEFORE UPDATE OR INSERT ON mfe_excuses
```

```
FOR EACH ROW
BEGIN
   IF UPPER (:NEW.title) LIKE '%HOMEWORK%'
   THEN
      :NEW.school_related := 'Y';
   ELSE
      :NEW.school_related := 'N';
   END IF;
END;
```

He runs some tests and verifies the behavior of the trigger. Off it goes to production, and on Jasper proceeds to his next assignment. Unfortunately, this trigger comes back to plague him over the coming weeks. Users report problems with the setting of the school_related column. Sometimes it is set properly. At other times, it is set to "N" when it should be set to "Y".

So Jasper goes back and tests some more, but is able to get the error to occur only once. In desperation, he looks at the mfe_excuses_bui_1 trigger, which has been in place for years, and finds this line of code:

```
IF INSTR (:NEW.title, 'homework') > 0
THEN
   :NEW.title := REPLACE (:NEW.title, 'homework', 'schoolwork');
END IF;
```

"OK," thinks Jasper, "that can definitely mess up my logic, but why doesn't it *always* (*or never*) cause the bug?" The apparent randomness seems so out of place in the world of software and Oracle. He turns to the wizened expert, Delaware, for help. Delaware cannot help but draw himself up straight-backed and act the guru:

> Ah, young Jasper, you have had a run-in with the Oracle Uncertainty Principle. Allow me to explain: while it is possible to create many DML triggers of the same type on a table, it is not possible to guarantee the order in which they fire. While several theories abound about firing order (including reverse order of creation or object ID), it isn't advisable to rely on theories when designing database triggers. Instead, you should consolidate into a single trigger all triggers that fire under the same conditions.

"You're kidding," says Jasper. "You are saying that the mfe_excuses_bui_1 might run first today, but then tomorrow take a back seat to my new trigger?"

Delaware nods sagely. "That is the way of Oracle: through ambiguity and controlled randomness, we retain the very core of the mystery of life."

Solution: Consolidate "same event" triggers or use the FOLLOWS clause.

Delaware continues: "Indeterminate firing order often doesn't matter, but in your case, you have a dependency between the two triggers. So you really have no choice but to take your new logic and integrate it into the existing trigger."

And then just as Delaware is feeling his wisest, Lizbeth pokes her head around the corner of his cubicle: "That's right," she says, "unless you've installed Oracle Database 11*g*. Didn't you see the memo, Delaware? In the new release, Oracle has now added a FOLLOWS clause so that you *can* dictate the order of execution! How cool is that?"

Delaware glares at Lizbeth, but grinds his teeth and nods. "Right, of course. The memo and FOLLOWS."

Luckily for Delaware, MFE is not yet using Oracle Database 11*g* as the company's base development version. When it does, however, Jasper could simply add the FOLLOWS clause to his trigger, as shown here:

```
CREATE OR REPLACE TRIGGER mfe_excuses_bu1_2
FOLLOWS mfe_excuses_bu1_1
.... same as above ....
END;
```

and then Oracle will always execute the new trigger after the original trigger.

Resources

You will find the following files on the book's web site:

multiple_triggers.sql
> Contains a detailed working version of an example of the indeterminate firing of triggers, plus the application of the FOLLOWS clause.

trigger_conflict.sql
> A simple query against the USER_TRIGGERS data dictionary view that helps you identify potentially conflicting triggers.

"One-stop triggering" is so much easier to understand and maintain.

Use Oracle Database 11g compound triggers to consolidate all related trigger logic on a table.

Problem: Lizbeth has created a dozen triggers and a support package on a critical database table.

Over the span of a year, Lizbeth has spent many hours building triggers for the mfe_activity table, a central log of all activity for a given customer. She has a trigger for just about every action (BEFORE UPDATE, AFTER UPDATE, row and statement level, etc.) and in a number of cases she must execute similar logic in multiple triggers. In addition, she needs to pass information between triggers and relies on collections declared at the package level to maintain "state."

To avoid duplicating logic, Lizbeth has created a new package to hold all of the code to be used in the triggers. Then she makes calls to the programs from within the triggers as shown in Figure 8-1. From the standpoint of code management, this is an excellent move on Lizbeth's part. She is, however, still left with all those different triggers and the package state requirement, which made her nervous, because if the BEFORE trigger raises an exception, the collection will not be cleaned up, and could consume lots of memory.

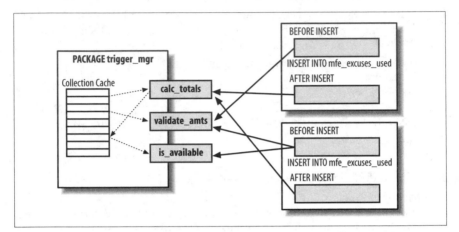

Figure 8-1. Use of a package to consolidate and encourage reuse of business logic

Solution: Consolidate all logic into a compound trigger, and lose the package if it is present only for trigger implementation.

Oracle Database 11g offers a new compound trigger that allows Lizbeth to move the logic from the package directly into a single trigger that combines all the previously distinct triggers. This new trigger has four *timing-point sections*:

BEFORE STATEMENT
> Consolidates all code that you need to run before the statement is executed. This would be the perfect place to reset any caching structures, for example.

BEFORE ROW
> Consolidates all code that you need to run before each row identified by the statement is executed.

AFTER ROW
> Consolidates all code that you need to run after each row identified by the statement is executed. If you are avoiding a mutating table error, you might take data from the row and place it in one or more collection caches.

AFTER STATEMENT
> Consolidates all code that you need to run after the statement is executed. This section, for example, is where you would place code to process DML operations that could not occur at the row level because of mutating table errors.

Here is a "skeleton" of the compound trigger body, showing the syntax for each of the sections:

```
CREATE TRIGGER full_mfe_excuse_transaction
BEFORE UPDATE ON mfe_customers
COMPOUND TRIGGER
   /*
   Declare any variables here; they can be accessed anywhere
   inside the trigger body.
   */

   BEFORE STATEMENT IS
   BEGIN
   ...
   END BEFORE STATEMENT;

   BEFORE ROW IS
   BEGIN
   ...
   END BEFORE ROW;

   AFTER ROW IS
   BEGIN
   ...
   END AFTER ROW;

   AFTER STATEMENT IS
   BEGIN
   ...
   END AFTER STATEMENT;

END full_mfe_excuse_transaction;
```

You can, of course, use the INSERTING, UPDATING, and DELETING functions within any of these sections so that you are able to write logic specific to the type of DML operation currently being executed.

You no longer need to rely on package-level collections to communicate between triggers. Instead, you declare a collection (or whatever sort of data structure you need) right in the declaration section of the trigger, as in:

```
CREATE TRIGGER full_mfe_excuse_transaction
BEFORE UPDATE ON mfe_customers
COMPOUND TRIGGER
   TYPE excuses_aat IS TABLE OF mfe_excuses%ROWTYPE
      INDEX BY mfe_excuses.title%TYPE;
   g_excuses excuses_aat

   BEFORE STATEMENT IS
   ....
```

You can then reference your variables anywhere inside the compound trigger. If the trigger fails with an unhandled exception, the memory for those variables is automatically cleaned up.

The compound trigger is a big step forward in terms of ease of writing and maintaining trigger logic. I look forward to using it frequently in my application development.

Your application should not be able to perform a "Houdini" with business rules.

Validate complex business rules with DML triggers.

Harry Houdini (1874–1926) was an escape artist who was famous for wiggling out of seemingly inescapable traps. Business rules express critical validation for your data; no part of your application should be able to escape from applying those rules.

Problem: There's more than one way to make an excuse.

My Flimsy Excuse management decides to expand their customer base by appealing to "high rollers," wealthy people who, when in need, are ready to pay big bucks for their flimsy excuses. At a meeting of users and frontend developers, a set of business rules are decided upon for a whole new class of excuses: those provided by CEOs to shareholders to justify their enormous compensation packages even as the stock price plummets.

The frontend developers implement the rules in their Java code and roll out their changes to the public web site. Meanwhile, another group of hotshot .NET developers build an applet that will be installed directly on CEOs' desktops to give them instant access to their flimsy excuses. That's all very wonderful, but those .NETters didn't get the memo about the business rules. As a result, the data inserted through the applet skips all validation and corrupts the database.

Which means that Delaware's beeper goes off at 2 A.M. on Wednesday morning and he spends hours fixing the data. When *that* fire is put out, he drinks another cup of Water Joe and angrily turns his attention to how this could have happened.

Solution 1: Apply the business rule at the lowest level possible, to ensure that it cannot be avoided.

A few hours later, Delaware has the .NET team lead on the phone and is chewing him out about the total lack of validation in the applet. Delaware concludes his rant: "And you know what? Keep your code just the way it is. *Leave* out the validation. That's fine with me, because that's not the place to do it, anyway." Delaware slams down the phone, wonders if perhaps he has ingested a bit *too* much caffeine, and starts thinking about database triggers.

Why triggers? The fundamental problem with the approach taken by those Java and .NET developers is that they assumed that they were the only way "in" to the underlying tables. Unfortunately, they cannot guarantee such a thing.

Someone else can always build *another* frontend web page or applet, and it will be virtually impossible to keep all those programs in synch when it comes to the necessary validation of the data.

A much better approach is to apply the logic and validation at the lowest level possible, as close as possible to the table itself—the database trigger. That way, no matter how a user tries to put data into the table, he will not be able to avoid the validation:

```
CREATE TRIGGER no_houdinis_allowed
BEFORE UPDATE ON mfc_customers
FOR EACH ROW
BEGIN
   IF new_business_rule_violated
   THEN
      /* Raise error to stop the transaction and
         communicate information back to the user. */
      ....
END;
```

Solution 2: Populate columns of derived values with triggers.

The same logic applies to dealing with derived column values. Some applications require that extra (that is, denormalized) information is stored in a row whenever it is inserted, updated, or deleted. This information is usually derived or computed from other column values. This step is usually taken to improve performance when retrieving information from the table.

If you want to make sure that the derived values are *always* computed properly and stored in the table, a database trigger is the most natural and effective place for this logic.

Suppose, for example, that the mfe_excuses table has title and upper_title columns. The upper_title column contains the same text as title, but the text is uppercased. The following trigger ensures that this derived value is always set correctly:

```
CREATE OR REPLACE TRIGGER denorm_mfe_excuses
BEFORE UPDATE OR INSERT ON mfe_excuses
FOR EACH ROW
BEGIN
   :NEW.upper_title := UPPER (:NEW.title);
END;
```

 Oracle also allows you to create and manage denormalized data with materialized views.

CHAPTER 9

My Code Runs Faster Than Your Code

Certainly one of the most frustrating experiences an application user can have is slow performance. Software is supposed to help people get things done faster and more easily. Ah, the gap between "supposed to" and reality!

This chapter offers many recommendations for helping you improve the performance of your PL/SQL programs. Of course, tuning PL/SQL is just a small part (and often not the most crucial part) of application tuning. Development teams (and their DBAs) must also optimize SQL statements (the most common source of performance issues) and overall database instance activity. Before diving into the details, I offer the following high-level advice regarding code optimization:

Performance optimization is never a theoretical exercise
> For example, I'll talk in this chapter about such specifics as the FORALL statement and how you could see an enormous increase in performance when you use this statement. The operative word here is "could." You need to verify the impact of this advice in *your* application, *your* installation of the Oracle database, *your* database server, and with your data. Don't assume that you will see the same results that I have experienced (hey, yours might be even better!).

Remember the 80-20 rule
> Most of the code you write will *not* be part of a performance bottleneck. So generally you should not obsess about optimizing every single line of code in your application. You will end up wasting a lot of time. Instead, you should prioritize writing code that meets user requirements and is easy to maintain. After that, you should analyze performance, identify bottlenecks that affect the user experience with the application, and *then* start tuning.

Tune your SQL statements before worrying about the PL/SQL code
> Most performance issues can be traced back to SQL, which after all directly manipulates the enormous quantities of data in your Oracle database. The gains from SQL tuning can easily overwhelm the gains of PL/SQL optimization. Note that this chapter does *not* offer advice for tuning SQL statements themselves.

Implement "straight" SQL when possible

If you can implement a requirement in straight SQL—without the need for procedural PL/SQL code—then you should do so. A SQL-only solution is usually faster and easier to optimize than a mixture of SQL and PL/SQL. Of course, there are any number of exceptions to this rule, and you will certainly encounter situations where you *need* to inject some SQL into your PL/SQL code to avoid a performance problem with a monster SQL statement.

I have separated the recommendations into three sections:

Best Practices for Finding Slow Code

Before you can tune your code, you have to figure out where it is running slowly. Also, you often need to be able to *compare* different implementations of the same program, to see which is faster. These best practices will help you with both tasks.

Best Practices for High-Impact Tuning

Presents best practices that can have an enormous impact (an order of magnitude or more) on elapsed time of PL/SQL programs. You should seek every opportunity to apply these tips first (after tuning the SQL, of course).

Best Practices for Other Tuning

Let's face it. Not all tuning tips are created equal. Most of the things you can do to tune PL/SQL code will have incremental impact (for example, 5 percent improvement, 10 percent improvement). You will want to look at these best practices after you apply the high-impact ideas.

This chapter does not attempt to provide a comprehensive review of all tuning possibilities for PL/SQL programs. Instead, I have focused on those ideas that are most likely to have a noticeable impact on your application's performance. You will find many more tuning tips in *Oracle PL/SQL Programming*. Oracle Corporation's *Oracle Database PL/SQL Language Reference* also contains a chapter devoted to this topic.

Best Practices for Finding Slow Code

As I mentioned, optimization is not an abstract, theoretical exercise. Before you can tune your application, you need to be able to identify which parts of that application are running too slowly. In addition, you often need to compare the performance of two or more implementations of the same functionality. This section offers guidance on how to achieve these ends.

First, I'll review the various options available to PL/SQL developers to trace globally the execution of their programs. It is outside the scope of this book to go into detail on any of these options, but I encourage you to check out the appropriate Oracle documentation (particularly the *PL/SQL Packages and Types References* guide) and leverage the Oracle utilities through the user interfaces provided in various PL/SQL editors.

Next, I'll describe a variety of additional utilities that you can use to trace and analyze performance in a very granular fashion (single-program execution or even portions of a program). These utilities will be especially helpful when you want to compare various implementations of the same functionality.

Take the guesswork out of optimization.

Use trace facilities to gather raw data about program performance.

The Oracle database offers a number of built-in trace capabilities that are very helpful in gathering raw data about program performance. You should familiarize yourself with the supplied packages and underlying tables for the PL/SQL Profiler, PL/SQL Trace, the PL/SQL Hierarchical Profiler, and the Application Data Profiler.

PL/SQL Profiler (DBMS_PROFILER)

The PL/SQL Profiler, accessible via the built-in DBMS_PROFILER package, calculates the time that your program spends on each line and in each subprogram. These runtime statistics are then written to a set of database tables. Profiling gives you an enormous number of data points; the hardest aspect of working with DBMS_PROFILER is extracting meaningful information. Most PL/SQL editors offer graphical interfaces (including graphs and charts) to help you understand the profile data. They also make it easy for you to turn on profiling.

You will not have to make any changes to your code to use this profiler; you will, though, need to start and stop the DBMS_PROFILER package. Here is an example of the kind of code you might write "around" your application code:

```
DECLARE
    profile_id PLS_INTEGER;
BEGIN
    DBMS_PROFILER.START_PROFILER (
        run_comment => '<profile descriptor>'
      , run_number => profile_id);

    my_application_code;

    DBMS_PROFILER.STOP_PROFILER ();
END;
```

PL/SQL Trace (DBMS_TRACE)

Oracle offers the built-in DBMS_TRACE package to allow you to control the tracing of the execution of subprograms in your application. You can also trace exceptions, SQL execution, and individual line execution. The information is then written to a set of tables owned by SYS (and created by the *tracetab.sql* script located in the *<Oracle_home>Rdbms\Admin* directory of the Oracle database installation).

You will not have to make any changes to your code to use this trace mechanism.

PL/SQL Hierarchical Profiler (DBMS_HPROF)

New in Oracle Database 11g, the Hierarchical Profiler (exposed through the built-in DBMS_HPROF supplied package) profiles program execution, but stores that data in a way that clearly reveals the hierarchical callstack of the application. The best way to understand the value of DBMS_HPROF is to contrast it to the original profiler (DBMS_PROFILER). DBMS_PROFILER tracks information down to the individual line, making it difficult for programmers to see the performance of distinct *units* of code (procedures and functions). The new DBMS_HPROF package, on the other hand, lets you see the performance of these units at a higher level.

You will not have to make any changes to your code to use this profiler.

Application Data Profiler (DBMS_APPLICATION_INFO)

You can use the built-in DBMS_APPLICATION_INFO package to trace the execution of specific programs and/or portions of programs. The output from this package is written to a variety of V$ views, which means that you can review and analyze trace information while the application is still running. This package is especially helpful in analyzing long-running programs.

You *will* have to make changes to your code to take advantage of this profiler.

There are so many ways to implement an algorithm; which is best?

Build or find tools to calculate elapsed time.

Problem: There are hundreds of ways to implement a requirement. How can Lizbeth find the fastest version?

Sunita has asked Lizbeth to write a program to determine whether there is at least one customer who has used a particular excuse. Lizbeth immediately realizes that there are a number of approaches she can take to do this and codes a few of them:

- Implicit query and use of exception section to return some of the results:

```
FUNCTION atleast1cust (mfe_excuse_id_in IN mfe_excuses.ID%TYPE)
   RETURN BOOLEAN
IS
   l_dummy   CHAR (1);
BEGIN
   SELECT 'x' INTO l_dummy
     FROM mfe_excuses_used
    WHERE mfe_excuse_id = mfe_excuse_id_in;

   RETURN TRUE;
EXCEPTION
   WHEN NO_DATA_FOUND THEN RETURN FALSE;
   WHEN TOO_MANY_ROWS THEN RETURN TRUE;
END atleast1cust;
```

- Use of implicit query and COUNT(*) to determine total number of rows:

```
FUNCTION atleast1cust (mfe_excuse_id_in IN mfe_excuses.ID%TYPE)
   RETURN BOOLEAN
IS
   l_count    PLS_INTEGER;
BEGIN
   SELECT COUNT (*) INTO l_count
     FROM mfe_excuses_used
    WHERE mfe_excuse_id = mfe_excuse_id_in;

   RETURN l_count >= 1;
END atleast1cust;
```

- Explicit cursor and single fetch:

```
FUNCTION atleast1cust (mfe_excuse_id_in IN mfe_excuses.ID%TYPE)
   RETURN BOOLEAN
IS
   l_return      BOOLEAN;

   CURSOR excuse_cur IS
      SELECT customer_id
        FROM mfe_excuses_used
       WHERE mfe_excuse_id = mfe_excuse_id_in;

   excuse_rec    excuse_cur%ROWTYPE;
BEGIN
   OPEN excuse_cur;
   FETCH excuse_cur INTO excuse_rec;
   l_return := excuse_cur%FOUND;
   CLOSE excuse_cur;

   RETURN l_return;
END atleast1cust;
```

They all get the job done—logically. But since this function is going to be used over and over again, Lizbeth needs to find the fastest one. So she creates a script that compiles a version of the atleast1cust function and then executes it for a particular excuse ID against a test table with 100 rows. She then starts up SQL*Plus, issues the SET TIMING ON command, and runs the script. And this is what she sees:

```
Elapsed: 00:00:00.03
Elapsed: 00:00:00.07
Elapsed: 00:00:00.02
```

Well, that's not very useful; variations in performance of hundredths of seconds can easily be caused by operating system activity, thereby telling us nothing about these programs themselves. And when Lizbeth turns to the DBMS_PROFILER package, she gets a lot more data points, but they all say pretty much the same thing: all three implementations are really, really fast! Lizbeth is pretty sure she knows which should be fastest—or at least, which should be slowest. But how can she verify her belief?

Solution: Use DBMS_UTILITY.GET_TIME and GET_CPU_TIME for very granular analysis.

Lizbeth is actually confronted by two problems:

- All of her programs run in a very small amount of time. She either needs to figure out a way to get them to slow down (lots and lots of data?) or needs to run each program lots of times to accumulate an elapsed time that isn't (more or less) 0.

- Her analysis is very focused: how does this one program run? Most of the built-in profiling mechanisms generate gobs and gobs of data that can actually make it *hard* to get answers to questions like "Which implementation is faster?"

Fortunately, Oracle's supplied package of miscellany, DBMS_UTILITY, offers two functions that will help Lizbeth resolve her dilemma.

DBMS_UTILITY.GET_TIME returns a point in time as an integer, with precision down to the hundredth of a second. DBMS_UTILITY.GET_CPU_TIME (introduced in Oracle Database 10g) returns the current CPU time as an integer, also with precision down to the hundredth of a second. You can use the GET_TIME function to calculate elapsed clock time and the GET_CPU_TIME function to compute elapsed CPU time (actual cycles used to perform work).

Generally, the way you use these utilities is to call the function once to get the start time, then run the program you want to time, then call the function a second time, and finally subtract the start time from the end time. The outcome is the number of hundredths of seconds that have elapsed in running the program (clock time or CPU time).

Here is an example of using the GET_CPU_TIME function:

```
DECLARE
    l_start PLS_INTEGER;

    PROCEDURE show_elapsed ( NAME_IN IN VARCHAR2 )
    IS
    BEGIN
        DBMS_OUTPUT.put_line (     '"'
            || NAME_IN
            || '" elapsed CPU time: '
            || TO_CHAR ( (DBMS_UTILITY.get_cpu_time - l_start ) / 100 )
            || ' seconds'
        );
    END show_elapsed;
BEGIN
    l_start := DBMS_UTILITY.get_cpu_time;

    DBMS_OUTPUT.PUT_LINE (atleast1cust (15783));

    show_elapsed ( 'At Least 1 using COUNT' );
END;
```

Now, if you ask me, that's a lot of code to write to use this function. Plus, there are several other issues:

- You still generally cannot run your program just once. It will usually need to be put inside a loop and run hundreds or thousands of times.
- In some operating systems, the GET_TIME and GET_CPU_TIME functions "roll over" and start counting up from 0. Thus, you can subtract start from end, and get a negative number. That's not a very useful elapsed time computation.

For these various reasons, I decided to make my life easier when it came to analyzing comparative performance specifically, and using the GET*TIME functions generally. I created a package, PLVtmr, and an object type (see the *plvtmr.pkg* and *tmr.ot* files on the book's web site), each of which encapsulates lots of the code and the baggage that comes with using these functions (see the "Resources" section at the end of this section).

Using PLVtmr, Lizbeth constructs a test driver procedure as follows:

```
PROCEDURE atleast1cust_test (description_in IN VARCHAR2)
IS
    l_result BOOLEAN;
BEGIN
    PLVtmr.capture;

    FOR indx IN 1 .. 1000
    LOOP
        l_result := atleast1cust (15786);
    END LOOP;

    PLVtmr.show_elapsed (description_in);
END atleast1cust_test;
```

Then she can compile a particular version of atleast1cust and run a block of code like this to obtain her timing:

```
BEGIN
    atleast1cust_test ('COUNT(*)');
END;
/
```

By the way, in case you were wondering, of the three implementations for atleast1cust shown above, the first (implicit SELECT with exception section) and third (explicit cursor with single fetch) are both generally more efficient than relying on COUNT(*) when the queries find precisely one row. If the query often identifies more than one match or none, then the first approach (relying on exceptions) will usually be slower than the third option, since exception handling is inherently slow. I find the explicit query and single fetch the best all-around way to implement the "at least one?" requirement.

Resources

You will find these packages, described in the previous section, on the book's web site:

plvtmr.pkg

The PLVtmr package was originally part of the freeware PL/Vision code library (available at *www.quest-pipelines.com*). It is available here as a stand-alone package.

tmr.ot

This is the object type version; it offers the advantage of instantiating and keeping track of multiple software "stopwatches" in a single session (the package version is limited to just one).

Best Practices for High-Impact Tuning

The ideas in this section have the *potential* to dramatically improve performance of your programs. Actual results will, of course, vary. So you should verify everything for yourself!

Let Oracle do most of the tuning for you.

Make sure your code is being optimized when compiled.

This is an easy one. Starting with Oracle Database 10g, the PL/SQL compiler will now also automatically rearrange our code to improve performance. In Oracle Database 10g, there are three different levels of optimization:

Level 2

This is the default and the most aggressive form of optimization. It applies the most rearrangements to your code elements, has the highest potential to improve performance, and also has the most impact on compile time (it increases it).

Level 1

The compiler performs basic optimizations on your code, but is not as aggressive as in Level 2. You will see limited performance improvements, but the compile time will also not be increased as dramatically.

Level 0

Optimization is disabled. The code is compiled just as it would be in Oracle9*i* Database.

And in Oracle Database 11g, Oracle now offers a new level:

Level 3

When you set compiler optimization to this level, the PL/SQL compiler will automatically "in-line" all calls to local subprograms in the current program. That is, it replaces the call to the subprogram with the code that is contained in that subprogram, resulting in additional optimization.

So, the best practice is simple: make sure that when your code base is compiled, you are using the highest possible optimization level. You should generally just stick with the default; I think it would be very unusual for you to run into a situation that calls for a reduced optimization level.

You can make sure that all your program units are compiled at the desired level by running this program (found in *whats_not_optimal.sp* on the book's web site):

```
PROCEDURE whats_not_optimal (level_in IN PLS_INTEGER DEFAULT 2)
IS
BEGIN
   FOR program_rec IN (SELECT owner, NAME, TYPE, plsql_optimize_level
                         FROM all_plsql_object_settings
                        WHERE plsql_optimize_level < level_in)
   LOOP
      DBMS_OUTPUT.put_line (   program_rec.TYPE
                            || ' '
                            || program_rec.owner
                            || '.'
                            || program_rec.NAME
                            || ' is optimized at level '
                            || program_rec.plsql_optimize_level
                           );
   END LOOP;
END whats_not_optimal;
```

You can also use conditional compilation to ensure that a particular program is optimized (or not) at a particular level. Here is an example:

```
PROCEDURE compute_intensive_program
IS
BEGIN
$IF $$PLSQL_OPTIMIZE_LEVEL < 2
$THEN
   $ERROR
      'compute_intensive_program must be compiled with maximum optimization!'
   $END
$END
   ... all the code ...
END compute_intensive_program;
```

Who has time for querying (or inserting or deleting or updating) one row at a time?

Use BULK COLLECT and FORALL to improve performance of multirow SQL operations in PL/SQL.

Problem: It worked so quickly in SQL*Plus. Why is it so slow in PL/SQL?

Jasper is at wit's end. He first learned about PL/SQL when he joined My Flimsy Excuse a year ago. It was certainly very different from C, his previous language. PL/SQL was *much* easier to learn and use, and of course it was so easy to write SQL statements within PL/SQL programs. Lizbeth also assured him that executing such SQL statements was very fast in PL/SQL.

Yet he is now facing a situation that seems to deny this assertion. He wrote a three-way join and executed it in SQL*Plus (connected to an Oracle9i database). It completed in less than a second. He then moved his query into a PL/SQL procedure and cursor FOR loop. The procedure now takes more than 10 seconds to completely iterate through the data returned by the query. How can this be? What is he doing wrong?

Solution: Sometimes you have to help PL/SQL integrate with SQL.

Oracle Corporation talks a good talk about how tightly integrated PL/SQL is with the SQL engine. But in some ways, that integration is only skin deep. And below the surface, a looser coupling between these two elements of Oracle technology results in reduced performance, both when *pulling* (querying) data from tables into program variables and when *pushing* data from a PL/SQL program into tables.

The cause for the delay that Jasper experienced when he moved the query into a PL/SQL block is the evil and much-to-be-feared *context switch*. When you run a PL/SQL program, the PL/SQL statements are executed with the PL/SQL statement execution engine. If, within that program, this engine encounters a SQL statement, it passes the statement over to the SQL engine (that's the context switch). Sure, both of these engines are located in the "backend," but there are different components of the backend, and Oracle must make the switch. Figure 9-1 shows this behavior for an UPDATE statement.

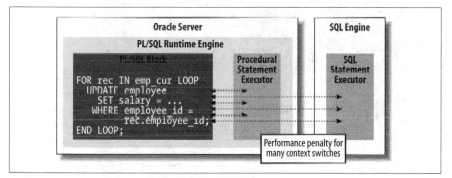

Figure 9-1. Many context switches with row-by-row SQL processing

Back in Oracle8 and Oracle8i, the overhead of a context switch was prohibitive—and very easy to identify. DBMS_SQL (the original dynamic SQL mechanism) was very inefficient because anything you did in DBMS_SQL involved multiple switches. Executing your own function within a SQL statement was horribly slow, especially if it was called in the WHERE clause—for the same reason.

Oracle Corporation has gone to great lengths to reduce the overhead of a context switch. As a result, DBMS_SQL is now pretty much as efficient as native dynamic SQL—and you don't pay a big penalty for calling your own function in SQL.

Still, these switches can be a significant bottleneck when your SQL statement processes many rows of data.

So in Oracle8*i*, Oracle introduced BULK COLLECT and FORALL, which in essence implement array processing for SQL operations in PL/SQL.

When you use BULK COLLECT, you request multiple rows of data in a single request (context switch) to the Oracle database. The SQL engine processes this request and returns all the data together (one context switch) to the PL/SQL engine, which deposits the data into one or more *collections* (array-like structures in PL/SQL).

For DML operations, you load *into* collections all the data you want to push back to your tables, and then FORALL batches up all the DML statements that need to be run to cover all the data in the collections. These statements are transferred over to the SQL engine in a single context switch.

Note that the SQL engine executes the same statements it would have run with row-by-row processing. Use of BULK COLLECT or FORALL does *not* change the SQL behavior. You are only changing the way that PL/SQL communicates *with* the SQL engine. See Figure 9-2 for a visualization of this process.

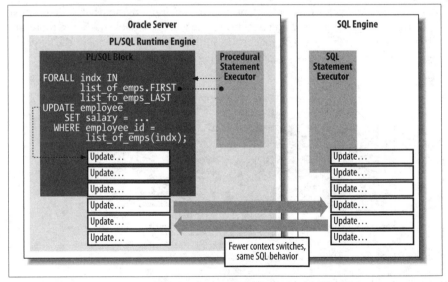

Figure 9-2. Fewer context switches with BULK COLLECT and FORALL

I offer in this section two short and simple examples of these statements, and then a set of recommendations for using BULK COLLECT and FORALL. If you are not familiar with these incredibly powerful PL/SQL enhancements, you will definitely want to study them (and the collections they depend on) further: *Oracle PL/SQL Programming* and the Oracle documentation both offer lots of background on these topics.

Here is an example of using BULK COLLECT to retrieve all of the excuses that have been requested by a customer:

```
1  PROCEDURE process_excuses (customer_id_in IN mfe_customer.ID%TYPE)
2  IS
3     CURSOR excuses_cur IS
4        SELECT * FROM mfe_excuses
5         WHERE customer_id = customer_id_in;
6
7     TYPE excuses_aat IS TABLE OF mfe_excuses%ROWTYPE INDEX BY PLS_INTEGER;
8     l_excuses    excuses_aat;
9  BEGIN
10    OPEN excuses_cur;
11    LOOP
12       FETCH excuses_cur BULK COLLECT INTO l_excuses LIMIT 1000;
13       ... do the processing ...
14       EXIT WHEN l_excuses.COUNT = 0;
15    END LOOP;
16 END process_excuses;
```

Line 12 shows the use of BULK COLLECT with a FETCH statement. In this example, I limit the number of rows I retrieve to 1,000 at a time (see the "Recommendations for BULK COLLECT" section, later in the chapter, for a motivation).

Here is an example of executing a *dynamic* SQL update within a FORALL statement. First, declare two schema-level nested table types to use in the PL/SQL procedure:

```
CREATE TYPE numbers_nt IS TABLE OF NUMBER;
/
CREATE TYPE customer_ids_nt IS TABLE OF INTEGER;
/
```

Now put them to use in a procedure that updates the specified column in the mfe_customers table to a value adjusted by the provided percentage. To verify what the new values are set to, add a RETURNING clause to retrieve the column value:

```
1  PROCEDURE update_customers (
2     column_in IN VARCHAR2
3     , cust_ids_in IN customer_ids_nt
4     , values_in IN numbers_nt
5     , pcts_in IN numbers_nt
6  )
7  IS
8     l_new_values    numbers_nt;
9  BEGIN
10    FORALL indx IN cust_ids_in.FIRST .. cust_ids_in.LAST
11       EXECUTE IMMEDIATE 'UPDATE mfe_customers SET '
12          || column_in
13          || ' = :value * :percentage WHERE id = :cust_id '
14          || ' RETURNING ' || column_in || ' INTO :new_values'
15       USING
16          values_in (indx), percentages_in (indx), cust_ids_in (indx)
```

```
17          RETURNING BULK COLLECT INTO l_new_values;
18
19     FOR indx IN 1 .. l_new_values.COUNT
20     LOOP
21        DBMS_OUTPUT.put_line (   'New value for customer ID '
22             || cust_ids_in (indx) || ' = ' || l_new_values (indx) );
23     END LOOP;
24  END update_customers;
```

I thought I might as well pack a whole bunch of interesting elements into this FORALL usage—specifically:

- In Oracle 9*i* Database Release 2 and above, you can use FORALL and BULK COLLECT with dynamic SQL statements.

- I can reference or bind into my statement more than one collection. Oracle will automatically synchronize the multiple data sources, using the same index values in each collection.

- Because my RETURN clause is executed within FORALL, it will be returning values for each distinct UPDATE statement executed. So the FORALL statement itself must have a RETURNING BULK COLLECT clause so that it can return a collection of those values.

Recommendations for BULK COLLECT. Here are my guidelines for BULK COLLECT:

More memory
> The memory consumed by PL/SQL collections comes out of the Process Global Area (PGA), not the SGA. This means that the memory consumption occurs on a per-session basis. Thus, if your BULK COLLECT program requires 5MB of data and you have 1,000 simultaneous connections, your application will need an extra 5GB of memory.

Cursor FOR loops
> When you compile your code with the PL/SQL optimization level set to 2 (the default) or higher, cursor FOR loops will be automatically optimized to run at the same speed as a BULK COLLECT operation. So, you do *not* need to rewrite your cursor FOR loops for Oracle Database 10*g* unless you are performing DML operations inside the loop. In this case, your query will have been optimized, but your DML operations will still execute on a row-by-row basis. In such cases, you should explicitly rewrite the cursor FOR loop into a BULK COLLECT and then use those collections to drive the DML operation.

LIMIT clause
> Always use the LIMIT clause when querying BULK COLLECT in production application code. Production data volume may (and likely will) grow dramatically. An unlimited BULK COLLECT that retrieves 100 rows today may retrieve 10,000 rows tomorrow. The resulting impact on per-session memory could have disastrous consequences for the application and user experience. You will need to try different LIMIT values to balance optimal performance with memory consumption.

No cursor attributes

> When using a LIMIT clause with an explicit cursor and loop, never rely on cursor attributes like %NOTFOUND or the NO_DATA_FOUND exception to terminate the loop. Instead, always and only examine the collection that was filled by the BULK COLLECT query. If no rows are returned, the collection is empty (COUNT = 0); the Oracle database will *not* raise NO_DATA_FOUND in this situation.

No string-indexed collections

> With BULK COLLECT, collections are always filled sequentially starting with index value 1. You cannot use string-indexed collections with BULK COLLECT.

Recommendations for FORALL. Here are my recommendations for using FORALL:

Exceptions

> By default, when the SQL engine raises an exception executing one of your many DML statements batched together by FORALL, it will pass that exception back to the PL/SQL engine, and the FORALL statement will terminate. You can tell the SQL engine to continue *past* exceptions, save them up, and return *all* of them when it is done by adding the SAVE EXCEPTION clause to your FORALL header.

Collections

> Prior to Oracle Database 10g Release 2, collections that are bound into your DML statements must be filled sequentially between the low and high index values specified in the FORALL range clause. Otherwise, Oracle will raise an exception. In Oracle Database 10g Release 2 and above, you can use the INDICES OF or VALUES OF clause to use collections that have gaps (index values between low and high that are not defined).

DML statements

> You can execute only one DML statement within each FORALL statement. If you have multiple DML operations, you will need to write a separate FORALL for each one—and you will need to write additional logic to synchronize activities between them. For example, suppose that I need to execute an INSERT followed by an UPDATE. If an exception is raised by one of my INSERT statements, I will not want to run the corresponding UPDATE statement.

If the SGA is so wonderful, why not emulate it?

Cache static data in the fastest memory location possible.

Problem: Jasper queries the same, unchanging data over and over and over again.

Like most applications, the MFE application contains lots of tables. Most of them contain data that is constantly changing. New customers are added almost every minute. Excuses are created, used by customers, edited, and so on.

Other tables change relatively infrequently, especially in comparison to the frequency of querying. An example of such a table is mfe_employees. Sure, people come and go, and their personal data changes, but the HR application on which mfe_employees is based queries the table thousands of times a day, while the data changes only once or twice a day.

And still other tables never change at all while users are running the application. One such table is the mfe_ref_codes dataset, a general "types" table that holds reference codes—for example, "O" is for "OPEN," "C" is for "CLOSED," etc.

One day, Jasper wrote a function to retrieve a description for a given code:

```
FUNCTION ref_code_description (
   category_in IN mfe_ref_codes.category%TYPE
 , code_in IN mfe_ref_codes.code%TYPE
)
   RETURN mfe_ref_codes.description%TYPE
IS
   l_description   mfe_ref_codes.description%TYPE;
BEGIN
   SELECT description INTO l_description
     FROM mfe_ref_codes WHERE category = category_in AND code = code_in;
   RETURN l_description;
EXCEPTION
   WHEN NO_DATA_FOUND THEN RETURN NULL;
END ref_code_description;
```

This function is called all over the application. In fact, it is called so often that Jasper receives a call from the production DBA:

> Jasper, I just did some performance analysis on the application. I discovered that the ref_code_description function is called more than 25,000 times in the span of a few minutes' time. Sure, each call is pretty fast, but the total elapsed time still amounts to 33 seconds.

Jasper is stunned. That's an awful lot of time to be spent retrieving this data. But he doesn't really see what he can do about it. "Doesn't the database automatically optimize such queries?" he asks the DBA.

"Sure," replies the DBA:

> That *is* the optimized performance. The query is preparsed and cached. The data is already sitting in the SGA; in fact, I moved the mfe_ref_codes table into the KEEP pool. I've even pinned the function into the shared pool. There's nothing more I can do. Are you sure you need to call the function so frequently?

Well, in fact, the application *does* need to call the function that often. Clean out of ideas, Jasper turns to Delaware for advice. And Delaware declares; "This calls for caching—the programmer way!"

Solution: If the normal SGA cache doesn't the trick, look for other ways to cache.

The whole point of the SGA is to store information in memory to avoid reading and writing to disk—the slowest step in the whole database round-trip. The MFE DBA is correct; the SGA is doing its job and is caching the information requested in this query.

We can also apply the concepts behind SGA caching to our PL/SQL code and achieve impressive decreases in elapsed time, but there is a downside: in the process we consume more memory.

Let's look at how we can employ the following caching options in the ref_code_description function; they are described in the following sections:

Per-session cache through PL/SQL package persistent data
> Through this cache we can store data in a package-level variable. The data persists for the entire session, but each session has its own copy.

Oracle Database 11g PL/SQL result cache
> A brand-new feature in the Oracle database, this new SGA memory cache avoids the overhead of the caching described in the Problem section and is shared across all sessions in the database instance.

Per-session cache in a PL/SQL package. When you declare data inside a package but not within any individual procedure or function in the package, that data persists for your entire session.[*] A package-level collection, for example, retains its values (say, 1,000 rows of data) until you delete one or more rows from the collection, close your connection, or recompile the package. This data persistence means that you can use package data as a *local* cache—local to that single session.

Here are some guidelines to help you decide how best to apply this technique:

- The data must be static for the duration of the session. It's possible to come up with ways to update the cache, but such efforts are likely to cancel out performance gains—and can be very complicated.

- Always remember that the memory consumed by package data comes out of the PGA and not the SGA. If this cache consumes 1 MB of data and you have 1,000 sessions connected to the Oracle database, your application will require an additional 1 GB of memory *in addition to* the SGA memory requirements.

- If your application uses connection pooling, you will need to make sure that each connection in a pool contains the same cached data. Otherwise, as your frontend application moves between sessions in the pool, it will work with different sets of data.

- You should declare the data structures inside the package *body* (make them private to the package use only) so that you can manage their contents and guarantee their integrity.

---

[*] You can insert the PRAGMA SERIALLY_REUSABLE statement into your package if you don't want package-level data to be persistent.

So how would Jasper apply these concepts to the ref_code_description function? First, he moves the function inside a package:

```
PACKAGE ref_code_cache
IS
    FUNCTION ref_code_description (
        category_in IN mfe_ref_codes.category%TYPE
      , code_in IN mfe_ref_codes.code%TYPE
      )
        RETURN mfe_ref_codes.description%TYPE;
END ref_code_cache;
```

Note that this means that he will either need to change all the existing calls to the function so they include the package name, or need to change the implementation of the original function to be a pass-through, as in:

```
FUNCTION ref_code_description (
    category_in IN mfe_ref_codes.category%TYPE
  , code_in IN mfe_ref_codes.code%TYPE
  )
    RETURN mfe_ref_codes.description%TYPE
IS
BEGIN
    RETURN ref_code_cache.ref_code_description (category_in, code_in);
END ref_code_description;
```

Next, Jasper implements the package body. Here is the code, followed by an explanation (you will also find this code in the *ref_code_cache.pkg* file on the book's web site):

```
 1  PACKAGE BODY ref_code_cache IS
 2     TYPE descriptions_for_code_aat IS TABLE OF
 3        mfe_ref_codes.description%TYPE
 4        INDEX BY mfe_ref_codes.code%TYPE;
 5
 6     TYPE codes_for_category_aat IS TABLE OF descriptions_for_code_aat
 7        INDEX BY mfe_ref_codes.category%TYPE;
 8
 9     g_cache    codes_for_category_aat;
10
11     FUNCTION ref_code_description (
12        category_in IN mfe_ref_codes.CATEGORY%TYPE
13      , code_in IN mfe_ref_codes.code%TYPE
14      )
15        RETURN mfe_ref_codes.description%TYPE
16     IS
17     BEGIN
18        RETURN g_cache (category_in) (code_in);
19     EXCEPTION
20        WHEN NO_DATA_FOUND THEN RETURN NULL;
21     END ref_code_description;
22  BEGIN
23     FOR ref_code_rec IN (SELECT * FROM mfe_ref_codes)
24     LOOP
25        g_cache (ref_code_rec.category) (ref_code_rec.code) :=
```

```
26                    ref_code_rec.description;
27    END LOOP;
28 END ref_code_cache;:
```

Line(s)	Significance
3–9	Declare two collection types: one to hold the description for a given code, the other to hold all the codes for a given category. Notice that I use the string columns as the collection indexes. I then declare my cache variable as one of these "collections of collections." Note that string-indexed and multilevel collections are supported only in Oracle9*i* Database Release 2 and above.
23–27	In the initialization section of my package, I query all the rows in the table and store the description in the cache, using the related category and code values to find the right place in the two-level collection.
18	Inside the description lookup function, I now replace the query with a simple (trivial, really, once you get used to the syntax of these multilevel collections) retrieval from the collection.

As you can see, the data is retrieved just once (per session) from the database. From that point on, all requests for descriptions are satisfied from the collection alone.

So what kinds of increases in performance are possible with this approach? To find out, Jasper can build another caching package that runs against the standard Oracle HR employees table, along with a procedure to compare the elapsed time of a number of different approaches to retrieving a row of data from the table. Here are the relevant files on the book's web site:

emplu.pkg

File that contains three *different* packages, showcasing different approaches to caching.

emplu.tst

Procedure that compares the performance and runs the test.

Here are the results for the standard query-driven function and a package-based cache (just two of the five approaches you will see compared in the *emplu.tst* script). As you can see, the improvement in performance can be quite dramatic!

Type of retrieval	Performance in seconds
Run query for each request for data	5.07
Cache entire contents of table into the associative array cache on initialization	.22

So be on the lookout for ways to apply this technique, but remember that your system must be able to accommodate the required per-session memory.

 This caching technique is also very handy when you execute long-running batch processes that must perform multiple passes through large result sets. In this case, you can usually afford to cache large amounts of data, because there is just a single process, as opposed to hundreds or thousands of sessions doing the same thing.

Oracle Database 11g PL/SQL function result cache. The package-based cache described in the previous section is a great technique, but it has two major limitations:

- The memory used by the cache is duplicated in each session.
- The cache makes sense only for completely static datasets.

These limitations greatly reduce the range of circumstances under which the caching can be applied. So, in Oracle Database 11g, Oracle has implemented a new kind of caching that combines the speed of the package-based PGA cache with the memory optimization and automatic cache management of the SGA.

Here is a rewrite of the original ref_code_description function using the PL/SQL function result cache:

```
 1  FUNCTION ref_code_description (
 2      category_in IN mfe_ref_codes.CATEGORY%TYPE
 3    , code_in IN mfe_ref_codes.code%TYPE
 4  )
 5      RETURN mfe_ref_codes.description%TYPE
 6      RESULT_CACHE RELIES_ON (mfe_ref_codes)
 7  IS
 8      l_description   mfe_ref_codes.description%TYPE;
 9  BEGIN
10      SELECT description INTO l_description
11        FROM mfe_ref_codes WHERE CATEGORY = category_in AND code = code_in;
12
13      RETURN l_description;
14  EXCEPTION
15      WHEN NO_DATA_FOUND THEN RETURN NULL;
16  END ref_code_description;
```

In other words, the only change made to the function was to add a new clause to the header (line 6):

```
RESULT_CACHE RELIES_ON (mfe_ref_codes)
```

This clause tells the Oracle database that it should remember (store in a special in-memory result cache) each record retrieved for a specific category-code combination. And when a session executes this function and passes in a combination that was previously stored, the PL/SQL runtime engine will *not* execute the function body, which includes that query. Instead, it will simply retrieve the record from the cache and return that data immediately. The result is much faster retrieval time.

 This caching *does* differ slightly from the package implementation in that the manual caching preloaded all of the rows when the session started, while the function result cache loads the required data as needed.

In addition, by specifying "RELIES_ON (mfe_ref_codes)", we inform the Oracle database that if any session commits changes to that table, any data in the result cache drawn from the table must be invalidated. The next call to the ref_code_description function would then have to execute the query and retrieve the data fresh from the table.

Finally, note that this cache is not per-session, but is available to all sessions connected to the instance.

Well, that is certainly is a whole lot easier to write than the package-based implementation! But how does it compare in performance? Jasper could modify his original "emplu" files to include the result cache technique. You can find the code for these files on the book's web site in the following:

11g_emplu.pkg
Source code for the various packages containing the different approaches.

11g_emplu_compare.sp
Procedure that compares the performance of each approach, using PLVtmr.

11g_emplu.tst
Script that runs the above two files, compiling all the necessary code, and then runs the test.

Type of retrieval	Performance in seconds	PGA memory consumed
Run query for each request for data	4.5	None (or very little)
Package-based cache	.11	~130,000 bytes
PL/SQL result cache	.27	None (or very little)

What's the conclusion of all this testing? The per-session PGA-based cache is still the fastest (it is simply more efficient to read from PGA memory than from SGA memory), but the PL/SQL function result cache is dramatically faster than repetitive querying. Plus, the new cache minimizes the amount of memory needed to cache and share this data across all sessions. This low memory profile, plus the automatic purge of cached results whenever changes are committed, makes this feature of Oracle Database 11g a very practical method for optimizing performance in our applications.

When waiting is not an option...

Use pipelined table functions to return data faster and to parallelize function execution.

Problem: Users hate to wait.

Not that those users are any different from we programmers—we hate to wait, too: for our programs to compile, for our tests to finish, or to get our next promotion (and raise). Unfortunately, there are many more users than there are programmers, and those users directly and indirectly pay our salaries.

So we need to do everything we can to keep them happy. At this moment, users of the My Flimsy Excuse web site are complaining bitterly about one particular web page. On this page, the visitor selects various criteria that result in a WHERE clause to identify the rows of data they want to see. Those rows are then displayed on the page. The problem is that sometimes the criteria result in a dataset of thousands of rows, and it takes minutes to return all the data. Minutes in the 21st century seem to equate to an "eternity."

Sunita asks Lizbeth to fix the problem. She analyzes the SQL statement that is being generated on the fly, and it is completely optimized. That's not the problem. Instead, the delay is simply that it takes a while to return all that data over the network, and the frontend process is blocked, waiting, until all of the data is returned.

What's a programmer to do in such a situation? Think "pipelining."

Solution: Design your function to return data while it is still running!

Suppose the function that returns data to the web page looks like this (I am simplifying what would surely be a very complicated and lengthy program):

```
CREATE TYPE numbers_nt IS TABLE OF NUMBER
/

/* Accept SQL query and return nested table with data. */
FUNCTION dynamic_query (query_in IN VARCHAR2) RETURN numbers_nt
IS
   l_cursor    SYS_REFCURSOR;
   l_return    numbers_nt;
BEGIN
   OPEN l_cursor FOR query_in;
   FETCH l_cursor BULK COLLECT INTO l_return;
   CLOSE l_cursor;

   FOR indx IN 1 .. l_return.COUNT
   LOOP
      manipulate_data (l_return (indx));
   END LOOP;

   RETURN l_return;
END dynamic_query;
A nested table to return a set of numbers */
```

This function is itself then called in a query, which returns the actual data:

```
SELECT * FROM TABLE (dynamic_query ('SELECT * FROM mfe_customers'))
```

When dynamic_query is used in a FROM clause like this, it is referred to as a *table function*.

As you can see, with dynamic_query defined this way, all the data must be retrieved and then manipulated before the function returns data (and control) to the query, which can in turn convert that data to a table format and then return the rows to the host environment from which it was called. And the user waits....

You can, however, take advantage of a fascinating alternative mechanism for returning data from within a function: *pipelining*. Here is a rewrite of dynamic_query using this feature:

```
 1  FUNCTION dynamic_query (query_in IN VARCHAR2) RETURN numbers_nt PIPELINED
 2  IS
 3     l_cursor    SYS_REFCURSOR;
 4     l_return    numbers_nt;
 5  BEGIN
 6     OPEN l_cursor FOR query_in;
 7     FETCH l_cursor BULK COLLECT INTO l_return;
 8     CLOSE l_cursor;
 9
10     FOR indx IN 1 .. l_return.COUNT
11     LOOP
12        manipulate_data (l_return (indx));
13        PIPE ROW ( l_return (indx) );
14     END LOOP;
15
16     RETURN;
17  END dynamic_query;
```

Here is an explanation of the new syntax in this rewrite.

Line	Significance
1	PIPELINED
	The addition of this keyword tells the Oracle database that you are defining a pipelined function, which allows you to use the constructs explained in the rest of this table.
13	PIPE ROW
	This statement says, in effect, "Send this data back from the function *now*, even though the function is still running."
16	RETURN
	Return nothing but control. The PIPE ROW statements have already returned all the data. This construct (a RETURN that does not return data) is allowed only in a procedure, unless the function is pipelined.

To get a sense of the performance impact of pipelining, I built a script (based on examples provided by Oracle Corporation) that compares pipelined and nonpipelined performance for a *streaming function* (see the *tabfunc_pipelined.sql* file on the book's web site). A streaming function is one that takes data in one format, transforms it, and passes it back to the calling query (which may then perform additional transformations). Here is the way that query looks:

```
INSERT INTO tickertable
   SELECT *
     FROM TABLE (stockpivot (CURSOR (SELECT * FROM stocktable)))
```

This script loads 20,000 rows into stocktable. The stockpivot function pivots each stocktable row into two rows to be inserted into tickertable. To test the impact of pipelining, I then added a ROWNUM clause so that I would insert only 9, rather than 40,000, rows as follows:

```
INSERT INTO tickertable
   SELECT *
     FROM TABLE (stockpivot (CURSOR (SELECT * FROM stocktable)))
   WHERE ROWNUM < 10;
```

I then ran this process for both pipelined and nonpipelined versions, and I saw these results:

```
Pipelined function, returning first nine rows: 0.1 seconds
Non-pipelined function, returning first nine rows: 10.13 seconds
```

Pipelining really does work! As soon as nine rows had been returned from the pipelined function to the calling query, the "ROWNUM < 10" clause was satisfied and the query was terminated. Without pipelining, the full pivoting of 20,000 to 40,000 rows was performed, and then the query said, in effect, "Thanks, but I really only wanted the first 9 of those 40,000." This is a very cool technology, indeed!

And that's not all!

You can also use a special variation of the pipelined function for parallel queries. A *parallel query* is one in which a query involving large amounts of data is partitioned to run on multiple processors simultaneously. The results from each partition are then merged and returned to the user.

If a PL/SQL function is called in the FROM clause of that query, however, it will cause serialization of the query. The Oracle database will not be able to partition its execution—unless you add the PARALLEL_ENABLE clause to the header of the function. This clause tells Oracle that the dataset being passed into the table function can and should be partitioned so that it can execute simultaneously on different processors for the various partitions. You can specify the type of partitioning, as well. Check the Oracle documentation for more details on enabling PL/SQL table functions for parallel execution.

Best Practices for Other Tuning

The tuning best practices described in this section are not likely to have the dramatic performance impact of those presented earlier. Under the right circumstances, however, following these guidelines may result in noticeable improvements in performance.

Sometimes "safe programming" is a little too slow.

Use NOCOPY with care to minimize overhead when collections and records are OUT or IN OUT parameters.

Problem: Delaware wants to use collections as parameters, but they are causing a bottleneck.

Collections get Delaware's heart racing. They are so useful, so elegant, so incredibly efficient. He has written code that scans collections containing hundreds, or even thousands, of elements in subsecond time. He uses them wherever he can, and he certainly uses them in the following procedure, which changes the descriptions of excuses according to a complex formula:

```
PACKAGE BODY manage_excuses
IS
   TYPE descriptions_aat IS TABLE OF mfe_excuses.descriptions%TYPE
      INDEX BY PLS_INTEGER;

   PROCEDURE change_descriptions (descriptions_io IN OUT descriptions_aat)
   IS
   BEGIN
      FOR indx IN 1 .. descriptions_in
      LOOP
         descriptions_io (indx) :=
            complex_adjustment (descriptions_io (indx));
      END LOOP;
   END change_descriptions;
END manage_excuses;
```

He runs a test or two on this procedure using a collection containing a dozen descriptions, and it works just fine. The program is rolled into production and, much to his chagrin, while out shopping for a new suit the next Saturday afternoon, he gets a call from the production DBA:

Delaware, what is going on with that new program you wrote? It is running incredibly slowly. I am cancelling the job. When you look it over and really test it thoroughly, I will be happy to run it for you.

Well, that call certainly ruined Delaware's day—and he is sorely vexed. Iterating through a collection is blazingly fast. What could be causing the problem?

Solution: Turn off the default copying that comes with IN OUT arguments.

Over the weekend, after mulling over the situation, Delaware decides that the performance issue must have something to do with the passing of that collection as an argument. He had certainly run lots of collection scans in the past (FOR indx IN 1 .. *collection*.COUNT) without any difficulties. Maybe it was that IN OUT collection argument. So the first thing Delaware does when he gets to the office on Monday morning is to check the Oracle documentation. There, he discovers that when you pass arguments through the parameter list of a program, those arguments can be passed by value or by reference:

By value
   Also known as "copy in, copy out." This means that the value of the argument is copied into the data structure of the program, and then is copied back out to the argument data structure if no exception occurs. If an exception propagates unhandled out of that program, the variable passed in for that argument remains unchanged.

By reference
   This means that the data structure manipulated inside the program points to the same location in memory that holds the value of the argument. Any changes made to the data structure take effect immediately and are not reversed by an exception.

Parameter passing in PL/SQL by default follows these rules:

- IN arguments are passed by reference.
- OUT and IN OUT arguments are passed by value.

Delaware groans loudly. He realizes instantly what this means for his program: he passed into change_descriptions a collection of 120,000 elements. The Oracle database then made an internal copy of those 120,000 rows of data, changed the data in that copy, and then, when the operation was completed, assigned all those changed elements back to his actual collection. No wonder the program was causing performance problems!

So how can he avoid all this copying? By including the NOCOPY hint* in the parameter definition:

```
PROCEDURE change_descriptions (
    descriptions_io IN OUT NOCOPY descriptions_aat)
```

When you specify NOCOPY for an argument, you tell Oracle to pass the argument by reference instead of by value. There are two consequences of this request:

- Oracle will not copy in or copy out, so the overhead of running your program will be reduced and performance will improve.
- If your program makes changes to your IN OUT argument and then the program raises an exception, those changes will *not* be reversed. This means that the contents of your variable could be corrupted or at least not be consistent.

The second consequence is rather severe. If you are going to use NOCOPY, you should not allow unhandled exceptions to propagate out of the program. You should trap errors and explicitly write the code necessary to ensure that the IN OUT argument's contents are OK.

Run the *nocopy.tst* script (available on the book's web site) to confirm for yourself the performance and data "corruption" aspects of NOCOPY. On Oracle Database 10*g*, I found that the version with NOCOPY ran in 18 seconds, while the program that performed copies ran in 33 seconds.

PL/SQL loops should not resemble hamsters running in circles.

Move static expressions outside of loops and SQL statements.

Problem: Lizbeth lost her focus as she wrote her loop.

Lizbeth usually pays close attention to detail as she writes her programs. She keeps her execution sections small, names her variables according to the coding standard, and above all avoids writing SQL statements (instead, calling prebuilt functions and procedures to do the work for her). This morning, however, she is

---

* NOCOPY is referred to as a *hint* because under a variety of circumstances (check the Oracle documentation for details), the compiler might silently decide that it can't fulfill your request to avoid copying.

very distracted—she has just been told by Sunita that she is being considered for the new Application Architect position. It's just what she's been wanting to do!

That doesn't stop her from writing code, of course, and she spins off this new procedure to display information about customers in a given state or province:

```
PROCEDURE show_customers (prefix_in IN VARCHAR2, state_in IN VARCHAR2)
IS
    CURSOR customers_cur IS
        SELECT last_name, first_name, city
          FROM mfe_customers WHERE state = UPPER (state_in);
BEGIN
    FOR customer_rec IN customers_cur
    LOOP
        DBMS_OUTPUT.PUT_LINE (
            TO_CHAR (SYSDATE, 'Mon DD, YYYY') || ' ' ||
            UPPER (prefix_in) || ' ' ||
            UPPER (state_in) || ' ' ||
            customer_rec.first_name || ' ' || customer_rec.last_name);
    END LOOP;
END show_customers;
```

The program works, but it is inefficient. How can this program be tuned up?

Solution: Avoid executing anything inside a loop that doesn't change in that loop.

Lizbeth's problem is that she includes several expressions in her loop that are based on static data, in particular:

TO_CHAR (SYSDATE, 'Mon DD, YYYY')
> Assuming that the program is not run right at midnight!

UPPER (prefix_in)
> IN arguments never change inside a program.

UPPER (state_in)
> IN arguments never change inside a program.

In this particular situation, the impact of these static expressions will not be great, but it certainly does make sense to avoid the extra cycles. Lizbeth could easily change her program as follows:

```
PROCEDURE show_customers (prefix_in IN VARCHAR2, state_in IN VARCHAR2)
IS
    /* Used inside query and in call to DBMS_OUTPUT.PUT_LINE. */
    c_state CONSTANT mfe_customers.state%TYPE := UPPER (state_in);

    /* Combine all static elements into single string. */
    c_output_prefix CONSTANT VARCHAR2(32767) :=
        TO_CHAR (SYSDATE, 'Mon DD, YYYY') || ' ' ||
        UPPER (prefix_in) || ' ' ||
        c_state;

    CURSOR customers_cur IS
        SELECT last_name, first_name, city
          FROM mfe_customers WHERE state = c_state;
```

```
BEGIN
   FOR customer_rec IN customers_cur
   LOOP
      DBMS_OUTPUT.PUT_LINE (
         c_output_prefix || ' ' ||
         customer_rec.first_name || ' ' || customer_rec.last_name);
   END LOOP;
END show_customers;
```

From this exercise, we can draw the following general advice:

> Whenever you set out to tune your PL/SQL programs, you should first take a look at your loops. Any inefficiency inside a loop's body will be magnified by the multiple executions of that code.

A common mistake is to put code that is static or unchanging (for each iteration of the loop) inside the body. When you can identify such situations, extract the static code, assign the outcomes of that code to one or more variables, and then reference those variables inside the loop.

Tailor-made datatypes are the best fit for your programs.

Choose datatypes carefully to minimize implicit conversions of data.

Problem: Oracle goes out of its way to make it easy for us to write PL/SQL programs.

I can just imagine the PL/SQL product manager reading that sentence and writing me an email that would go like this:

> And exactly how is that a problem, Steven? Think about everything PL/SQL does for the developer: it lets you code in high-level, very readable constructs; provides the ability to write SQL statements natively; and automatically optimizes your code when you compile it.

And I would agree: that is all good stuff. To which I would add one additional thing Oracle does for us that is perhaps not so wonderful: implicit datatype conversions. Oracle doesn't mind one bit when I write code like this:

```
DECLARE
   l_string   VARCHAR2 (10) := 1000;
   l_number   NUMBER := '500.5';
BEGIN
   l_number := l_string + l_number;
   DBMS_OUTPUT.put_line (l_number);
END;
```

When I run this code, I will see the string "1500.5" displayed on my screen. But in the process of getting to this point, the following data conversions will have been performed implicitly:

1. Convert 1000 to '1000' and assign the result to the l_string variable.
2. Convert '500.5' to 500.5 and assign the result to the l_number variable.

3. Convert l_string to a number, and assign it to the l_number variable.

4. Convert l_number to a string, and display it using the DBMS_OUTPUT. PUT_LINE function.

Well, that's awfully nice of Oracle and very convenient...but that implicit conversion has a price: it incurs some overhead, and under a variety of circumstances, that overhead can become prohibitive. This is especially the case when implicit conversions occur inside SQL statements and have the effect of disabling the use of indexes.

The bottom line is that implicit conversions let us get away with being lazy about how we write our code. In lots of cases, it won't really matter. In other cases, these conversions carry a severe performance penalty.

Solution: Avoid implicit conversions and choose your datatypes carefully.

Sometimes you need to convert between datatypes. When this is the case and when you expect to be executing such code in performance-sensitive areas, use the built-in functions Oracle provides to perform those conversions, as in:

```
DECLARE
    l_string    VARCHAR2 (10) := 1000;
    l_number    NUMBER :- TO_NUMBER ('500.5');
BEGIN
    l_number := TO_NUMBER (l_string) + l_number;
    DBMS_OUTPUT.put_line (TO_CHAR (l_number));
END;
```

In addition, you should choose carefully among the datatypes Oracle provides to make sure you use the datatype that will provide the best performance. Here are some guidelines to follow:

- When manipulating integers whose values fall between $-2^{31} + 1$ to $-2^{31} - 1$ (approximately -2.13 billion to 2.13 billion) and you are running Oracle Database 10g and below, then declare the variable as PLS_INTEGER. Starting with Oracle Database 11g, use the new SIMPLE_INTEGER datatype. It is faster, but its behavior is a bit different, so check the Oracle documentation for details.

- The NUMBER datatype (and its subtypes) are represented in an internal format designed by Oracle for portability and not performance. If you need to coax more performance out of your numeric computations, consider using the (new to Oracle Database 10g) BINARY_FLOAT and BINARY_DOUBLE types—they can use native hardware arithmetic and consume less memory.

- Avoid datatypes like NATURAL and POSITIVE that contain in their definitions declarative constraints (such as "must be greater than or equal to 0" and "must be greater than 0," respectively). These constraints are checked at runtime, with every usage of a variable based on these types.

Best Practices Quick Reference

The *Best Practices Quick Reference* provided in this appendix compiles the best practice titles across all the chapters into a concise list; for each best practice, the first, sometimes tongue-in-cheek title of each best practice appears in the left column and the second, more serious title in the right column. Once you have studied the individual best practices, you can use Table A-1 as a checklist, to be reviewed before you begin coding a new program or application.

Table A-1. Best Practices Quick Reference

Chapter 1, *The Big Picture*	
Successful Applications	
Software is like ballet: choreograph the moves or end up with a mess.	Put into place a practical workflow that emphasizes iterative development based on a shared foundation.
Deferred satisfaction is a required emotion for best practices.	Hold off on implementing the body of your program until your header is stable and your tests are defined.
Contracts work for the real world; why not software, too?	Match strict input expectations with guaranteed output results.
Don't act like a bird: admit weakness and ignorance.	Ask for help (or at least take a break) after 30 minutes on a problem.
Five heads are better than one.	Review and walk through one another's code; then do automated code reviews.
Don't write code that a machine could write for you instead.	Generate code whenever possible.
We need more than brains to write software.	Take care of your "host body": fingers, wrists, back, etc.
Chapter 2, *Real Developers Follow Standards*	
Developing and Using Standards	
It's a free country; I don't have to use carriage returns in my code.	Adopt a consistent format that is easy to read and maintain.

Table A-1. Best Practices Quick Reference (continued)

Too much freedom is a very bad thing.	Adopt consistent naming conventions for subprograms and data structures.
Good names lead to good code.	Name procedures with verb phrases, and functions with noun phrases.
Put your checklists into your code.	Define templates to foster standardization in package and program structure.
Who needs comments? My code is self-documenting!	Comment tersely with value-added information.

Chapter 3, *Life After Compilation*

Testing, Tracing, and Debugging

Thanks, but no thanks, to DBMS_OUTPUT.PUT_LINE!	Avoid using the DBMS_OUTPUT.PUT_LINE procedure directly.
Assume the worst, and you will never be disappointed.	Instrument your code to trace execution.
Users really don't want to be programmers.	Test your programs thoroughly, and as automatically as possible.
Do you take road trips without a destination in mind?	Follow the test-driven development methodology.
For every test you can think of, there are 10 tests waiting to be performed.	Don't worry about getting to 100 percent test coverage.
Sherlock Holmes never had it so good.	Use source code debuggers to hunt down the cause of bugs.

Chapter 4, *What's Code Without Variables?*

Declaring Variables and Data Structures

That column's never going to change!	Always anchor variables to database datatypes using %TYPE and %ROWTYPE.
There's more to data than columns in a table.	Use SUBTYPEs to declare program-specific and derived datatypes.
I take exception to your declaration section.	Perform complex variable initialization in the execution section.

Using Variables and Data Structures

This logic is driving me crazy!	Replace complex expressions with well-named constants, variables or functions.
Go ahead and splurge: declare distinct variables for different usages.	Don't overload data structure usage.
Didn't your parents teach you to clean up after yourself?	Clean up data structures when your program terminates (successfully or with an error).
Programmers are (or should be) control freaks.	Beware of and avoid implicit datatype conversions.

Declaring and Using Package Variables

Danger, Will Robinson! Globals in use!	Use package globals sparingly and only in package bodies.
Packages should have a strong sense of personal space.	Control access to package data with "get and set" modules.

Table A-1. Best Practices Quick Reference (continued)

Chapter 5, *Developer As Traffic Cop*

Conditional and Boolean Logic

Reading your code should not require mental gymnastics.	Use IF...ELSIF only to test a single, simple condition.
KISS (Keep it Simple, Steven).	Use CASE to avoid lengthy sequences of IF statements.
Beware the hidden costs of NULL.	Treat NULL conditions explicitly in conditional statements.

Loop Processing

There's a right way and a wrong way to say goodbye.	Never EXIT or RETURN from WHILE and FOR loops.
Don't take out "programmers' insurance"...and don't worry about SkyNet.	Never declare the FOR loop index or any other implicitly declared structure.
There is more than one way to scan a collection.	Use FOR loops for dense collections, WHILE loops for sparse collections.

Branching Logic

Maze-like programs are never a good thing.	Use GOTO and CONTINUE only when structured code is not an option.

Chapter 6, *Doing the Right Thing When Stuff Goes Wrong*

Understanding Error Handling

Ignorance is bad exception management.	Study how error raising, handling, and logging work in PL/SQL.
All exceptions are not created equal.	Distinguish between deliberate, unfortunate, and unexpected errors.
One error management approach for all.	Use error-management standards to avoid confusion and conflicts.

Nitty-Gritty Everyday Exception Programming

Your code makes me feel dumb.	Use the EXCEPTION_INIT pragma to name exceptions and make your code more accessible.
Avoid programmer apathy.	Never use WHEN OTHERS THEN NULL.

Coding Defensively

You weren't supposed to do that with my program!	Use assertion routines to verify all assumptions made in your program.

Chapter 7, *Break Your Addiction to SQL*

General SQL

The best way to avoid problematic code is to not write it.	Hide your SQL statements behind a programmatic interface.
You may write PL/SQL code, but SQL always takes precedence.	Qualify PL/SQL variables with their scope names when referenced inside SQL statements.
When one transaction is not enough.	Use autonomous transactions to isolate the effect of COMMITs and ROLLBACKs.
I don't always want to save my changes.	Don't hardcode COMMITs and ROLLBACKs in your code.

Querying Data from PL/SQL

It's always better to fetch items into a single basket.	Fetch into cursor records, never into a hardcoded list of variables.
Answer the question being asked; that is, be a good listener.	Use COUNT only when the actual number of occurrences is needed.
Your code makes my head spin.	Don't use a cursor FOR loop to fetch just one row.

Changing Data from PL/SQL

Assume the worst!	Don't forget exception handlers for your DML statements.
Things only get more complicated over time.	List columns explicitly in your INSERT statements.
Timing is everything in the world of cursors.	Reference cursor attributes immediately after executing the SQL operation.

Dynamic SQL

Make it easy to untangle and debug your dynamic SQL statements.	Always parse a string variable; do not EXECUTE IMMEDIATE a literal.
Give the RDBMS a break.	Avoid concatenation of variable values into dynamic SQL strings.
So you think you know what users might do with your code?	Do not allow malicious injection of code into your dynamic statements.
It's rude to drop someone else's objects.	Apply the invoker rights method to stored code that executes dynamic SQL.

Chapter 8, *Playing with Blocks (of Code)*

Parameters

Once a program is in use, you can't change it willy-nilly.	Ensure backward compatibility as you add parameters.
What the heck do those parameter values mean?	Use named notation to self-document subprogram calls and pass values more flexibly.
Where'd that data come from?	Functions should return data only through the RETURN clause.

Procedures and Functions

Write tiny chunks of code.	Limit execution section length to no more than 50 lines.
Every program should be an island (of purpose).	Minimize side effects and maximize reuse by creating programs with narrowly defined purposes.
Gifts should always come tightly wrapped.	Hide business rules and formulas inside functions.
One way in, one way out: multiple exits confuse me.	Limit functions to a single RETURN statement in the execution section.

Black or white programs don't know from NULL.	Never return NULL from Boolean functions.

Packages

Where there is one program, there will soon be two.	Avoid schema-level programs; instead, group related code into packages.
"Easy to use code" is code that is used—and reused.	Anticipate programmer needs and simplify call interfaces with overloading.

Triggers

Uncertainty in trigger execution is a most unsettling emotion.	Consolidate "overlapping" DML triggers to control execution order, or use the FOLLOW syntax of Oracle Database 11*g*.
"One-stop triggering" is so much easier to understand and maintain.	Use Oracle Database 11*g* compound triggers to consolidate all related trigger logic on a table.
Your application should not be able to perform a "Houdini" with business rules.	Validate complex business rules with DML triggers.

Chapter 9, *My Code Runs Faster Than Your Code*

Finding Slow Code

Take the guesswork out of optimization.	Use trace facilities to gather raw data about program performance.
There are so many ways to implement an algorithm; which is best?	Build or find tools to calculate elapsed time.

High-Impact Tuning

Let Oracle do most of the tuning for you.	Make sure your code is being optimized when compiled.
Who has time for querying (or inserting or deleting or updating) one row at a time?	Use BULK COLLECT and FORALL to improve performance of multirow SQL operations in PL/SQL.
If the SGA is so wonderful, why not emulate it?	Cache static data in the fastest memory location possible.
When waiting is not an option…	Use pipelined table functions to return data faster and to parallelize function execution.

Other Tuning

Sometimes "safe programming" is a little too slow.	Use NOCOPY with care to minimize overhead when collections and records are OUT or IN OUT parameters.
PL/SQL loops should not resemble hamsters running in circles.	Move static expressions outside of loops and SQL statements.
Tailor-made datatypes are the best fit for your programs.	Choose datatypes carefully to minimize implicit conversions of data.

Resources for PL/SQL Developers

As you will no doubt have gathered from reading this book, I believe that in order to write high-quality applications, you need to take advantage of the resources out there. I refer to many such resources throughout the book, and this appendix collects information on how to get hold of them.

This is *not* intended to be a complete guide to any and every resource that could be useful to a PL/SQL developer. Rather, it reflects my own personal experience: tools and content that I have used myself or that have been recommended by others I respect.

Book Example Files

Throughout the text, I've made reference to files I've written specifically for this book. Some of these files contain reusable code you can put to use immediately in your applications. Others contain performance analysis scripts or simply demonstrations of techniques. You will find in Table B-1 a list of these files in alphabetical order, offering a brief description of the contents of each file, and where it is referenced in the book. See the "About the Code" section in the Preface for information on downloading these files.

 This software is provided to you on a "user beware" basis. I give you permission to use and change this code as desired. You can put this code in your production applications, but it is entirely your responsibility to fully test the code you use and make sure that it meets your requirements.

Table B-1. Book example files

File name	Description	Referenced in
11g_emplu.pkg *11g_emplu.tst* *11g_emplu_compare.sp*	Demonstration of the performance of the Oracle Database 11*g* function result cache	Chapter 9
assert.pkg	Simple assertion package you can use to validate assumptions and pre- and post-conditions in Design By Contract	Chapters 1 and 6
atleast1cust.tst	Comparison of different ways to answer the question "Is there at least one row that satisfies the condition?"	Chapter 9
boolean_utils.pkg	Boolean-VARCHAR2 conversion utility package	Chapter 5
bpl.sp	"Display Boolean value" utility procedure	Chapter 3
callstack.sql	Demonstration of the approach of "dumping" package state through a standardized error package	Chapter 3
case.sql	Showcase of CASE expression usage to simplify logic	Chapter 5
dbc_demo.sql	Demonstration of Design by Contract in pre- and post-conditions	Chapter 1
display_clob.sp	Utility to display the contents of a CLOB value	Chapter 8
dropwhatever.sp	Powerful, dangerous, and very flexible utility to "drop whatever" using dynamic SQL	Chapter 7
emplu.pkg *emplu.tst*	Comparison of different ways of querying rows of data, leveraging various kinds of caching	Chapter 9
excquiz.sql*	Quizzes to test and reinforce your understanding of exception handling in PL/SQL	Chapter 6
excuse_tracker.pkg	Demonstration of multilevel, string-indexed collections, combined with assertion programs, to track strings that have been used	Chapter 6
genlookup.sp	Generation of functions to look up single rows of data, showing the value of code generation of standardized code	Chapter 1
mfe_customer_rules.pkg *mfe_customer_rules.qut*	Demonstration of a package containing rules and a Quest Code Tester export of a test definition that exercises this code	Chapter 8
multiple_triggers.sql	Demonstration of the problems of having multiple triggers on the same trigger point, and the use of the compound trigger (new in Oracle Database 11*g*)	Chapter 8
my_commit.pks *my_commit.pkb*	Encapsulation package for COMMIT, allowing developers to "hide" the commit from your code, and flexibly turn it on and off	Chapter 7
nocopy.tst	Demonstration of the NOCOPY hint to avoid copying the contents of collections and other data structures passed as IN OUT arguments	Chapter 9

Table B-1. Book example files (continued)

File name	Description	Referenced in
overdue.pkg	Demonstration of building tracing into your package to show (when needed) what is happening inside that package	Chapter 3
p.pks *p.pkb*	Encapsulation of DBMS_OUTPUT.PUT_LINE that is much more flexible and easier to use	Chapters 3, 7, 8
pl.sp	Single-procedure encapsulation of DBMS_OUTPUT.PUT_LINE, handy for pasting into another program for a local substitute for that built-in	Chapter 3
plvtmr.pkg	Elapsed time computation package, a part of the PL/Vision library (but installable all by its lonesome); use it to time the elapsed time of PL/SQL blocks down to the hundredth of a second	Chapter 9
ref_code_cache.pkg	Demonstration of the use of a package-based collection to cache data in the database and improve query performance	Chapter 9
select_into_template.sql	Template for a function that returns one row of data, and offers flexibility on the handling of the NO_DATA_FOUND exception	Chapter 6
serial_package.sql	Demonstration of the use of the serialization pragma for packages	Chapter 7
standards.zip	Collection of files that offer a set of standards and naming conventions for writing PL/SQL code	N/A
stdhdr.pkg	Utility package to work with standard package headers based on an XML format	Chapter 2
stdpkg_format.sql	Template for a standard package format that you can use as a starting point for development of new packages	Chapter 2
string_to_list.sf *string_to_list.qut*	Generic utility to parse a delimited string into a collection of individual items, as well as an export of a Quest Code Tester test definition to exercise the utility	Chapter 8
string_tracker.pks *string_tracker.pkb*	Utility to keep track of strings that have been used in a given session	Chapter 6
tabfunc_pipelined.sql *tabfunc_streaming.sql*	Demonstrations of table functions, both pipelined and streaming	Chapter 9
topdown.zip	The topdown package offers refactoring to create local modules as you specify; includes Word documentation explaining why this is so useful and how to use this package	Chapter 8
tmr.ot	Elapsed time computation object type; use it to time the elapsed time of PL/SQL blocks down to the hundredth of a second	Chapter 9
trigger_conflict.sql	Simple query against the USER_TRIGGERS data dictionary view that helps you identify potentially conflicting triggers	Chapter 8
watch.pkg *watch.tst* *watch_noplv.pkg*	Replacement for DBMS_OUTPUT as a tracing mechanism for "watching" what is happening inside a program; the "noplv" version removes any dependencies on the PL/Vision library	Chapter 3

File name	Description	Referenced in
whats_not_optimal.sp	Program that displays all program units whose optimization level is less than the specified value	Chapter 9
workaround_comment.sql	Template comment to document a workaround in your code	Chapter 2

Books and Other Content

In this section I list a number of books that you may find helpful. The first subsection references other books on the PL/SQL language. (Certainly, this relatively short book on best practices for PL/SQL cannot give you all the information you need to build applications with this language.) In the next subsection I provide descriptions of some of my favorite non-PL/SQL books. Finally, I list references to helpful online content.

Oracle PL/SQL Books

Let's start with my own oeuvre, the Oracle PL/SQL Series from O'Reilly Media. The major books are listed here. For full information on these and other books, see the O'Reilly web site at *www.oreilly.com*.

Oracle PL/SQL Programming, by Steven Feuerstein with Bill Pribyl
>A fairly complete language reference for Oracle PL/SQL. Now in its fourth edition, it is also known as "the ant book" since the cover showcases ants.

Oracle PL/SQL Developer's Workbook, by Steven Feuerstein with Andrew Odewahn
>A workbook containing problems (and accompanying solutions) that will test (and help you develop) your knowledge of Oracle PL/SQL language features.

Learning Oracle PL/SQL, by Bill Pribyl and Steven Feuerstein
>A comparatively gentle introduction to the PL/SQL language, ideal for new programmers and those who know a language other than PL/SQL.

Oracle PL/SQL for DBAs, by Arup Nanda and Steven Feuerstein
>PL/SQL isn't just for developers. This book offers guidance on a variety of topics critical for database administrators (and very useful to developers as well), including security, performance, and scheduling.

Oracle PL/SQL Language Pocket Reference, by Steven Feuerstein, Bill Pribyl, and Chip Dawes
>A quick reference to the PL/SQL language syntax.

Other Helpful Books

I think you will find these books on programming and other topics helpful and interesting.

Code Complete, by Steven McConnell (Microsoft Press)
> A classic text, this "practical handbook of software criticism" should be on the bookshelf of every developer (or at least in your team's library). Chock-full of practical advice for constructing code, it shows examples in many languages, including Ada, which is enough like PL/SQL to make learning from McConnell a breeze. Don't start coding without it! The web site for Steven McConnell's consulting practice, *http://www.construx.com*, is also packed with lots of good advice.

Refactoring: Improving the Design of Existing Code, by Martin Fowler (Addison-Wesley Professional)
> According to this book, "refactoring is the process of changing a software system in such a way that it doesn't alter the external of the code, yet improves its internal structure." Sound great or *what?* This excellent book uses Java as its example language, but the writing is clear and the Java straightforward. There is much to apply here to PL/SQL programming.

Extreme Programming Explained, by Kent Beck (Addison-Wesley Professional)
> This book is a highly readable and concise introduction to Extreme Programming (XP), a lightweight software development methodology. Visit *http://www.xprogramming.com* or *http://www.extremeprogramming.org* for a glimpse into the world of this interesting approach to development.

Thinking in Java, by Bruce Eckels (Prentice Hall PTR)
> I believe that every PL/SQL developer should learn enough Java to be able to read the code comfortably and write basic wrappers on top of underlying Java functionality. If you like the way I write, I think you will also enjoy Eckel's book. Lots of examples, a sense of humor, and an accessible way of presenting Java concepts all helped me learn Java quickly.

Code and Other Laws Of Cyperspace, by Lawrence Lessig (Basic Books)
> Laws constrain the behavior of human beings. And when you are in cyber-space, software constrains what you can do. In this sense, code is like a new form of law. Lessig's somewhat dense but very insightful book analyzes the ramifications of code as a form of law. This book greatly enhanced my understanding of the critical role of software developers in the big world "out there."

The Timeless Way of Building, by Christopher Alexander (Oxford University Press)
> Christopher Alexander is an architect (real buildings in the real world) who is sharply critical of how most buildings are designed and built. This book takes a deep look at what makes for a high-quality environment for human beings. From his analysis, Alexander concludes that it is possible to come up with an objective *pattern language* to help architects create beautiful, life-enhancing structures. This is a beautiful read, and I strongly encourage you to check it out.

Horton Hears a Who, by Dr. Seuss (MGM/UA)
> OK, so this one's not about technology. It's "just" about life and compassion. This book is one of my favorites in the whole wide world of books. If you have children, I encourage you to get this book and read it to them a whole lot.

Online Content

You can't beat books for learning a language intensively, but there is lots of online content to help PL/SQL developers ask and get answers to questions quickly. Some of my favorites are listed here:

Complete Oracle Documentation Set (http://tahiti.oracle.com)

That's right: all of Oracle's documentation for every supported version of the database is available online. Just visit the link above, type in the keyword for the functionality in which you are interested, and search. Oracle will show hits across all versions, and off you go. You can also download whole documents as PDF files.

Quest Pipelines (http://www.quest-pipelines.com)

The Quest Pipelines are *noncommercial*, online communities for developers and DBAs who work with Oracle, DBA, SQL Server, or mySQL. This site is hosted and supported by Quest Software, but the company does not push its commercial products on this site. The Oracle Pipeline offers extensive discussion forums (containing content provided by developers and DBAs for the last five-plus years), free downloads, tips, and much more.

Oracle Technology Network (http://www.oracle.com/technology)

OTN is one of the most important online resources for Oracle technologists generally, and PL/SQL developers in particular. I author a Best Practice PL/SQL column, and the PL/SQL product manager loads up the PL/SQL pages with lots of excellent white papers and related resources.

Obsession for PL/SQL (http://ToadWorld.com/SF)

ToadWorld provides a portal for Toad users and PL/SQL developers. I have built a "second home" here called Obsession for PL/SQL to offer my latest ideas on best practices for PL/SQL. You will also find and can download all my presentations, demonstration code, quizzes, puzzles, Qusefuls, ILovePLSQLand, so much more.

Free Software

There is an incredible amount of very useful software out there that comes without a license fee. Here are some of my favorites, mostly things that I have contributed.

In this appendix, I have decided to list only freeware products, and avoid listing commercial products to minimize perceived or actual conflicts of interest (being a Quest employee and all that jazz). You will find a number of references to commercial tools throughout the book, and they should be more than enough to steer you to products that you think may be helpful.

Quest CodeGen Utility (http://www.ToadWorld.com [click on Downloads] or http:// www.qcgu.net)

Freeware from Quest Software, the CodeGen utility is, in essence, a very generalized "Design Pattern Factory." That is, you can use the Code Generation Markup Language (CGML) to capture a *pattern* in your code (a piece of code you find yourself writing over and over again). Then you generate the code (in PL/SQL, Java, HTML, XML…whatever!) based on that pattern for your specific database object. CodeGen comes with hundreds of predefined patterns or templates, including the Quest Development Architecture (QDA) templates that implement a table API for your underlying datasets.

Quest Error Manager (http://www.ToadWorld.com [click on Downloads])

When I built CodeGen, I included in its table API templates for a generic error management framework. To make it easy for you to take advantage of this framework, I extracted it from CodeGen and packaged it as its own standalone utility. Use QEM to raise, handle, log, and communicate errors to your users in a consistent and effective manner. The most important concept inside QEM is that you trap and log information about *instances* of errors, not just the Oracle error.

PL/Vision (http://quest-pipelines.com/pipelines/dba/PLVision/plvision.htm)

From the web site: "The PL/Vision Code Library provides more than 1,000 PL/SQL functions and procedures that extend the capabilities of the PL/SQL language. Easily mastered by developers with any level of PL/SQL experience, PL/Vision integrates seamlessly into your development environment. PL/Vision's reusable and cleanly encapsulated packages dramatically accelerate development, simplify maintenance, and increase program reliability." PL/Vision is old, but you will still find lots of handy utilities in it. You are welcome *and encouraged* to change it to meet your needs.

utPLSQL (http://utplsql.sourceforge.net/)

utPLSQL is PL/SQL's analog of Java's Junit. It is, in other words, an open source unit testing framework, based on Extreme Programming principles. I wrote utPLSQL back in 1999 and released it to the world. Since then hundreds, and perhaps thousands, of PL/SQL developers have used it to write extensive test packages and achieve a high level of regression testing in their applications. The major downside of utPLSQL is that you still have to writes lots of test code. Access this URL for the software as well as links to forums and other resources.

log4plsql (http://log4plsql.sourceforge.net/)

Written by Guillaume Moulard, log4plsql is "a framework for logging information from PL/SQL program units. It uses the underlying log4j utility (a widely used standard logging facility for Java)."

Index

We'd like to hear your suggestions for improving our indexes. Send email to *index@oreilly.com*.

Dawes, Chip (Oracle PL/SQL Language Pocket Reference), 255
DBMS_APPLICATION_INFO package, 52, 57, 221
DBMS_DEBUG package, 72
DBMS_ERRLOG package, 118, 135
DBMS_HPROF package, 221
DBMS_OUTPUT.PUT_LINE procedure, 15, 52, 54, 209–211
DBMS_PROFILER package, 220
DBMS_SQL package, 168
DBMS_SQL.EXECUTE function, 208–211
DBMS_SQL.TO_CURSOR function, 170
DBMS_SQL.TO_REFCURSOR function, 170
DBMS_TRACE package, 13, 220
DBMS_UTILITY.FORMAT_BACK_TRACE function, 118
DBMS_UTILITY.FORMAT_ERROR_STACK function, 117
DBMS_UTILITY.GET_CPU_TIME function, 223
DBMS_UTILITY.GET_TIME function, 223
DDL statements, automatic execution of, 209
debugging, 52, 53
    bugs reported by users, handling, 14
    program iterations, 14
    source code debugger, 71
    tools for, 53
declarations, 73
    anchoring variables to database datatypes, 73–76
    errors not trapped in, 78–80
    grouping, 42
    subtypes, creating, 76–78
    variable initialization in, avoiding, 78–80
    (see also variables)
Delaware character, xii
DELETE statement (see DML statements)
deliberate exceptions, 119, 120, 122
design
    Design by Contract, 19–24
    resources for, 256

structure of code, ensuring maintainability with, 4
top down design, 188
Design by Contract, 19–24
developers (see software developers)
display_clob.sp file, 209
DML errors, continuing past, 118
DML statements
    columns listed explicitly in INSERT, 164
    encapsulating in procedures, 147
    exception handlers for, 163
    in subprograms, 198
DML triggers, validating business rules with, 216–217
documentation, Oracle online, 257
dropwhatever.sp file, 178
dynamic SQL, 168
    DBMS_SQL package, 168
    EXECUTE IMMEDIATE, parsing string for, 170
    implementations of, 168
    invoker's authority used to run, 176
    malicious code injection, preventing, 174
    methods of, 169
    native dynamic SQL (NDS), 168
    variable concatenation for SQL strings, avoiding, 172

E

Eckels, Bruce (Thinking in Java), 256
emplu.pkg file, 235
emplu.tst file, 235
entity-relationship diagram (ERD), 143
ergonomic workspace, 34
error management
    assertion routines, verifying assumptions with, 136–139
    continuing past DML errors, 118
    continuing past exceptions in bulk bind, 118
    declaration section, errors not trapped in, 78–80
    DML operations requiring, 147, 163
    exception section, not having application logic in, 122
    formalizing and automating, 10

error management (*continued*)
line number of most recent
exception, retrieving, 118
messages associated with errors,
retrieving, 117
naming exceptions, 132–134
for Oracle database instance, 118
package initialization, errors in, 117
propagation of exceptions, 117
resources for, 119
saving logs separately from business
transactions, 154
scope of exception section, 117
severity of exceptions,
categorizing, 119–127
single component for, 129–131
SQL statements, runtime errors
caused by, 140
standards for, defining, 9, 127–131
tools for, 258
traces when errors occur, 58–60
types of errors, 119–122
WHEN OTHERS THEN NULL,
avoiding, 134
Error Manager, Quest, 131, 258
examples (see code examples)
EXCEPTION_INIT pragma, 132–134
exceptions (see error management)
excquiz files, 119
excuse_tracker.pkg file, 137, 139
EXECUTE function, DBMS_SQL
package, 208–211
EXECUTE IMMEDIATE
statement, 170
exercise, 34
EXIT statement, 102–105
Extreme Programming
pair programming as part of, 29
Test-Driven Development associated
with, 18, 69
utPLSQL based on, 63, 258
Extreme Programming Explained
(Beck), 29, 256

F

Feuerstein, Steven
Learning Oracle PL/SQL, 255
Oracle PL/SQL Developer's
Workbook, 119, 255
Oracle PL/SQL for DBAs, 255
Oracle PL/SQL Language Pocket
Reference, 255
Oracle PL/SQL Programming, 119,
219, 255
ToadWorld Obsession for PL/SQL
web site, xvii, 257
FOLLOWS clause, 212
fonts used in this book, xvii
FOR loop, 101
for collections, 107–111
exiting from, 102–105
index of, not declaring, 105
when to use, 101, 162
FORALL statement
INDICES OF clause, 111
performance improved by, 226–231
SAVE EXCEPTIONS clause, 118,
132, 135
formal code walkthroughs, 29
formal parameters, 180
FORMAT_BACK_TRACE function,
DBMS_UTILITY
package, 118
FORMAT_ERROR_STACK function,
DBMS_UTILITY
package, 117
formatting, consistent, 38–40
formulas, hiding in functions, 198–201
Fowler, Martin (Refactoring: Improving
the Design of Existing
Code), 256
free country (metaphor), 38–40
free software, 257
Freedman, Daniel (Handbook of
Walkthroughs, Inspections,
and Technical Reviews), 29
freedom, too much (metaphor), 40–43

function result cache, 233, 236–237
functions, 186
    Boolean, not returning NULL, 20, 204
    business rules in, 198–201
    formulas in, 198–201
    implementing SQL behind, 144–151
    length of, 186–195
    local subprograms, 188, 191–192
    naming conventions for, 42, 43
    overloading, when to, 181
    package-level subprograms, 192–195
    purpose of, narrowly defined, 196–198
    returning data from, 184–186
    schema-level, 192, 205–207
    side effects from, avoiding, 198
    simplifying complex expressions with, 81–82
    single exit points in, 201–203

G

generated code, 30–33, 195, 258
genlookup.sp file, 32
GET function, in package specification, 92
GET_CPU_TIME function, DBMS_UTILITY package, 223
GET_TIME function, DBMS_UTILITY package, 223
global package variables, 89–92
global search-and-replace, checking, 152
GOTO statement, 111, 112

H

Handbook of Walkthroughs, Inspections, and Technical Reviews (Freedman, Weinberg), 29
hardcoding
    avoiding, 142
    SQL as, 143

headers
    comments in, 49
    implementing first, 16
health, maintaining, 33
help, when to ask for, 24–27
Horton Hears a Who (Seuss), 256
Houdini, Harry (as metaphor), 216
housekeeping, 32

I

IDE (Integrated Development Environment)
    automatic formatting feature of, 39
    tools for, 39
IF statement
    handling NULL in, 100
    replacing with CASE statement, 97–99
    simplifying, 96
implicit datatype conversions, avoiding, 87, 244
initialization section of package, errors in, 117
inputs
    contract requirements for, 21
    defining, 16
    naming conventions for, 16, 42
    (see also parameters)
INSERT statement (see DML statements)
instrumentation (see tracing)
insurance for programmers (metaphor), 105
Integrated Development Environment (IDE)
    automatic formatting feature of, 39
    tools for, 39
iterative development, 6–15
iterative testing, 68

J

Jasper character, xiv
Java Debug Wire Protocol (JDWP), 72
JDWP (Java Debug Wire Protocol), 72
join logic, encapsulating in views, 146

L

Learning Oracle PL/SQL (Pribyl, Feuerstein), 255
Lessig, Lawrence (Code and Other Laws of Cyberspace), 256
Lizbeth character, xiv
local subprograms, 188, 191–192
log4plsql framework, 258
logging
    example implementation of, 153
    saving logs separately from business transactions, 154
    tools for, 118, 135, 258
    in WHEN OTHERS, 135
    (see also error management)
logic, simplifying, 81–82
logical thinking, by programmers, x, xi, 9, 16, 37, 144
loops
    exiting from, 102–105
    scanning collections, 107–111
    static expressions in, affecting performance, 242–244
    type of, choosing, 101

M

maintainability
    analyzing, 11
    as criteria for success, 3, 4
malicious code injection, preventing, 174
McConnell, Steve (Code Complete), 113, 256
MFE (My Flimsy Excuse) fictional company, xii
mfe_customer_rules.pkg file, 200
mfe_customer_rules.qut file, 200
multiple_triggers.sql file, 213
My Flimsy Excuse (MFE) fictional company, xii
my_commit.pkb file, 158
my_commit.pks file, 158

N

named notation, 182–184
naming conventions, 9
    formalizing and automating, 10
    functions, 43
    list of, 40–43
    parameters, 16, 42
    procedures, 43
    programs, 16
Nanda, Arup (Oracle PL/SQL for DBAs), 255
native dynamic SQL (NDS), 168
nested subprograms (see local subprograms)
nested table types, naming conventions for, 42
NNINNO (NOT NULL IN, NOT NULL OUT) contract, 20
NOCOPY parameters, 240–242
nocopy.tst file, 242
NOT NULL IN, NOT NULL OUT (NNINNO) contract, 20
NULL
    handling in conditional statements, 100
    not returning from Boolean functions, 20, 204
    in WHEN OTHERS, 134

O

object types, naming conventions for, 42
Obsession for PL/SQL web site, 257
Odewahn, Andrew (Oracle PL/SQL Developer's Workbook), 119, 255
OPEN-FOR statement, 170
Oracle Database 10g
    BINARY_FLOAT and BINARY_DOUBLE datatypes, 245
    cursor FOR loops, 230
    DBMS_SQL package, 169
    DBMS_UTILITY.GET_CPU_TIME function, 223

performance
    analyzing
        for application iteration, 11
        on granular level, 223
        for multiple
            implementations, 221–224
    bottlenecks, identifying first, 218,
        219
    caching static data in
        memory, 231–237
    of collections or records as
        parameters, 240–242
    as criteria for success, 3, 4
    datatypes, choosing based on, 245
    implicit datatype conversions,
        minimizing, 244
    of multirow SQL
        operations, 226–231
    optimizing code during
        compilation, 225
    pipelined table functions, 237–240
    SQL statements affecting, 140, 218
    of static expressions in
        loops, 242–244
    tracing, gathering performance data
        with, 220
    variable concatenation for dynamic
        SQL affecting, 172
per-session cache, 233–235
personal space, of package
    (metaphor), 92
PGA (Process Global Area), 230
PIPE ROW statement, 239
pipelined table functions, 237–240
pl.sp file, 55
PL/SQL Developer
    automated code review feature
        of, 29, 119
    automatic formatting feature of, 40
PL/SQL Hierarchical Profiler, 221
PL/SQL Profiler, 220
PL/SQL Trace, 220
PL/Unit testing framework, 63
PL/Vision Code Library, 258
PLVtmr package, 225
plvtmr.pkg file, 224, 225
positional notation, 183
postconditions, in Design by
    Contract, 21
p.pkb file, 55, 211

p.pks file, 55, 211
preconditions, in Design by
    Contract, 21
Pribyl, Bill
    Learning Oracle PL/SQL, 255
    Oracle PL/SQL Language Pocket
        Reference, 255
    Oracle PL/SQL Programming, 119,
        219, 255
private package subprograms, 192
procedures, 186
    implementing SQL behind, 144–151
    length of, 186–195
    local subprograms, 188, 191–192
    naming conventions for, 42, 43
    package-level subprograms, 192–195
    purpose of, narrowly
        defined, 196–198
    schema-level, 192, 205–207
    side effects from, avoiding, 198
    when to use instead of
        functions, 186
Process Global Area (PGA), 230
programmers (see software developers)
programs
    debugging (see debugging)
    header for, 16, 49
    iterations of, building, 13
    name for, 16
    overloading, 16, 208–211
    preparation for coding, 12, 15–19
    testing (see testing)
    tracing execution of (see tracing)
    workflow for, 12–15
    (see also functions; procedures;
        software applications)
public package subprograms, 192
PUT_LINE procedure, DBMS_
    OUTPUT package, 15, 52, 54,
    209–211

Q

q$error_manager package, 55
Q##MY_COMMIT.qut file, 158
QUAD (QUick And Dirty)
    "methodology", 1
queries (see SQL)
Quest Code Tester for Oracle, 63, 66
Quest CodeGen Utility, 33, 149, 258

software developers (*continued*)
  intelligence required for, 37
  logical thinking by, x, xi, 9, 16, 37,
        144
  responsibilities of, x
  role in defining user requirements, 9,
        16
source code control (SCC), 32
source code debugger, 53, 71
SQL
  in application-level code,
        avoiding, 146
  COUNT function, when to
        use, 160–162
  cursors, retrieving attributes
        immediately from, 166–168
  custom statements, separate package
        for, 150
  disadvantages of using in code, 140,
        141–144
  DML errors, continuing past, 118
  DML statements
    columns listed explicitly in
          INSERT, 164
    encapsulating in procedures, 147
    exception handlers for, 163
    in subprograms, 198
  DML triggers, validating business
        rules with, 216–217
  FOR loop, for fetching rows, when to
        use, 162
  generating, 148–150
  as hardcoding, 143
  implementing behind procedures and
        functions, 144–151
  join logic, encapsulating in
        views, 146
  qualifying variables used in, 151–153
  rows returned by, type of data
        structure for, 147, 158–159
  transactions
    autonomous, 153–155
    not hardcoding end of, 155–157
  when to use in code, 9, 10
  (see also dynamic SQL)
SQL injection, preventing, 174
SQL Navigator, automatic formatting
        feature of, 39
SQL%BULK_EXCEPTIONS
        pseudocollection, 118, 132

SQLERRM function, 117
standards, 38
  automating, 10
  in code templates, 45–48
  comments, 48–50
  consistent formatting, 38–40
  defining, 9
  ensuring use of, with code
        reviews, 27–29
  formalizing, 10
  naming conventions, 40–43
static polymorphism (see overloading)
stdhdr.pkg file, 48
stdpkg_format.sql file, 47, 86
stdpkg.pkg file, 48
step-wise refinement, 188
streaming function, 239
string_to_list.qut file, 206
string_to_list.sf file, 205
string_tracker files, 139
strongly typed language, 73
structure definitions, name indicating
        type of, 42
structure of code, ensuring
        maintainability with, 4
subprograms (see functions; procedures)
subsystems, 188
SUBTYPE statement, 76–78
Sunita character, xii
System Global Area (SGA), 231–237

T

tabfunc_pipelined.sql file, 239
TDD (Test-Driven
        Development), 67–69
templates for code, 45–48
test cases, 70, 71
Test-By-Hand Coma State, 69
Test-Driven Development
        (TDD), 67–69
testing, 52
  automating, 63–66
  building code for, 18
  cost of, 63
  defining required tests, 17
  ensuring user requirements by, 3
  importance of, 61, 63
  iteratively, 68
  number of tests, 69

W

watch.pkg file, 55
WBS (Why Bother Syndrome), 70
We, xi
web sites
    for code examples, xvii
    for online communities, 257
    for Oracle documentation, 257
    for PL/SQL developers, 257
    for Quest CodeGen Utility, 33
    for Safari Books Online, xix
    for Set game, 33
    for Steven McConnell, 256
    for TDD (Test-Driven
        Development), 18
    for this book, xviii, 255
    list of, 257

Weinberg, Gerald M. (Handbook of
    Walkthroughs, Inspections,
    and Technical Reviews), 29
whats_not_optimal.sp file, 226
WHEN OTHERS statement, 134, 148
WHILE loop, 101
    for collections, 107–111
    exiting from, 102–105
    when to use, 102
Why Bother Syndrome (WBS), 70
workaround_comment.sql file, 47
workflow, 6–15
    application-level, 7, 8–11
    single-program, 7, 12–15
workspace, ergonomic, 34

About the Author

Steven Feuerstein is considered one of the world's leading experts on the Oracle PL/SQL language, having written 10 books on PL/SQL (all published by O'Reilly Media), including *Oracle PL/SQL Programming*. Steven has been developing software since 1980, spent five years with Oracle (1987–1992), and has served as PL/SQL Evangelist for Quest Software since January 2001. He is also an Oracle ACE director. He writes regularly for *Oracle Magazine*, which named him the PL/SQL Developer of the Year in both 2002 and 2006. Steven's online technical cyberhome is located at *www.ToadWorld.com/SF*; explore the non-PL/SQL side of his life at *www.StevenFeuerstein.com*.

Colophon

The animal on the cover of *Oracle PL/SQL Best Practices*, Second Edition, is a red wood ant. Red wood ants (*Formica aquilonia*) are often the dominant ants of forests throughout the northern hemisphere. *F. aquilonia* can build nest mounds of dried spruce needles and twigs that are three feet or more in diameter and height. Each nest can contain thousands of ants as well as several queens. The insects have no sting but can defend themselves by firing formic acid from their rear ends when disturbed.

The workers vary in size up to about half an inch in length with a red thorax, black abdomen, and red and black marked head. The ants are both scavengers and general predators of insects, carrying many soft-bodied caterpillars, flies, and sawflies along their several major trails back to the nest.

Red wood ants are a keystone species (i.e., without them the ecosystem changes fundamentally). When red ants disappear from a system, herbivorous insects can subsequently damage forest trees. In forests weakened by pollution and acid rain in central Europe, red wood ant populations are often endangered, which in turn causes further imbalances in predator-prey dynamics and the ecosystem. These rare ants are protected by law in some European countries because of their great value in destroying forest pests.

For 28 years, Professor Seigo Higashi has been studying a supercolony of Japanese red wood ants (*Formica yessensis*), which dwell along a strip of shoreline on the Ishikari coast of northern Japan. When first discovered in 1973, the colony consisted of approximately 45,000 nests with connecting tunnels extending nearly 12.4 miles along the shore of the Japan Sea. It was estimated that the colony had about 306 million workers and 1.1 million queens, and is thought to be about 1,000 years old. Since 1973, the colony has been under siege, threatened by the development of infrastructure for a new port on Ishikari Bay, which has occurred on top of 30 percent of the ant megalopolis. This has reduced the number of red wood ants living there by more than half.

The Ishikari ants are one of only two known ant supercolonies in the world. The other, smaller one is in the Swiss Jura mountains.

The cover image is a 19th-century engraving from the Dover Pictorial Archive. The cover font is Adobe ITC Garamond. The text font is Linotype Birka; the heading font is Adobe Myriad Condensed; and the code font is LucasFont's TheSans Mono Condensed.

Related Titles from O'Reilly

Oracle PL/SQL

Learning Oracle PL/SQL

Oracle PL/SQL Best Practices

Oracle PL/SQL for DBAs

Oracle PL/SQL Language Pocket Reference, *3rd Edition*

Oracle PL/SQL Programming, *4th Edition*

Oracle Books for DBAs

Oracle DBA Checklists Pocket Reference

Oracle DBA Pocket Guide

Oracle RMAN Pocket Reference

Unix for Oracle DBAs Pocket Reference

Oracle SQL and SQL Plus

Mastering Oracle SQL, *2nd Edition*

Oracle SQL* Plus: The Definitive Guide, *2nd Edition*

Oracle SQL Tuning Pocket Reference

Oracle SQL*Plus Pocket Reference, *3rd Edition*

Oracle

Building Oracle XML Applications

Optimizing Oracle Performance

Oracle Application Server 10*g* Essentials

Oracle Essentials: Oracle Database 10*g*, *3rd Edition*

Oracle in a Nutshell

Oracle Regular Expressions Pocket Reference

Perl for Oracle DBAs

SQL Cookbook

SQL Hacks

SQL in a Nutshell, *2nd Edition*

SQL Pocket Guide, *2nd Edition*

TOAD Pocket Reference for Oracle, *2nd Edition*